Louisiana and the Gulf South Frontier, 1500–1821

LOUISIANA
and the
Gulf South Frontier
1500–1821

F. TODD SMITH

Louisiana State University Press
Baton Rouge

Published by Louisiana State University Press

Manufactured in the United States of America
First printing

Designer: Barbara Neely Bourgoyne
Typeface: Ingeborg
Printer and binder: Maple Press

Library of Congress Cataloging-in-Publication Data are available at the Library of Congress.

ISBN 978-0-8071-5710-7 (cloth: alk. paper)— ISBN 978-0-8071-5711-4 (pdf) — ISBN 978-0-8071-5712-1 (epub) — ISBN 978-0-8071-5713-8 (mobi)

The paper in this book meets the guidelines for permanence and durability of the Committee on Production Guidelines for Book Longevity of the Council on Library Resources. ♾

For Sophie

CONTENTS

MAPS

ACKNOWLEDGMENTS

I would like to thank the many people who helped me—mainly by agreeing to play tennis, racquetball, and guitar with me, in addition to the eating, drinking, and smoking that usually followed—during the writing of this book. They include Charles Bittner, Neilesh Bose, Marianne Bueno, Patricia Burton, Mike Campbell, Kent Calder, Gregg Cantrell, Erica Charters, Guy Chet, Don Chipman, Sam Haynes, Rick McCaslin, Jill Montgomery, Chris Morris, Aaron Navarro, Lisa Siraganian, Jennifer Wallach, and The Mike Wise Experience. Of course, most of my thanks and love go to Sophie Burton, who, along with Allie, Sammie, Luna, Blue, and the late Toby and Wiley—not to mention all the fish, frogs, salamanders, and newts—made it all worthwhile.

Louisiana and the Gulf South Frontier, 1500–1821

Introduction

For the past two decades or so, scholars have put forth a number of highly acclaimed studies of the people of Native American, European, and African descent who coexisted in the Lower Mississippi Valley and surrounding regions between the sixteenth and early nineteenth centuries. When considered together, these works have conclusively established that the Gulf South area, stretching northward from the Gulf of Mexico to the Tennessee and Arkansas Rivers, and westward from the Suwannee River to the Trinity River, constitutes a distinctive historical region that should be studied as a whole, regardless of international boundaries. The Gulf South is characterized by extremely well-watered, fertile soil that, with a sufficient labor force, is one of the most productive agricultural areas in the world. Native Americans originally settled in the Gulf South and developed the most complex culture in North America prior to the arrival of Europeans and Africans in the sixteenth century. Basing their economic development on the production of food crops, various powerful indigenous states emerged in which a small population of hereditary elites resided in an exalted status far above the more numerous commoners. Ultimately, people of European ancestry came to supplant the Indians and, through the use of forced African slave labor, raised commercial crops alongside foodstuffs to establish the wealthiest region in the United States by the early nineteenth century.

Although similar scenarios emerged in eastern North America—an area much more familiar to students of early U.S. history—during the same era, for various reasons, the Gulf South stands out as a region distinct from the four zones—New England, Middle Colonies, Chesapeake, and Low Country—that made up British North America. First, the Indians of the Gulf South were wealthier and more powerful than any other indigenous groups in North America. Although they suffered intense population decline following the invasion from the Eastern Hemisphere, tribes such as the Apalaches, Creeks, Choctaws, Chickasaws, Caddos, Quapaws, Osages, and Wichitas adapted—due, in part, to an influx of mixed-bloods—to their changing circumstances and remained powerful, independent entities well into the nineteenth century. Although there were exceptions, most notably the Iroquois and the Cherokees, the Native Americans located near the Atlantic Coast were overwhelmed and quickly succumbed to the numbers of Europeans and Africans (and their diseases) that began to arrive in the early seventeenth century. As a result, the far more numerous Europeans in British North America established hegemony over the dwindling number of Indians much quicker than their brethren in the Gulf South.

Second, whereas English-speaking (Anglo) Protestants made up an overwhelmingly large proportion of the European settlers in the thirteen British colonies located along the Atlantic Coast, the Gulf South's Europeans were much more heterogeneous. Although Catholics from France and Spain had originally established the colonies of Texas, Louisiana, and Florida, a variety of people of European ancestry, including Germans, Acadians, Canary Islanders, and Anglos, resided in the Gulf South by the end of the eighteenth century. In addition to ethnic, linguistic, and religious differences, the absolute monarchs of France and Spain ruled over their subjects with little interference from below throughout the era, while the Anglos on the eastern seaboard obtained representative government at an early date. The Gulf South colonies, unlike their stable Atlantic Coast counterparts, experienced disruptive political transfers as Spain, France, and Great Britain exchanged the various provinces at one time or another before the United States finally obtained exclusive possession of the entire region (except for Texas) in 1821. Also, in contrast to the prized British colonies on the East Coast, European officials always considered Texas, Louisiana, and Florida to be backwaters, far down the list—if not at the very bottom—of their Western Hemisphere possessions.

Finally, the nature of African slavery that developed in the Gulf South differed—albeit in subtle ways—from bondage in British North America. Almost from the start, slaves made up a majority of the population of French Louisiana; only South Carolina had a black majority among the thirteen colonies. Most of the slaves initially came from the same region in Africa and, concentrated together on large plantations, were able to form a culture unique to Louisiana. Also, French and Spanish laws recognized the slaves as Crown subjects and granted them legal rights, as well as membership in the Catholic Church, unlike the situation in the English provinces, where slaves were considered more straightforwardly as property. The right of self-purchase, along with fewer cultural prohibitions on interracial sex, spurred the formation of a large caste of free people of color in the Gulf South toward the end of the eighteenth century. While the creation of the three-caste system in Louisiana was part of a similar development in other French and Spanish holdings in the Western Hemisphere during the period, it stood in direct contrast to the strict biracial polarity that existed in British North America at the same time.

The persistent strength of the Gulf South's Indian tribes, the relatively low number of European settlers, the colonial powers' lack of interest in the area, and the large percentage of African slaves resulted in the creation of what scholars now term a frontier zone of interaction. In the early twentieth century historians portrayed a boundary between civilization (embodied by people of European descent) and barbarism (represented by indigenous peoples all over the world) as being a frontier. During the past thirty years or so, the historical definition of frontier has undergone a radical conceptual transformation; it is now classified as a zone of interaction where different groups or polities are relatively equal in power, and either contend for resources and control, or establish an interdependence with one another. The few early twentieth-century historians who studied any aspect of the Gulf South region accepted as fact the superiority of Western European culture and portrayed the era prior to 1821 as being a struggle that justly and inevitably resulted in the triumph of white over red and black. Whereas a few scholars might have professed admiration for the French and Spanish efforts in the region, most historians, publishing at the height of American power throughout the world, unconsciously cast the United States' acquisition of the Gulf South as a positive and beneficial extension of Manifest Destiny, as they were themselves products of this thought process.

The civil rights movement, America's faltering foreign policy, and the revolutionary demographic transformation that has taken place in the United States over the past few decades has encouraged more recent historians to alter the triumphal interpretation of the colonial past. Heavily influenced by the many studies of British North America that began in the 1960s, over the past two decades scholars working on the Native Americans, Europeans, and Africans in the Gulf South have interpreted their findings through the prism of frontier interaction, contention, and interdependence. They have put a stop to the tendency to privilege the standing and experiences of white people over the "other." However, despite the outpouring of excellent works on the Gulf South region in the last twenty years, most of the studies have been unnecessarily restricted by political divisions and chronological eras. As a result, most of the extant works are confined to one province—Texas, Louisiana, or Florida—and only rarely consider the region as a distinct social and economic entity—as the British colonies are often grouped—beyond the artificial political boundaries. In addition, most of these studies tend to open with the French occupation of the Gulf South around 1700, resulting in the neglect of the Native American tribes that dominated the region prior to the eighteenth century. Moreover, almost all of these works conclude with the Louisiana Purchase, assuming that the frontier era of the region's history came to a close with the United States' acquisition in 1803.

Taking into account the sudden increase in the number of publications on the region that have emerged in the past two decades, I have produced a history of Louisiana and the Gulf Coast frontier from 1500 to 1821. This work begins at the turn of the sixteenth century in order to provide an overview of the various Indian groups that resided in the region on the eve of the earliest European intrusion, while concluding at the point that the United States gained possession and hegemony of all the provinces east of Texas. An epilogue then traces, in lesser detail, the removal of the Indians from the Gulf South, the Anglo Protestant conquest of Texas, and the continuing spread of African slavery. This work is rooted in the conviction that the affairs of the entire region—from East Texas to West Florida and from the Gulf of Mexico to the mouth of the Arkansas River—were interrelated and connected to such an extent that the area, despite its political divisions, must be considered as a whole to gain a true understanding of its nature. In fact, after 1718 the Gulf South could be defined as being New Orleans and its hinterlands, as what tied the entire region together—even West Florida and East Texas—was the gravitational pull of the Mississippi River and the Crescent City port, no matter which country possessed the town. In keeping with the nature of recent works, this book strongly emphasizes demographic, economic, social, and cultural concerns as well as examining matters such as diplomatic and military affairs. I have also followed the laudable tendencies of the new frontier history and have included the various Native American tribes, the different European groups, and the African slaves on a relatively equal basis without favoring or privileging one polity over the other. This study purposefully characterizes the Gulf South as a frontier from the beginning of the sixteenth century to the early years of the nineteenth century—even after the United States' acquisition of Louisiana in 1803—for the Americans were forced to contend with the Gulf South's various groups for nearly two decades before obtaining hegemony in 1821. Only during the course of the following twenty years were the Americans able to remove most of the Indian tribes, come to overwhelm Louisiana's French creoles numerically and politically, and impose a racial system that was in accordance with the rest of the Deep South. Finally, this study places colonial Louisiana and the Gulf Coast frontier in the context of the Spanish, French, and British colonial empires rather than limiting the view through comparisons with the history of the United States. Although many specialized works have been consulted to produce this study, I have aimed the narrative at upper-level undergraduate and graduate students who are unfamiliar with the early history of Louisiana and the Gulf South. As a result, I have forsaken the use of footnotes, choosing instead to list the excellent secondary works that have made this study possible.

1

Initial Encounters, 1500–1670

During the four centuries prior to the arrival of newcomers from the Eastern Hemisphere, the native inhabitants of the Gulf South—of various linguistic affiliations—had established powerful chiefdoms, led by a class of hereditary elites, throughout the region stretching from West Florida to East Texas. Although many chiefdoms had gone into decline and were abandoned around 1350, a number of impressive polities continued to exist in the Gulf South by the time Catholic Spaniards, along with a few Africans, arrived during the first half of the sixteenth century. These Spaniards ravaged and plundered many of the Indian states in their fruitless pursuit of the type of wealth that other Iberians had uncovered in Central and South America. Although the character of the Spanish effort in America transformed to the desire to spread Christianity among the natives by the beginning of the seventeenth century—resulting in the establishment of an evangelical colony in Florida—most of the chiefdoms collapsed and suffered huge population losses in the wake of the Spaniards' brutality. Consequently, by 1670, when Europeans from Britain and France began to enter the Gulf South, most of the region's Indians had reorganized themselves into smaller sedentary, agricultural communities that were more egalitarian in nature than the chiefdoms that had existed in the past.

The Native Inhabitants

Humans had lived in the Gulf South for fifteen thousand years or so before Europeans and Africans began arriving half a millennium ago. For the first ten thousand years, during which the climate was hot and humid, the residents were hunters who lived in small family groups. Around five thousand years ago the climate became cool and drier, resulting in the establishment of the plants and forests, and the animals that lived in them, that exist in the Gulf South today. Accordingly, over the course of the next three thousand years or so, the region's indigenous residents developed horticulture, pottery, a sedentary lifestyle, and the long-distance exchange of goods. By the beginning of the current era the Gulf South people dramatically intensified these developments, creating what scholars have termed the Woodland tradition. Most people occupied villages year round, in part because of their increasing dependence on horticulture. In addition to squash, which had previously been grown domestically, the residents added corn to their list of garden crops during this period. As more food became available, hierarchies and social ranking emerged. People celebrated death and burial publicly, constructing small earthen mounds to inter the deceased elites, along with large quantities of valuable and rare imported goods.

Whereas some groups stopped participating in this elaborate mortuary cult and became a bit more egalitarian around 700, people living in the interior expanded on the trends characteristic of the Woodland tradition to create the most complex culture in North America prior to the European and African arrival. This tradition, known as Mississippian, began taking shape between 700 and 900 along the middle course of the Mississippi River, developing earliest and most spectacularly at Cahokia in the tremendously rich American Bottoms, near the mouths of the Illinois and Missouri Rivers. At its height, between 1050 and 1200, Cahokia covered six square miles, with a population of around twenty thousand and more than one hundred mounds of various sizes. From Cahokia, the Mississippian tradition spread southward, resulting in the development of a number of hierarchical chiefdoms located between East Texas and West Florida. Intensified corn cultivation was the key to the development of Mississippian culture, and the Gulf South people, despite lacking metal or domesticated animals other than dogs, made the transition from raising crops in small gardens to clearing forests in order to create extremely large fields of maize. Once the natives had made the shift, food production increased dramatically and the population rose accordingly. Agricultural innovation continued as beans were added to corn and squash staples around 1000. Gathering wild plants, nuts, and berries, as well as hunting and fishing, continued to be important sources of food, but they quickly assumed a secondary role to agriculture. Mississippians were matrilineal, meaning that they traced descent only through the female line. Women played the most important economic role, as they were in charge of the fields that formed the basis of their tribe's wealth. Men spent most of their time hunting white-tailed deer and other game, in addition to acting as soldiers in the chronic warfare that existed among the Mississippians.

Along with the intensification of corn and bean agriculture in the Gulf South came the further development of chiefdom forms of government. Throughout the region, powerful states emerged with a small number of hereditary chiefs, nobles, and priests who ranked in an exalted status far above the more numerous commoners. Within each chiefdom there was a multiple-town political organization in which the elites lived on top of an earthen platform mound in a capital center. A cluster of secondary administrative centers, often containing smaller earthworks, were located nearby, with other towns spread throughout a river valley. A typical town contained from forty to sixty households, consisting of a total population of around five hundred people living in domiciles constructed of wooden frames covered with bark or cane mats. Generally, a simple chiefdom consisted of five to eight such towns. In some instances throughout the Gulf South during this period, one chiefdom conquered or formed alliances with others, resulting in a paramount chiefdom. Between 1100 and 1350 impressive variations of Mississippian paramount chiefdoms developed throughout the region, most dramatically at ceremonial sites similar to Cahokia, such as Etowah in northwestern Georgia, Moundville in northwestern Alabama, Bottle Creek in southern Alabama, Winterville in western Mississippi, and Spiro near the Arkansas-Oklahoma border.

Due to the wealth that had been developed within the paramount chiefdoms, warfare was a constant, and most Mississippian towns were fortified with palisade walls and ditches. In the capital town, the chief's house and other public buildings were placed on large flat-topped mounds, which served as a symbol of power and as the center of the chiefdom. They also served as important symbols of a religious cult devoted to renewal rituals. One of the public buildings was usually employed as a mortuary temple where the physical remains of the chief's ancestors were buried or stored in baskets. Next to these public buildings was a rectangular plaza that served as an outdoor public space. Surrounding it were the homes of the high-ranking people, with the commoners living in houses on the outskirts of the town. Among the elites was a man designated as a war chief and diplomat, who served as an advisor to the principal chief and as the leader of military endeavors. Chiefs were treated as divine, entitled to a special

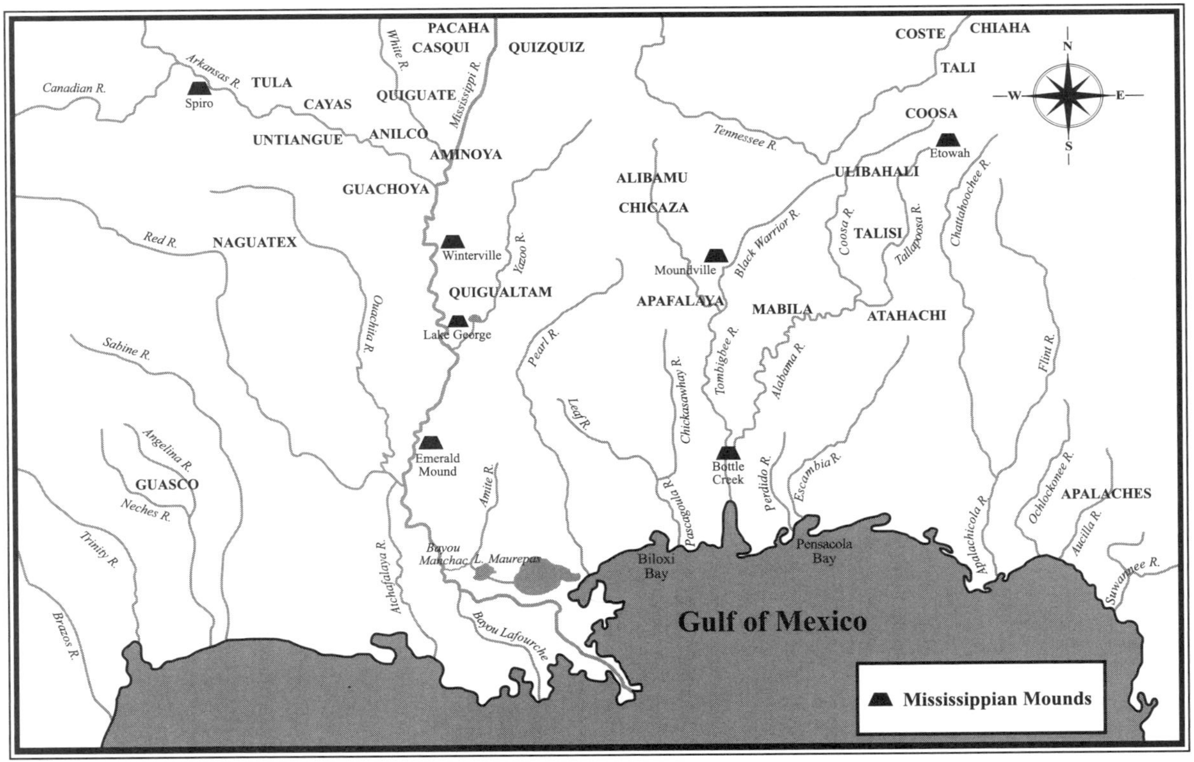

MAP 1. THE GULF SOUTH, CA. 1500

diet provided by the commoners, and often were carried on litters borne on the shoulders of the people so their feet never touched the ground. They displayed symbols of their elite status, including large plates of copper worn on the head, feather garments, and shell ornaments. The subsidiary towns paid tribute to the chief, who controlled food surpluses, luxury artisanal goods, and exotic trade materials obtained through exchanges with other chiefdoms.

Despite the power and influence of the complex chiefdoms, there was a constant pattern of rise and fall among the Mississippian groups. Certain stresses, such as soil exhaustion, drought, depletion of core resources, military defeats, and contested claims to leadership often caused the chiefdoms to collapse. The overall regional stability of the Mississippian world, however, allowed for the establishment of new chiefdoms following a period of adjustment after a fall, as people joined other existing polities or new areas opened for the settlement and development of new chiefdoms. In the middle of the fourteenth century the climate became colder and drier, causing the transformation of most of the major paramount chiefdoms. Around 1350 mound building began to decrease and there was an outmigration from many of the ceremonial centers. While many paramount chiefdoms had been abandoned by 1500, a few remained in the Gulf South at the beginning of the sixteenth century, often situated near a series of simple chiefdoms.

Chiefdoms located along the Tombigbee and Alabama river systems that flow into Mobile Bay were among the most impressive that existed in the 1500s. Coosa, located in present Georgia, Alabama, and Tennessee, was perhaps the largest paramount chiefdom in the Gulf South. Coosa's antecedents emerged around 1000 along the Coosawattee and Etowah Rivers, upper tributaries of the Coosa River, on the ecotone boundary where the streams poured forth from the Appalachian Mountains and entered a valley rich in alluvial soils. Many Gulf South chiefdoms were established on ecotone boundaries, thus allowing the people to raise crops in the valley's fertile soils while also being able to hunt and collect nuts and berries in the nearby hills. Often shoals were present in the streams at the fall line near the ecotone boundary, providing good fishing sources and an easy place to cross the rivers. By 1200 the main center of power was located on the Etowah River, and six large mounds were constructed at the capital site, with eleven other dependent towns located along the stream. Around 1350, however, Etowah began to lose power, allowing the people in the nearby Coosawattee Valley to establish dominance. By 1475 a capital had been established about fifteen miles upstream from the Coosa River at the Little Egypt site, consisting of two or three mounds arranged around a plaza area, with eight dependent settlements in the Coosawattee Valley. Like many people in the Gulf South east of the Mississippi River, the Coosas spoke Muskogean, in particular the subgroup known as Eastern Muskogean. This subgroup is further divided into Alabama, its similar variant Koasati, Muskogee, and Mikasuki (with two dialects—Hitchiti and Mikasuki). These Eastern Muskogean languages are mutually intelligible, except for Hitchiti. Linguistic diversity throughout the Gulf South, however, led the indigenous people to use a pidgin language known as Mobilian to communicate with one another. During its rise to prominence in the fifteenth century Coosa became a paramount chiefdom by extending its dominance over various groups of Eastern Muskogean speakers, including the Chiaha, Coste, and Tali—as they were called by intruding Spaniards at the time—chiefdoms in the Tennessee River Valley over one hundred miles to the north, as well as the Ulibahali and Abihka chiefdoms along the Coosa River and the Talisi chiefdom in the nearby Tallapoosa Valley.

Another paramount chiefdom, Tascalusa, was located near where the Coosa and Tallapoosa meet to form the Alabama River. Tascalusa emerged from the Moundville chiefdom—one of the grandest of all the Mississippian societies—which peaked during the thirteenth century in the Black Warrior Valley of northwestern Alabama. During the 1400s the once-thriving center of Moundville was radically transformed to a largely vacant and unpalisaded ceremonial site, as many people abandoned the Black Warrior Valley to establish independent chiefdoms elsewhere. Tascalusa formed around 1450 on the Lower Tallapoosa and Alabama Rivers, with its capital situated at Atahachi, on the Alabama, just three miles below present Montgomery. Like the people of Tascalusa, the founders of the nearby province of Mabila were also descendants of Moundville, having moved down the Black Warrior River to settle near Mobile Bay around 1100. In the fifteenth century, however, Mabila relocated farther up the Alabama River and established several towns near the mouth of the Cahaba River, about fifty miles downstream from Atahachi. Soon thereafter, the Tascalusa and Mabila chiefdoms, both consisting of Eastern Muskogean speakers, formed an alliance.

During the twelfth century, at about the same time the Mabilas moved to Mobile Bay, other groups of people migrated west from Moundville to establish a series of simple chiefdoms in the Black Prairie region located along the Tombigbee River. In the 1400s, during the decline of Moundville, the paramount chiefdom of Chicaza emerged along the middle reaches of the Tombigbee within the triangle formed in Mississippi near the present Starkville-Columbus-West Point area. Whereas the Chicazas spoke Western Muskogean, two Alabama-speaking chiefdoms, the Alibamu and Micalusa, resided just upstream and were considered subordinate to the Chicazas. Other Alabama-speakers, the Taliepacanas, Moculixas, and the Apafalayas, resided near the confluence of the Black Warrior and the Tombigbee in simple chiefdoms.

Although the chiefdoms located along the waterways that emptied into Mobile Bay were perhaps the most impressive in the Gulf South at the beginning of the sixteenth century, many others existed throughout the region. Relatives of the same people who were in the process of constructing Moundville in the twelfth century also established chiefdoms on the Lower Chattahoochee River. During the 1200s one group of Hitchiti-speakers moved south from the Chattahoochee to the Tallahassee hill region of the Florida panhandle, where they established the Apalache paramount chiefdom between the Aucilla and Ochlockonee Rivers. Instead of the population being concentrated in compact towns, as was the case with many Mississippian societies, the Apalaches developed a hierarchical system of principal villages dispersed throughout the territory, with the common people being spread across the hilltops between the region's coastal plain rivers. Prior to 1500 the principal Apalache chief lived at the multimound ceremonial center located along Lake Jackson, just north of present Tallahassee. Early in the sixteenth century, however, the Apalaches abandoned the Lake Jackson site and moved the seat of power southwestward to the moundless town of Anhayca. The Apalache country was very fruitful, and the inhabitants used the surrounding forests and swamp-like rivers to supplement the corn, beans, and squash staples that provided the foundation of their society. The Apalaches' wealth allowed them to develop a strong military tradition and, like many Mississippian chiefdoms, they created buffer zones on all sides of their territory.

Several large and impressive chiefdoms also existed along the central Mississippi River at the beginning of the sixteenth century. Between 700 and 1000 the native people living just downstream from the mouth of the Ohio River made the transition to intensive corn cultivation by establishing settlements and planting crops on the natural levees—which are particularly rich in fertile soil—created by the meandering Mississippi. In addition to the food raised in their meander zone soils, the settlers hunted in the nearby floodplain forest as well as in the prairies and hills located throughout the area. Between 1000 and 1350 the Mississippian way of life was consolidated and elaborated upon, as large ceremonial centers appeared along with palisaded towns and small dispersed farmsteads. Due to climate change and constant warfare, however, the region was abandoned in the late fourteenth century, and most of the people relocated southward to establish dense population centers in the fertile bottomlands located near present Memphis, Tennessee. Pacaha became the dominant paramount chiefdom in the area, with a principal town consisting of four mounds surrounded by a palisade and a ditch located on the west bank of the Mississippi about twenty miles north of Memphis. By 1500 the powerful people of Pacaha had brought the downstream chiefdoms of Quizquiz and Aquijo, located on opposite sides of the Mississippi, into their dominion. The Casqui chiefdom—enemies of the Pacahans and their allies—was located about twenty miles west of Pacaha, with its capital town on the east bank of the St. Francis River. Quiguate, one of the largest towns in the entire Gulf South, stood about fifty miles down the St. Francis from Pacaha. Other spectacular Mississippian polities, such as Anilco, Guachoya, and Aminoya, were located farther south near the mouth of the Arkansas River. Although the culture of the central Mississippi was similar to that of the Tombigbee-Alabama region, the residents spoke Tunican instead of Muskogean.

Quigualtam, one of the largest and most powerful paramount chiefdoms that existed in the early sixteenth century, was centered on the east bank of the Mississippi in the Lower Yazoo River basin. It was heir to yet another regional Mississippian development that emerged about 700 on both sides of the river, from just below the mouth of the Arkansas down to the mouth of the Homochitto River in southwestern Mississippi. Known as Coles Creek culture, these people constructed ceremonial centers between 1000 and 1200 despite not raising corn until the very end of the period. Between 1200 and 1350 the culture of the central Mississippi was introduced into the Yazoo basin, creating a hybrid called Plaquemine culture. Corn cultivation became well established during this time, and the Plaquemine people—mainly Natchezan-speakers—constructed many impressive ceremonial centers on both sides of the Mississippi River, including the Winterville site in northwestern Mississippi, the Emerald and Anna sites east of Natchez, and the Transylvania and Fitzhugh sites in the Tensas River basin in Louisiana. The Lake George site, consisting of thirty large and small mounds located on the lower reaches of the Yazoo River, was the most impressive ceremonial center in the region. Although the

Lake George complex was in decline by 1500, it seems to have remained one of the principal Quigualtam towns.

Less powerful chiefdoms, heavily influenced by the Mississippian world, also existed on the margins of the culture's core. Western Muskogean speakers, who resided on the lower reaches of the Mississippi River and along the Gulf of Mexico eastward to the Florida panhandle, relied on agriculture and marine resources and were organized into simple chiefdoms located near single mounds. Many of the groups, including the Quinipissas, Houmas, and Bayogoulas along the Mississippi River, as well as the Pascagoulas and Tohomes on the Gulf Coast, had contact with the great interior chiefdoms through trade in salt. Outlying, marginally Mississippian polities also existed west of the great river on the boundary between the eastern woodlands and the Great Plains. Due to the drier conditions in the region, these Tunican-speakers were only able to establish simple chiefdoms, including the Cayas and Untiangue, in central Arkansas near present Little Rock. Although these people raised corn and hunted white-tailed deer in the surrounding hills like the Mississippians of the Southeast, buffalo hunting and salt extraction and trading were also important to their economy.

Caddoan speakers resided in the westernmost chiefdoms, located in the hilly, forested region just east of the Great Plains. Between 700 and 1350 these people constructed large numbers of ceremonial sites in the various river valleys located between the Trinity and the Arkansas Rivers. The most impressive site, consisting of twelve mounds, emerged between 1100 and 1250 at Spiro, on the Arkansas River just west of Fort Smith. Although similar to other Mississippians, Caddoan societies were characteristically composed of dispersed farmsteads, more closely settled at places where there was good farming along the larger rivers, and less so on the smaller tributaries. The population was a bit less dense than the societies to the east, and no Caddoan communities were surrounded by fortifications. Although they built houses comparable to those in the Mississippian Gulf South, the Caddoans covered them with grass rather than barks and cane. Climate change and drought in the fourteenth century forced the people to stop building mounds, and by 1450 the chiefdom at Spiro had collapsed. Although a small chiefdom called Tula remained in the area, many of the Caddoan-speakers moved farther up the Arkansas to concentrate more on buffalo hunting than agricultural production. Others migrated southward to join their brethren in the Ouachita, Red, Sabine, and Neches Valleys. As a result, impressive Caddoan chiefdoms, such as the Naguatex at the bend of the Red River and the Guasco on the Neches, continued to function well into the sixteenth century and beyond.

The Spanish Invaders

Spaniards along with a few African slaves violently entered the Gulf South Mississippian world in the early 1500s. Although the peoples of the Iberian peninsula, like most of Western Europe's original inhabitants, were Celtic-speakers, six centuries of Roman rule—which came to an end in the 400s—resulted in the Latinization of the language and the culture. In the fifth century Germanic-speaking Vandals conquered Iberia and established several independent kingdoms while maintaining many of the institutions and laws of the late Roman Empire, including Christianity. In the 700s Arab Muslims from North Africa conquered nearly all of the Iberian peninsula, creating the province of Al-Andalus. While some Latinized inhabitants converted to Islam, the Muslim rulers of Al-Andalus tolerated their subjects who remained Catholic and Jewish, resulting in the development of a dynamic and highly educated state that became one of the leading cultural and economic centers of the Mediterranean world. Nonetheless, for much of its history Muslim Al-Andalus existed in conflict with the Latin Catholic kingdoms of northern Iberia that were determined to reconquer the entire peninsula. At once a military and religious enterprise, most of the *reconquista* had been completed by the mid-thirteenth century, with the Emirate of Granada being the only remaining Iberian Muslim state, coexisting with the independent Christian kingdoms of Portugal, Castile, and Aragon. In 1479, following the marriage of Ferdinand of Aragon to Isabella of Castile, two of these crowns were joined together, laying the foundations for the modern Spanish state. The reconquista was finally completed in January 1492 when the final Muslim ruler of Granada surrendered his kingdom to the royal couple, known as the Catholic Monarchs.

Flush with victory after more than seven centuries of war with Muslims, eight months later Ferdinand and Isabella backed Christopher Columbus, a Genoese sailor, in the endeavor that resulted in the Spanish conquest of much of the Western Hemisphere. Because of the timing of Columbus's "discovery," the Spanish effort to control the so-called New World and its peoples became, in effect, an extension of the reconquista. Much of the legal apparatus employed by Spain in the exploration and conquest of the Americas was based on medieval Iberian institutions that had been modified to meet the new circumstances. For instance, most military actions against the Iberian Muslims had been privately financed with Crown authorization through a contract awarding a military leader the title of *adelantado.* Similar arrangements were made with the conquerors of the New World, as the Crown licensed wealthy men to recruit the soldiers and pay for the supplies that would be used to overwhelm Native American societies. In return, the adelantado expected to share in wealth procured through conquest and in rights to conquered land, as well as receiving a noble title. As with the situation in feudal Spain, the soldiers were given a share in the conquest, with the high-ranking officials being awarded *encomiendas,* through which the conquered peoples would pay tribute. Although during the early reconquista the Christian rulers had allowed the vanquished groups to practice their faith without severe penalty, by the fifteenth century the Catholic Monarchs conceived of the reconquest as a religious crusade and were determined to force the conversion of Muslims and Jews. With the discovery of America, the Spaniards expanded this belief to include the conversion of New World pagans to Christianity through the offices of various religious orders, including the Franciscans and Dominicans.

Prior to the voyage of Columbus, however, Portugal had been the first Iberian Christian kingdom to promote overseas expansion. Throughout the fourteenth century Portuguese rulers employed Italian sailors to explore the west coast of Africa in search of a route to the Far East, and the riches that had been previously described by Marco Polo. In the course of their explorations the Portuguese developed relations with various West African kingdoms by which the Europeans exchanged cloth, weapons, and other goods in return for ivory, gold, and slaves, many of whom were then shipped to Italian-run sugar plantations that had been established on island chains such as the Azores and the Cape Verdes, in the eastern Atlantic Ocean. Columbus had sailed for the Portuguese for more than a decade before Bartholomew Dias, a fellow Italian, rounded the Cape of Good Hope in 1488, finally opening the sought-after sea route to the Indian Ocean. Four years later the Spanish rulers contracted with Columbus to support his scheme to reach the Indies by sailing west. Following the Genoan's return to Europe in early 1493 after encountering islands in the Caribbean, Portugal and Spain divided the world through treaty and papal ordinance, granting the Spaniards the exclusive right to spread the gospel and to establish settlements and trade among the inhabitants of most of the Western Hemisphere.

As a result of the agreements, over the course of the following two decades Spaniards—mainly from the impoverished southern and western Castilian provinces of Andalucia and Extremadura—subjugated the native populations on the large Caribbean islands of Hispaniola, Cuba, Puerto Rico, and Jamaica. Spanish officials awarded encomiendas to their supporters on all the islands, but the Indians—as they were called by the conquerors—died in huge numbers from overwork and disease. Lacking acquired immunity to Eastern Hemisphere diseases such as smallpox, measles, influenza, and whooping cough, the Caribbean Indians—namely Arawaks, who lived in chiefdoms similar to those in the Gulf South—succumbed quickly, leaving few natives to provide the Spanish *encomenderos* with the tribute they demanded. The Spaniards responded to the rapid depopulation of the Caribbean islands by intensifying their search for additional lands with fresh sources of Indian labor in the second decade of the sixteenth century.

The Spanish quest for new territory with large native populations began with the expedition of Juan Ponce de León, a nobleman from Vallodolid who had sailed with Columbus on his second voyage in 1493 and had subsequently helped conquer Puerto Rico in 1508. Hearing reports of an island to the north called Bimini, Ponce sought and received permission from the Crown to investigate in February 1512. A little over a year later he sailed from Puerto Rico in three vessels, one piloted by the experienced Antonio de Alaminos, a native of the Andalucian port city of Palos. Making landfall far up the Atlantic Coast near Daytona Beach, Ponce named the land for the day he went ashore, Easter Sunday, or the *Pascua Florida*. From there, the party turned south and maneuvered its way through the Florida Keys and sailed up the west coast as far as Charlotte Harbor before returning to Puerto Rico. In 1514 Ponce traveled to Spain and received the right to conquer what he believed to be the island of Florida. Seven years later he attempted his conquest but was killed by Indians shortly after landing at Charlotte Harbor.

While Ponce de León's attempt to conquer Florida had failed, the pilot Alaminos used his experience on the 1513 expedition to further Spanish knowledge of the Gulf of Mexico. In 1517 and 1518 he guided expeditions that revealed the entire western coastline of the Gulf from the Yucatán Peninsula to the Pánuco River, near the future site of Tampico. In 1519

Alonso Álvarez de Pineda completed the work of Alaminos by filling in the gap between Charlotte Harbor and the Pánuco. Setting out from Jamaica with four ships in March, Álvarez de Pineda sailed northward up the west side of Florida, following the coast as it turned toward Mexico. Along the way the Spanish pilot noted bays and several large rivers, including the Mississippi. The flotilla continued down the east coast of Mexico past the Pánuco River before returning to Jamaica in late fall 1519. In addition to proving that Florida was not an island, Alvarez de Pineda sketched a map showing the character of the Gulf of Mexico in more or less accurate proportions. By 1520 then, the Spaniards had developed a firm understanding of the geography of the Caribbean and the Gulf of Mexico as well as their relation to the Atlantic Ocean.

Soon thereafter news traveled throughout the Spanish world that Hernán Cortés, an Extremaduran who had been one of the original conquerors of Cuba, had successfully invaded the Aztec empire of mainland Mexico and had taken possession of its capital, Tenochtitlán, bringing enormous riches to himself and to a few of his followers. The conquest of Mexico set off dozens of Spanish expeditions throughout the Western Hemisphere in search of indigenous empires comparable to that of the Aztecs. Most sought to follow the blueprint Cortés had used in conquering the Aztecs, that of establishing strategic Indian alliances and taking native rulers hostage while setting up residence in the empire's capital city. In an attempt to control the expeditions and the resulting conquests, Carlos I, the Austrian Habsburg ruler who had become the King of Spain in 1516, established the Council of the Indies in 1524 and gave it the responsibility of overseeing colonial affairs. Over the course of the following three decades the Council authorized various Spanish expeditions throughout the Western Hemisphere that established control over numerous Indian polities, a few of which were extremely wealthy.

Two of these expeditions followed up on the previous exploits of the Spanish explorers in the Gulf of Mexico by landing huge armies on the North American mainland. These armies made the first direct contacts with the Gulf South Mississippians. In December 1526 the Council of the Indies awarded Pánfilo de Narváez the royal contract to explore the Gulf Coast from Pánuco to Florida and to establish two towns and three fortresses in the land. Narváez, a Spaniard from Valladolid, was a veteran of the conquest of Cuba who felt that he had been illegally deprived of the right to conquer Mexico. He had lost an eye to Cortés in a battle fought on the coast near Veracruz in 1520. Hopeful of finding an Indian empire in Florida as wealthy as that of the Aztecs, Narváez financed an expedition that sailed from Spain in June 1527. It included five ships, eighty horses, and six hundred people, including ten women and African servants. However, by February 1528, when the ill-fated expedition headed toward Florida after first landing in Hispaniola and Cuba, only about four hundred people remained with Narváez, as nearly one-third of the voyagers had deserted. Among those who remained on board was Alvar Núñez Cabeza de Vaca, the Andalucian royal treasurer who would survive the expedition to compose one of the most famous accounts of all the numerous Spanish *entradas* in the Western Hemisphere.

Two months after leaving Cuba, the Narváez flotilla landed on the coast of Florida, a few miles south of Tampa Bay. After reconnoitering the region for a few days, scouts encountered an indigenous village, probably that of the agricultural Tocobagas, whose lightly gold-adorned leaders informed Narváez through sign—or at least, he believed they told him—that the Apalache province to the north contained enormous amounts of the precious metal the Spaniards so desired. Learning of this exciting news, Narváez made the fateful decision to divide the expedition in two. All able-bodied men and horses would proceed on foot, going inland at times but keeping parallel to the coast, until they reached Apalache, after which they would proceed on to the Pánuco. At the same time the ships, carrying only crew members and the women, would sail up the coast hoping to rendezvous with the overland party. In early May Narváez began marching northward with about three hundred men, a few Africans, and the surviving forty horses. The party would never encounter the ships again. The vessels fruitlessly scoured the Gulf Coast for any sign of the land expedition for an entire year before giving up and heading for Cuba.

In the meantime, following a grueling month and a half of marching northward, in which the hungry Spaniards encountered only a couple of Indian villages that provided them with corn, Narváez and his men arrived at a small outlying Apalache town, consisting of "forty low, small thatch houses . . . surrounded by dense woods and many little lakes." They quickly took possession of the village and forced the inhabitants to flee, except for the town chief, whom they held as hostage. Finding huge stores of food, the starving group remained in the village for about four weeks, fending off constant guerrilla attacks in which the Apalaches tried to dislodge the intruders and force the release of their leader. Three scouting parties failed to find the main Apalache town of Anhayca or any other village reminiscent of the Aztec capital of Tenochtitlán. Therefore, when captive

Indians informed the Spaniards that Ochete, a nearby town located on the coast, had ample corn, beans, and squash, the disappointed Narváez abandoned his desire of conquering the Apalaches and headed toward the Gulf in hopes of somehow encountering his ships.

The nine-day march to Ochete was disastrous, as the Apalache warriors, who "loomed big and naked and from a distance looked like giants," ambushed the Spaniards while they laboriously made their way through nearly impassable swamps and lagoons. By the time the Spaniards finally reached the hastily abandoned Ochete, located on the Lower Wakulla River, nearly a third of the expedition had fallen sick and could barely walk. Realizing they would never be found in this area of shallow inlets, coves, and swamps, the Spaniards decided to slaughter their horses for food and constructed five rafts on which they hoped to float toward Mexico. In late September the 250 survivors set off from the so-called Bay of Horses and headed west along the coast. After encountering fresh water being discharged into the Gulf of Mexico by the Mississippi River, the forlorn fleet became separated. By November 1528 all five of the vessels had miraculously landed on the Texas Gulf Coast between Corpus Christi Bay and Galveston Bay. Soon thereafter most of the expedition members were either killed or enslaved by the coastal Karankawa Indians. In 1534 Cabeza de Vaca and three survivors escaped together and, after traveling through Texas and northern Mexico, reached fellow Spaniards.

Learning of the fate of the Narváez expedition following Cabeza de Vaca's arrival in Mexico City, Hernando de Soto, an Extremaduran veteran of the conquest of Nicaragua and Peru, sought and received a contract from the Crown in April 1537 to explore and establish settlements in Florida, what the Spaniards then defined as the land between Delaware Bay and the Pánuco River. De Soto easily recruited six hundred or so eager men, mainly from Extremadura and Andalucia, as well as their servants and a few wives. The men had convinced themselves that new Perus and Mexicos lay in the interior of the Southeast. De Soto's fleet of ten ships left Spain in April 1538 and, after stopping first in Cuba to gather more supplies, landed in Tampa Bay in May 1539. In addition to the soldiers recruited in Spain, De Soto now had a few priests and skilled tradesmen, as well as two hundred horses, numerous pigs, and huge mastiff dogs under his command. Four men later left accounts of the De Soto expedition.

As with Narváez, De Soto planned to feed his army by moving through native villages and taking stored food as needed, in addition to using local women as consorts and captured men and boys as guides and bearers. The Spaniards spent two months investigating the Tampa Bay area before deciding that the soil was too sandy for settlement and that the local Indians did not have enough wealth for their tastes. Therefore, De Soto decided to leave a small garrison at the landing site while he and five hundred men headed north in search of wealthier Indian kingdoms. Traveling farther inland than Narváez, De Soto's party crossed through the territory of Timucuan speakers near the confluence of the Santa Fe and Suwannee Rivers before heading due west toward Apalache, which they had been informed was the richest and most powerful province in the region. Although the Spaniards occasionally had to use force as they made their way up the peninsula, once they crossed the Aucilla River in September and entered the territory of the Apalache chiefdom the fighting became fierce, as the well-organized Indians closely contested the invaders' progress. Following a week or so of intense fighting, however, the Spaniards finally gained possession of the principal town of Anhayca, forcing its residents to flee.

The fall harvest having been collected, De Soto set a precedent the Spaniards would follow throughout their search. He decided to take advantage of the huge stores of food and spend the winter in the natives' well-stocked capital. Although the Apalaches constantly harassed the intruders, small groups of Spaniards scouted around the area and encountered the Bay of Horses, where Narváez had built his rafts eleven years before. Another party traveled by hastily constructed boats and found the excellent harbor of Pensacola Bay about two hundred miles to the west. Learning from a captive Indian that Cofitachequi, a province supposedly immersed in pearls and gold, lay to the northeast, De Soto decided to move his army there in the spring of 1540. The Spaniards departed from Anhayca in early March and traveled up the Flint River before crossing out of the Gulf South toward waters that flowed into the Atlantic Ocean about three weeks later. Following another month's travel northeastward, De Soto's force reached Cofitachequi, located on the Wateree River near present Camden, South Carolina. Although they did find freshwater pearls at the large Indian town, there was no gold. De Soto decided to push onward after only a couple weeks. In order to force the Indians' compliance, De Soto took the native leader hostage, thereby establishing another pattern the Spaniards would continue as they made their way through the region over the course of the next few years. The Cofitachequi queen led the Spaniards up the

Catawba River before slipping away as the travelers crossed the Blue Ridge Mountains and reentered the Gulf South region by way of the Tennessee River Valley.

In June they reached the Indian town of Chiaha on the French Broad River, the northernmost chiefdom that was subject to the paramount chief of Coosa. The residents of Chiaha allowed the Spaniards to rest for three weeks and then provided them with a peaceful entry into the principal town of Coosa, located along the Coosawattee River, which flowed southward toward the Gulf of Mexico. Despite the hospitality, De Soto seized the Coosa chief—who had welcomed the Spaniards in a "chair borne on the shoulders of his principal men, seated on a cushion, and covered with a robe of marten skins"—and put him and his followers in chains in order to ensure the good behavior of his tributaries. They also enslaved some of the Coosa commoners and forced them to serve as laborers. The Spaniards and their hostages continued down the Coosa until they reached the chiefdom of Tascalusa and its central town of Atahachi. Although the Tascalusa chief—a "very dignified" man, who was "greatly feared by his neighbors and vassals"—peacefully complied with De Soto's demands for women and laborers, thousands of his armed followers ambushed the Spaniards in mid-October after they entered the allied town of Mabila. The Indians initially had the advantage, killing twenty Spaniards and wounding about 150. However, the Spanish horses and armor allowed the invaders to withstand the ambush and to counterattack successfully. De Soto and his troops nursed their wounds at Mabila for about a month before heading northwest. In December the Spaniards crossed the Tombigbee River and took possession of the well-stocked town of Chicaza, where they spent a hard, cold winter being constantly harassed by the dislodged natives. Upon De Soto's abandonment of the village in March 1541, the Chicazas attacked the Spaniards and killed a dozen men as well as a number of pigs and horses.

Although many of the Spaniards were utterly demoralized and desired to give up and head for Mexico, De Soto doggedly pushed on in his quest to find a wealthy Indian kingdom. Heading northwest, the Spaniards encountered many towns and people in the area between the Yazoo River east of the Mississippi and the St. Francis River on the west bank, and unwittingly got involved in the warfare between the Pacaha and Casqui chiefdoms. Although this area contained some of the most complex societies that the Spaniards had encountered in all of their travels, none of the chiefdoms possessed the riches De Soto desired. Therefore, the Spaniards continued westward across the White River before reaching Tula on the Arkansas River near present Fort Smith in October. The Caddoan-speaking Tulas were different than the Mississippians the Spaniards had encountered since Apalache, for they resided in small, dispersed settlements and hunted buffalo in addition to deer. Realizing that little wealth lay to the west, De Soto turned back down the Arkansas and spent his third winter in North America at Utiangue, an Indian town near present-day Little Rock. Continuing down the river toward the Mississippi in the spring of 1542, De Soto learned from the local natives that no great cities like Tenochtitlán existed anywhere in the vicinity. Disheartened by this news, De Soto became ill and died in May.

De Soto's field marshal, Luís de Moscoso y Alvarado, took command of the three hundred or so surviving Spaniards, who agreed to give up their search for riches and attempt to reach Mexico by traveling overland. Heading west from the Mississippi, the group crossed the Ouachita River and reentered the Caddoan-speaking area. Continuing on through dense populations who unwillingly provided the Spaniards with food, Moscoso reached the Trinity River in October. Their Indian captives informed them that the groups to the west had no settled towns and did not practice agriculture. Understanding they would not be able to find the stores of corn on which they depended, the Spaniards reluctantly decided to retreat toward the Mississippi once again. The party spent the winter at Aminoya, a community near the Mississippi that consisted of two large palisaded towns about a mile apart and upstream from the mouth of the Arkansas. Forcibly occupying one of the towns, the Spaniards tore down the second to obtain building materials for additional houses and to construct boats. In July 1543 they began their journey toward Mexico and set sail down the Mississippi. Just above the mouth of the Yazoo River a fleet of one hundred large canoes from the chiefdom of Quigualtam, located on the east bank, attacked them. The Spaniards were able to elude this force, only to be assaulted by another fifty canoes farther downstream. The attackers gave up near Natchez, after which Moscoso and his men encountered no other Indians until they reached the Gulf of Mexico two weeks later. Unlike the Narváez expedition, Moscoso kept his small fleet together on the ocean, and they reached the Spanish settlement near the mouth of the Pánuco River in September, four years and four months after they had sailed from Havana.

Following a decade of inactivity in the region, the Spaniards renewed their interest in Florida during the 1550s, mainly in response to the French insistence that Giovanni da Verrazzano had claimed the Atlantic coast of North America for France in 1524. In order to more firmly establish Spanish possession of North America, the Council of the Indies put forth an ambitious plan in December 1557 calling for the landing of a large force at Pensacola Bay that would be sent inland to Coosa and eventually to Santa Elena, present Port Royal Sound, South Carolina, where Lucas Vázquez de Ayllón had established a short-lived colony in 1526. By stages, the Spaniards planned to build a chain of towns along a road that would connect the Gulf of Mexico and the Atlantic. The viceroy of New Spain named Tristán de Luna y Arellano, an Aragonese veteran of the 1539 Coronado expedition to New Mexico, to head the operation. The Luna expedition finally got under way in June 1559 when fifteen hundred people, including Mexican Indians, five hundred soldiers, settlers, and clergy, set sail from Veracruz in eleven ships.

Two months later the fleet reached Pensacola Bay, which Luna deemed to be one of the best ports yet discovered in America—"so secure that no wind could ever do any damage whatsoever." Luna was proved dramatically wrong in mid-September when a hurricane struck the unloaded fleet, still anchored in the bay. In addition to drowning many colonists, the storm sank seven ships and ruined most of the provisions. Realizing that the small local native population could not supply sufficient food, Luna sent out three expeditions to find Indian towns in the interior. One group, consisting of men who had marched through the region with De Soto in 1540, encountered Nanipacana, a town of about eighty houses, on the Alabama River not far from where the Mabila village had existed two decades earlier. Seeing no alternative, Luna ordered that the colony move from the coast to Nanipacana. By the time most of the colonists had relocated in spring 1560, however, the Indians had managed to hide what remained of their stored food, harvest the first corn crop, and flee, leaving the Spaniards with a largely uninhabited district. In April 1560, on the verge of starvation, Luna sent a troop of soldiers northward in the hope of locating the wealthy native province of Coosa. The Spanish force reached Coosa in July, traveling through many towns with extensive fields but encountering few people, as most of the Indians had left prior to the soldiers' arrival.

In the meantime Luna's officers rebelled, and the settlers at Nanipacana returned to Pensacola Bay, where they were soon joined by the troops who had ventured to Coosa. Learning of the disasters befalling the expedition, in early 1561 the viceroy sent Ángel de Villafañe to Pensacola with orders to take command and move the colonists, now reduced to only about three hundred people, to Santa Elena on the Atlantic Coast. Arriving in April, Villafañe took over from Luna and transferred over two hundred people to Havana, leaving seventy soldiers at Pensacola. Understandably, most of the Luna expedition's colonists chose not to accompany Villafañe to Santa Elena and remained in Cuba when four ships sailed north from Havana in the summer. Villafañe had no better luck than Luna, as he lost two ships in a storm upon arriving at Santa Elena, after which he retreated to Cuba and eventually withdrew the men from Pensacola as well.

Four years after Luna's dismal failure on the Gulf Coast of Florida, the Spaniards took steps to establish a more permanent presence on the Atlantic Coast. As a result of these efforts, Spanish soldiers and priests would return to the Gulf South in a more peaceful manner early in the following century. In March 1565 the Spanish Crown responded to the establishment of a French Huguenot colony at the mouth of the St. John's River near present-day Jacksonville by authorizing Pedro Menéndez de Avilés to remove the Gallic intruders and to found settlements in Florida. Within two years of receiving his contract, Menéndez had destroyed the French Protestant post and established the principal towns of Santa Elena and St. Augustine, in addition to five other small settlements on the Florida peninsula. However, over the course of the following two decades, neglect, Indian attacks, and English raids forced the Spaniards to abandon all of these settlements except for St. Augustine, which consisted of only a small garrison of troops and a few priests.

Franciscans among the Apalaches

In the meantime the character of the Spanish effort in the Western Hemisphere had changed dramatically. Having subjugated most of the wealthy Indian kingdoms in America through military force, in 1573 the Spanish Crown issued the Royal Orders for New Discoveries, giving missionaries the central role in the exploration and pacification of new lands. Preaching the holy Gospel to heathens theoretically became the principal purpose for new discoveries and settlements in America. Pacification rather than conquest would be the new order of the day, and missionaries, their expenses paid by the Crown, were to enter new lands before all others. The Royal Orders particularly benefited the Order of St. Francis, whose members had worked to seek Christian converts since the thirteenth century. The first Franciscans had come to America in 1493 and had been successful in converting the Indians of central Mexico following the conquest. By the late sixteenth century, however, the Crown cut costs by replacing the Franciscans with secular clergy—nonmonastic priests—and transformed the missions into self-supporting diocesan parishes. Dislodged from the settled region of central Mexico, the Franciscans were given the opportunity to move into fringe areas in North America that were marginal to the economic life of the Spanish empire and minister to the Indians without much competition from civilians, soldiers, or secular priests. As a result, over the course of the following century the Franciscans successfully transformed Florida into a colony whose main purpose was the evangelization of the indigenous tribes.

The Franciscan effort in Florida effectively got under way in 1595 when the missionaries began seeking converts among the Guale Indians along the present Georgia coast and the Timucuans, who lived near St. Augustine and in the interior of Florida. By 1608 the Franciscans had established six missions among the Guales and the Timucuans, and convinced the Spanish Crown to continue to provide an annual subsidy, or *situado,* to support the friars and the three hundred soldiers stationed at the capital of St. Augustine. Assured of continued royal backing, the Franciscans ambitiously expanded their work in Florida, and by 1630 thirty-three missions existed in the province, half of which were located in the Timucuan interior between the Suwannee and the Aucilla Rivers. Although the Indians struggled with the missionaries at times, their leaders accepted Christianity and colonization in return for personal prestige, gifts, payments, and the chance to be allied with the powerful Spaniards and their new religion. Embracing Catholicism offered a chief and his people access to the knowledge, abilities, and material goods that the Spaniards displayed.

The Franciscans' work in the Florida interior brought them into contact with the Timucuans' chief enemy, the Apalaches, in the early seventeenth century. In 1608 Father Martín Prieto and an entourage of Timucuans traveled to the Apalache town of Ivitachuco, just west of the Aucilla River, and met with over thirty thousand tribal members from one hundred or so towns. Seventy Apalache leaders accepted the priest's overtures for peace with the Spaniards and their Timucuan allies and sent the principal chief from Anhayca to St. Augustine to meet with the Spanish governor. The peace agreement allowed the Franciscans to establish more firmly their presence among the Timucuans and led to further contact with the Apalaches over the next quarter of a century. Throughout the 1620s the wealthy Apalaches sent corn to St. Augustine to help relieve the food shortages that the capital periodically faced. As a result of these exchanges, in 1633 the Apalaches allowed the Franciscans to establish a mission at Ivitachuco. Over the course of the next six years, two other missions were founded in Apalache, the most important being San Luís de Talimali at the principal town of Anhayca. In the 1640s the Apalaches agreed to the establishment of seven more Franciscan missions, with another one constructed in the following decade and a final mission added in the 1660s. In addition to the twelve Apalache missions, the Spaniards sent a deputy governor and a garrison of soldiers to the province. In order to make it easier to send supplies from St. Augustine and Havana to the isolated soldiers and missionaries in Apalache, in 1639 the Spaniards established a post, called San Marcos de Apalache, near the mouth of the St. Marks River, about twenty miles from San Luís de Talimali.

The goal of the Franciscan missions was to save the Apalache souls while shaping their minds and controlling their bodies, all in support of Spanish interests. The friars' strategy for Christianizing the Indians was first to convert and co-opt the chiefs and then to use the leaders' influence to convert their people. After successfully attaining this goal, the missionaries taught the Apalaches Catholic doctrine in addition to transforming their daily lives through the introduction of many items from the Spanish world. As a result, over the course of four decades of evangelization, by the late seventeenth century the Apalaches had transformed their world and, like many natives throughout the Western Hemisphere, had become moderately Hispanicized Christian Indian subjects of the Spanish Crown.

Throughout the Spanish empire it was standard procedure to favor and Hispanicize the native leaders, protecting their hereditary status and rank. In Apalache, the Franciscans obtained acceptance by regaling the leaders with gifts such as food, metal goods, European clothing, and symbols of office. After gaining the approval of the principal town's elites, the friars established a mission in the main plaza opposite the native council house. The twelve Apalache missions that existed by mid-century were called *doctrinas,* and they featured churches where religious doctrine was taught to Indian villagers. Generally, only one resident friar lived at each doctrina, but he periodically traveled to the principal town's satellite villages, called *visitas,* to celebrate mass and indoctrinate the inhabitants. For instance, the friar at San Luís de Talimali was responsible for about fourteen hundred people, including the three or four satellite villages that lay outside of the doctrina. In each doctrina, Apalache villagers constructed churches while working under the watch of the Franciscan friars. Most churches combined native techniques with Spanish ones, including the use of iron tools and hardware. In contrast with the Apalaches' round dwellings, the churches were rectangular buildings with peaked roofs supported by wooden wall beams and interior support posts. The walls were made of whitewashed wattle and daub, the roofs consisted of palm or palmetto fronds, while the floors were packed earth and clay. Whereas most of the churches in Apalache were about sixty by thirty-five feet, San Luís de Talimali, the principal village for the province, was nearly twice that size and was the largest mission in all of Florida.

Once the church was constructed, the Franciscan friar attempted to Christianize and Hispanicize his Apalache flock, which often consisted of more than one thousand people per missionary. Working first with the elites and their children, the friars achieved their greatest successes with the second generation of converts. Apalache children were taught the catechism and baptized as Catholics, just as steeped in the faith as other Spaniards and Indians throughout the empire. A few tribespeople learned to read and write, and many Apalaches took Christian first names while maintaining their native surnames, as in the case of Patricio Hinachuba, chief of Ivitachuco. The friars denounced Apalache practices such as multiple wives, and by mid-century most tribal members had accepted the idea of monogamy. By the late seventeenth century, as cloth became more prevalent in Florida, most Apalaches had abandoned traditional deerskin clothing and had adopted Hispanicized forms of dress. Due to the Franciscan ministrations, observers characterized the Apalaches as being "good Catholics who attended Sunday mass dressed in silk cloaks and cloth overcoats."

In other material matters, the Spanish intrusion had its greatest impact in agriculture—not so much in changing the Apalaches' methods of farming or their basic crops, but in enriching them. In addition to traditional corn, beans, and squash, under the Spanish influence the Apalaches began raising European vegetables, such as wheat, barley, and chickpeas in addition to establishing peach orchards and vineyards. Metal farm implements such as hoes, plows, axes, and knives made it easier for the Apalaches to plant and harvest the crops. The Franciscans also provided the Apalaches with domesticated animals. Soon after the establishment of peace with the Timucuans in 1608, the Apalaches obtained hogs and chickens through trade with their new allies. Cattle arrived with the missionaries in the 1630s, and by mid-century the Apalaches had become herdsmen who had learned how to make tallow, ham, and bacon. The Franciscans also taught the women how to manufacture lard, butter, and jerky. Horses were the last domesticated animal to be brought into Apalache, but they were never numerous.

The friars also introduced new crafts and skills to the Apalaches. Because of their distance from St. Augustine, the Franciscans established a few forges and taught some of the natives the practice of blacksmithing. As a result, the Indians learned to repair small iron tools and forge nails and spikes for construction projects. Larger metal tools, such as saws, augurs, and chisels, were sent from the capital, allowing the Apalaches to develop further their skills in carpentry, as evidenced in the construction of the churches and meeting houses. Although the Apalaches were already experienced leather tanners, the Spanish presence enhanced their abilities through the introduction of new methods. On the other hand, the Franciscans had little impact on the making and use of pottery, and the friars adopted the Apalaches' fine earthenware cooking and eating utensils. Although Spanish policy attempted to restrict the natives' access to guns, most of the Apalache leaders were able to obtain firearms. The majority of the warriors continued to rely on the traditional bow and arrow, while also carrying metal hatchets and knives.

Despite the religious and technological innovations the Franciscans introduced to the Apalaches, there were serious drawbacks to the Spanish presence on the Florida Gulf Coast. One problem was work, as the Franciscan friars in Florida tapped into the native labor and tribute system known as the *sabana*. Prior to contact with the Spaniards, it was the prerogative of the Apalache chiefs to demand that their vassal villagers provide labor for various projects, such as mound building and planting fields especially for the use of the principal leaders and their families. With the acquiescence of the chiefs, Spanish authorities expanded the sabana system to include fields for themselves. The Franciscans, who had introduced the Indians to new agricultural tools, techniques, and crops, quickly went to the head of the line of sabana system beneficiaries. Although the rich soil between the Aucilla and the Ochlockonee provided the Apalaches with more than enough food for the priests and the soldiers who began to arrive in the 1630s, the commoners also had to provide the friars with periodic labor as "service to the convent." Men hunted and fished for the Franciscans and acted as boatmen, guides, bodyguards, and couriers. Women and children collected firewood, prepared food, and cleaned the church and its grounds for the priests. While the onerous service to the convent at least allowed the Apalaches to remain near their homes, the Spanish officials also implemented a labor draft, or *repartimiento,* that required a few men from each village to travel to St. Augustine on a rotating basis to work for months at a time on various projects to support the governor and the soldiers. Apalache women complained bitterly about the departure of their husbands for such long periods, and a number of the men did die while working at the capital.

The Apalaches found their duties as cargo bearers for the Spaniards even more demanding and degrading than the sabana or the repartimiento. Provisioning the friars was a major exercise in logistics, as their annual supplies had to be transported across the peninsula from St. Augustine. Because Florida lacked horses and mules early in the seventeenth century, Indians were forced to carry the heavy burdens for the Franciscans. Not only did they transport goods from the capital, the Apalaches also took their own province's products to St. Augustine as part of the annual sabana. At first Apalache men carried cargo on their backs from St. Augustine along the royal road that the Spaniards established from the capital through the Timucua province and on to the Aucilla River. Indian towns were established about every twenty miles along the road so that the burdeners had a place to rest and eat after a long day's journey. By mid-century a partially amphibious route was opened, as goods were transported from St. Augustine overland to the Suwannee River, where they were transferred to canoes and floated downstream to the Gulf of Mexico before they entered the St. Marks River to be unloaded in Apalache province. Although the burdeners were paid a small amount for their labor, the work was socially demeaning as well as tremendously hard. The bearers often suffered from cold and hunger, and many died while on the trips from the missions to St. Augustine.

In the middle of the seventeenth century the Apalaches responded violently to the Spaniards' increasing labor demands. In 1645 Governor Benito Ruíz de Salazar established a wheat farm and cattle ranch just east of the Aucilla River. Although the operation was located in Timucuan territory, Apalache men constituted most of the native work force. Salazar, like a few of the Franciscan friars, used the Apalache labor not only to work on his farm and ranch, but also to transport the produce to San Marcos de Apalache, where it was loaded on ships and transported illegally to Havana rather than St. Augustine. Disgruntled by the Spanish officials' labor demands, in February 1647 a group of Apalaches who had yet to accept Christianity rose up and killed three friars along with the governor's lieutenant and his family. They also burned seven churches located in their territory. The surviving Franciscans and soldiers retreated eastward, where Spanish troops and Timucuan allies had gathered to counterattack. Before this force reached Apalache, a much larger rebel group engaged them in a nine-hour struggle that resulted in a Spanish-Timucuan victory. Soon thereafter the Christian Apalache converts convinced the rebels to surrender and allow the Franciscans and soldiers to return. By February 1648 all seven burned churches had been rebuilt. Over the course of the following decade most of the recalcitrant Apalaches converted to Christianity, and many tribesmen joined with Spanish troops to put down a Timucuan rebellion in 1656.

Despite the establishment of peace and the nearly universal acceptance of Christianity and Hispanicization, the Apalache population continued to decline following the Timucuan rebellion. Whereas thirty thousand or so Apalaches had greeted the first Franciscans in the early seventeenth century, by 1670 their population had declined by two-thirds to about ten thousand, mainly from disease. Throughout the seventeenth century a series of epidemics, including smallpox and measles, struck Florida as the colony was brought into increasing contact with the Atlantic World. Ships landing at St. Augustine delivered the germs to Florida, which were then distributed through the colony by native cargo bearers delivering supplies to the missions. Ironically, the Spanish-instituted peace between the Apalaches, Timucuans, and Guales had erased traditional buffer zones, thus allowing people and deadly germs to travel freely across the peninsula. Not only did the chain of missions heighten the opportunities for the Indians to become exposed to new diseases, the intensified labor demands further deteriorated health and diminished the ability to fight off infection. In addition to epidemic disease, part of the Apalache depopulation was simply the result of flight, as many tribal members ran away from the Catholic missions.

Seventeenth-Century Native Migrations

Most of the Apalache runaways headed north into the Gulf South interior, an area that had experienced profound changes since the Spaniards had last visited in the mid-sixteenth century. De Soto's entrada had destabilized many of the region's chiefdoms, accelerating the decline that the Mississippian world had been experiencing since the fourteenth century.

With only a few exceptions, most chiefdoms collapsed from depopulation by the beginning of the 1600s, resulting in the end of mound building, a leveling of the social and political hierarchy, and migrations and regroupings throughout the region. For instance, toward the end of the sixteenth century the people of Coosa abandoned northern Georgia and began a series of southward movements as the hierarchical chiefdom organization crumbled. For nearly a century the people of the chiefdom migrated farther down the Coosa River every thirty years or so, concentrating the decreasing population into fewer towns with each relocation. By the late 1600s they had established several villages on the Coosa along the ecotone boundary, about fifty miles upstream from its junction with the Tallapoosa. Abihka, which had been subject to Coosa in the 1500s, was at the center of this province, and the descendants of the former paramount chiefdom would be known by this name in the future.

The Mabila and Tascalusa chiefdoms collapsed at about the same time as Coosa. Sometime in the early seventeenth century most of the people from the former chiefdom moved downstream into the Mobile-Tensaw delta, where they became part of the tribe known as the Mobilians. Located nearby was a group called the Tohomes, who, like the Mobilians, established agricultural villages on small bluffs overlooking the delta. They were situated close enough to the coast to take advantage of its rich fishing sources but far enough away to be protected from spring floods and autumn hurricanes. The Pascagoulas, Biloxis, and Moctobis, who resided between Mobile Bay and the Pearl River to the west, lived in settlements similar to those of the Mobilians and Tohomes. By the late 1600s the five tribes consisted of about eight thousand people.

Most of Tascalusa's inhabitants, on the other hand, remained in various towns located near the juncture of the Coosa and the Tallapoosa Rivers. In the mid-1600s Alabama-speaking refugees from the simple chiefdoms located along the Tombigbee River moved eastward and joined the Tascalusans, establishing the towns of Pakana and Mucclassa, among others. Soon thereafter Koasati-speaking relatives from the Coste chiefdom of the Tennessee Valley—former members of the Coosa paramount chiefdom—established the village of Coushatta among this group, which became known collectively as the Alabamas. The people of Talisi, yet another chiefdom formerly tied to Coosa, remained along the Lower Tallapoosa River following its decline in the late sixteenth century. In the 1600s a collection of towns, such as Tallassee and Tukabatchee, were established in the bend of the river to the east, forming the group that would be called

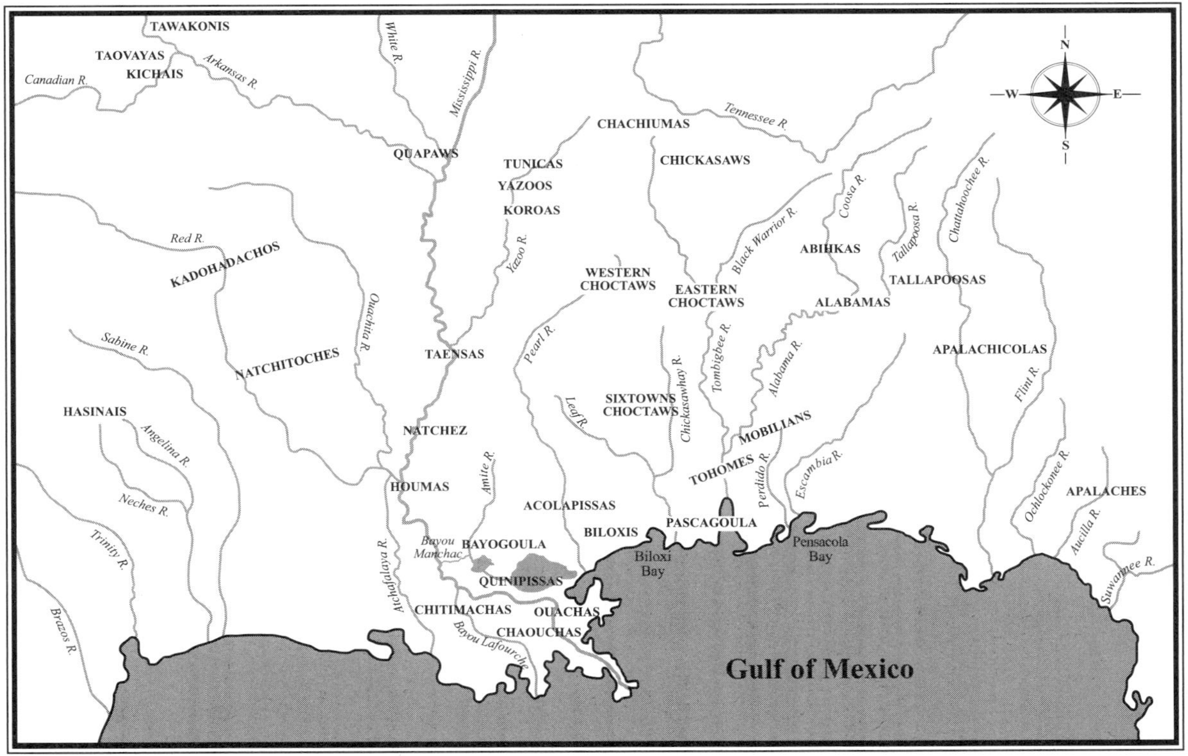

MAP 2. THE GULF SOUTH, CA. 1700

the Tallapoosas. Together, the Abihkas, Alabamas, and Tallapoosas would become collectively known as the Upper Creek Indians.

Muskogeans from other fallen chiefdoms established towns to the east of the Upper Creeks along the Chattahoochee River. In the late sixteenth century the Hitchiti-speakers living on the Chattahoochee abandoned several mound sites and moved a bit farther down the river to settle in smaller villages. At about the same time Eastern Muskogean speakers from the Cussita chiefdom, previously located on the lower reaches of the Coosa River and subject to the influence of Tascalusa, began to migrate eastward toward the Chattahoochee. Following a period during which they resided on the Lower Tallapoosa River, in the early 1600s the Cussitas moved to the Chattahoochee and established towns on the northern frontier of the Hitchiti's domain. In the mid-seventeenth century a group known as the Cowetas followed their Cussita kinsmen and moved from central Alabama to the Chattahoochee, with both peoples establishing town sites on abandoned mounds located on either side of the river near present Columbus, Georgia. Eventually the Hitchitis and Eastern Muskogeans would join into one multilingual polity that became known as Apalachicola, which would later become the core nucleus of the group known as the Lower Creeks. Despite the huge population losses, by the latter half of the 1600s about ten thousand people still lived along the Chattahoochee River, while twice as many people resided among the Upper Creeks.

The Creek culture that emerged out of the Mississippian system that preceded it was similar to that of most other Gulf South Indian groups of the period. The Creeks deemphasized the cult of the chief in favor of establishing the balance and the harmony of the group. One of the most important changes that came out of the Mississippian collapse for the Creeks and others was the enhanced importance of individual towns. Creek towns, or *talwas,* of which there were about sixty by the late seventeenth century, were essentially autonomous political entities, each with its own political hierarchy, free to make independent political decisions. Each town contained a ceremonial plaza, which included a ball yard, enclosed by four buildings. The town chief, known as a *mico,* resided in the building located on the western side of the plaza, which was a much more accessible and egalitarian public space than the platform mounds of the earlier era. The micos were supported by a group of secondary chiefs, as well as a *fani miço,* or "Squirrel King," who served as the town's official ambassador. Although the political offices continued to be hereditary in nature, and passed through the maternal line, the Creeks generally came to decisions through consensus. In keeping with the relatively egalitarian nature of the post-Mississippian system, the Creek mico was indistinguishable in dress and appearance from other tribal members. In addition to towns, Creeks and the other Gulf South Indians were divided into clans, extended kinship networks of families traced through the female line. People of the same matrilineal clan had strong, proscribed relations and obligations to one another, one of the deepest being to avenge the death of a fellow member. Clan leaders, as well as political headmen, controlled most ceremonial and luxury goods, and distributed them to the rest of their lineage, thereby reinforcing the ties among kin.

The experience of the Chicazas was similar to that of the Creeks following the De Soto entrada of the mid-sixteenth century. Due to population loss, the chief-based hierarchy broke down and the ancestors of the modern Chickasaws migrated from the bottomlands of the Tombigbee River northward to settle in the upland areas along the Black Prairie in Lee County, Mississippi. The Chickasaws were culturally and politically similar to the Creeks, but spoke a western variant of the Muskogean language. By the late seventeenth century about ten thousand Chickasaws lived in twenty or so villages situated along the ridge that separates Kings Creek from Town Creek, western tributaries of the Tombigbee River located near present Tupelo. Closely associated with the Chickasaws were the Chachiumas, a group of about two thousand people who resided in towns to the west along the Upper Yazoo River.

Whereas most of the descendants of the chiefdoms located along the Tombigbee, Alabama, and Chattahoochee Rivers migrated within the region following the Spanish entradas, the people living in the great chiefdoms of the central Mississippi Valley—Casqui, Pacaha, Quiguate, Quizquiz, and Aminoya, among others—abandoned the area altogether and moved southward. By the late seventeenth century a group of Tunican-speakers, who were probably the descendants of several of the fallen chiefdoms, had settled in villages along the Yazoo River about thirty miles above its mouth. Although they spoke a different language than their Muskogean neighbors, the five thousand or so Tunicas, Yazoos, and Koroas had a culture and political system that was similar to those of the Creeks and Chickasaws. Just downstream from the mouth of the Yazoo, about five thousand Natchezan-speaking Taensa Indians lived in eight to ten villages located on an ox-bow lake a few miles west of the Mississippi.

The Taensa towns surrounded a ceremonial mound center, and the tribe shared a culture and language with the Natchez Indians, who lived about fifty miles downstream on the opposite side of the Mississippi.

The Natchez were descendants of the powerful Quigualtam paramount chiefdom. Although Quigualtam declined during the late sixteenth century, the fall was not as steep as in the other Mississippian chiefdoms, and the hierarchical structure remained intact by the late 1600s. Following the De Soto entrada Natchez-speakers maintained populated villages near five mound centers, including Emerald Mound, the second largest earthwork in North America. Over the course of a century, however, the population dropped to about six thousand people, and four mounds were abandoned, leaving only the Grand Village of the Natchez, located on St. Catherine's Creek about ten miles upstream from the Mississippi River, as the capital center. The Natchez leader, called the Great Sun, was similar in power and stature to a Mississippian chief, lived at the Grand Village, and had supreme jurisdiction over the tribe's civil affairs. The Great Sun's brother, called the Tattooed Serpent, conducted diplomacy and also resided at the capital mound center. Both men were members of a hereditary elite who, like the Mississippian nobles of the previous century, were supported by the common people who resided in the nearby Flour and Tioux villages. Other nobles ruled over commoners at the White Apple, Grigra, and Jenzenaque villages, located a few miles to the east along the headwaters of St. Catherine's and Fairchild's Creeks. Although these settlement districts were allied with the Grand Village, their Suns maintained a large degree of political autonomy, in the manner of a Mississippian simple chiefdom.

Newcomers from outside the Gulf South moved into the abandoned central Mississippi Valley at some point in the early seventeenth century. Prior to 1650 or so a large group of farming Dhegiha Siouan-speaking people migrated from the Ohio River to the Mississippi Valley, forced out of their homeland by Indians armed with weapons obtained from Dutch, French, and English colonies located on the Atlantic Coast. Whereas the Dhegihan groups known as the Osages, Kansas, Omahas, and Poncas moved up the Missouri River and established towns along its tributaries, the Quapaws began cultivating the extremely rich soils located near the juncture of the Arkansas and Mississippi Rivers, where the Aminoya and Guachoya chiefdoms had once stood. By the late seventeenth century about five thousand Quapaws lived in three villages—Kappa, Osotouy, and Tourima—located on the west bank of the Mississippi, while the town of Tonginga lay just across the river. In contrast to the descendants of the

Mississippian chiefdoms, the Quapaws were patrilineal, and decision-making was shared broadly among the egalitarian community, and no hereditary elite directed the population. However, the Quapaws were similar to the Mississippians in that the women were accomplished horticulturalists, raising three different corn crops a year, in addition to beans, squash, and melons. Quapaw men hunted game, including buffalo, bear, white-tailed deer, and fowl in the forested regions near their villages. The Quapaws also brought to their new home the calumet ceremony, a ritual that was used to create and sanctify alliances and other forms of friendly relations. The ceremony consisted of the communal smoking of the pipe, or calumet, along with a feast, gift exchanges, and dances, which served to extend fictive kinship ties to esteemed outsiders. By the late seventeenth century most of the Lower Mississippi Valley Indians began including the calumet ceremony in their own diplomatic rituals.

Among these groups were seven distinct Western Muskogean-speaking tribes, numbering perhaps fifteen thousand people, who occupied the lower reaches of the Mississippi River. The Houmas resided on the east bank bluff overlooking the large bend in the Mississippi just below its junction with the Red River. In the fields surrounding their villages, Houma women raised staple native crops, while the men hunted in the uplands on both sides of the Mississippi downstream for about fifty miles. Near the present site of Baton Rouge stood a tall pole painted red with fish heads and bear bones tied to it, signifying the boundary between the hunting grounds of the Houmas and those of the Bayougoulas, who lived in villages located along the Mississippi near the mouth of Bayou Lafourche. A group known as the Acolapissas lived east of the Houmas in the area between the Mississippi and Pearl Rivers north of Lake Pontchartrain, while the Chitimachas resided between Bayou Lafourche and the Atchafalaya River to the west. The Quinipissas lived along the Mississippi downstream from Bayou Manchac to the vicinity of the future site of New Orleans. Two tribes, the Ouachas and the Chaouachas, inhabited the southernmost banks of the Mississippi downstream from the Quinipissas, maintaining their villages on the natural levees formed by sediment deposited during annual flooding. These groups also hunted and fished in the lakes and bayous west of the Mississippi toward Bayou Lafourche.

By the mid-1600s about twenty thousand Caddoan speakers, descendants of Spiro and Tula who would come to be known as the Wichitas, had settled in present eastern Oklahoma. Three major Wichita groups—the Taovayas, Tawakonis, and Kichais—established agricultural settlements along the Arkansas River just upstream from its junction with the Canadian. The Wichitas used their recently obtained horses—spread throughout North America from New Mexico, a Spanish colony established in 1598—to travel west to the nearby plains to hunt buffalo and to enter the Ozark and Ouachita Mountains to the east. Fearing the newly arrived Dhegiha Siouan-speaking Osages, who settled to the east in the prairies on the headwaters of the Osage River in Missouri, the Wichitas began to arrange their grass houses in compact villages surrounded by stockades and ditches, as the Mississippians had done in the previous era. Nonetheless, the Wichitas' political system had become relatively open and egalitarian, with each village headed by a chief chosen for his leadership and physical prowess by a council of warriors.

In contrast to their Wichita linguistic kinsmen, the fifteen thousand or so remaining Caddos continued to maintain a political-religious system dominated by a hereditary elite, much in the same manner as the Natchez. By the late seventeenth century the Caddos resided in three collections of villages located in the forested region between the Red and Neches Rivers in western Louisiana and eastern Texas. The group known as the Kadohadachos lived in towns established near the bend of the Red River around present Texarkana, while the Natchitoches clustered in villages located two hundred miles downstream in Louisiana. The largest Caddo assemblage, the Hasinais, lived to the west along the upper reaches of the Neches and Angelina Rivers in Texas. A paramount religious authority, known as the *xinesí,* presided over each of the three Caddo groups, residing in a temple complex with a sacred fire that was maintained by commoners. Whereas each Caddo group followed the spiritual guidance of its own xinesí, a hereditary chief, or *caddí,* along with a group of advisers known as *canahas,* presided over each individual village. In recognition of these authority positions, commoners followed a protocol of deference and obligation that included supplying the elites with food and other provisions, as well as yielding to authorities who organized community-wide activities such as house building and planting. As with the Wichitas, by the late 1600s the Caddos had also incorporated horses into their economy, using them to expand their hunting range westward to the plains region inhabited by huge herds of buffalo.

Despite the huge population losses incurred by the Gulf South Indians during the century and a half that followed the initial Spanish intrusion, over one hundred thousand natives continued to thrive in the region by 1670. Unfortunately for the Gulf South's residents, however, new Europeans and Africans would arrive over the course of the following four decades, bringing death and destruction that reduced the Indian population even further. This decline in indigenous numbers would enable the Old World newcomers to form permanent settlements in the Gulf South during the early eighteenth century, forcing the remaining Indians to dramatically alter their culture just in order to survive.

2

Initial European Settlements, 1670–1712

Europeans established their first long-lasting colonies in the Gulf South during the four decades after 1670, as Frenchmen built a small settlement on Mobile Bay and Spaniards successfully erected a fort to the east on Pensacola Bay while failing in their effort to establish missions in East Texas. Nonetheless, the English colony of Carolina, established on the Atlantic Coast in 1670, had a much greater impact on the region than the small French and Spanish outposts. Carolinians—the colony was not divided between North and South until 1729—initiated trade with the large interior tribes, who then used their new European weapons to conduct raids throughout the Gulf South, obtaining Indian women and children to be sold as slaves to the English plantations located near Charleston and in the West Indies. The slave trade greatly weakened the Gulf South tribes—including the slave raiders—who succumbed to a smallpox epidemic that swept through the area in the late 1690s, reducing their numbers even further. Warfare continued to plague the Gulf South in the early eighteenth century, as the English used indigenous allies to attack their European enemies at Mobile, Pensacola, and Apalache. By the end of the period—when violence in the Gulf South caused by the War of the Spanish Succession came to an end—Apalache had been completely destroyed while the French at Mobile and the Spaniards at Pensacola struggled just to survive.

British Carolina

Although the English began exploring throughout the Western Hemisphere soon after the return of Columbus in 1493, successful colonization did not take place until after Queen Elizabeth I calmed the country's religious strife, caused by the Protestant Reformation, in the late sixteenth century. Following the queen's death in 1603 her Scottish Stuart successor, James I, authorized the Virginia Company to establish a colony on Chesapeake Bay. Although Virginia struggled during its first decade, the settlers eventually learned from the local Indians how to raise tobacco, which became the colony's economic mainstay by 1620. Over the course of the next five decades thousands of British people arrived in Virginia as indentured servants to work on tobacco plantations. A few hundred Africans were also brought to the Chesapeake, where they toiled as slaves alongside the indentured servants and Indian bondspeople, obtained through trade with Virginia's indigenous allies. The tobacco boom led other English companies to develop colonies on small Caribbean islands—ignored by the Spaniards following the conquest of Mexico—such as Barbados, St. Kitts, Nevis, and Jamaica. These colonies initially employed indentured servants to raise the increasingly unprofitable crop of tobacco, but by the middle of the seventeenth century British planters in the West Indies had converted to the cultivation of high-priced sugar and were using black slaves brought by Dutch traders who had recently taken over Portuguese posts in West Africa. By 1660 or so sugar plantations covered most of the small English islands in the Caribbean, causing settlers to search elsewhere in the Western Hemisphere for lands that might yield sugar or other profitable crops. Despite their growing number of colonies, the English—in direct contrast to the Spaniards—did little to establish central institutions such as the Council of the Indies to direct overseas expansion.

The English became involved in the Gulf South region of North America in 1663 when King Charles II issued a royal charter establishing the boundaries of Carolina as stretching north from the Florida peninsula to Virginia and west from the Atlantic Ocean to the Pacific, despite the grant's overlap of Spanish territorial claims. The king then gave control of the province to eight of his closest friends and supporters—the Lords Proprietors of Carolina—who soon authorized several voyages of exploration to ascertain the best ways to start settling, subduing, and exploiting their new colonial possession. These efforts resulted in the establishment of Charleston at the junction of the Ashley and Cooper Rivers in 1670, leading to the arrival of colonists in Carolina soon thereafter. The first English settlers largely hailed from other colonies, namely Barbados in the West Indies, and they moved to Carolina in search of rich land and commercial opportunities, looking to use their African slave laborers to produce goods for export and profit. Establishing commercial agricultural enterprises, however, took a long time as the land needed to be cleared, crops planted, and seed experimented with until colonists found what would thrive in the Carolina soil. Furthermore, the cultivation of staples for export meant that labor had to be purchased, which in turn required capital. To obtain revenue, the colonists looked to the Indian trade, where investments brought quicker returns. Soon after the arrival of the first colonists in Carolina, a commerce developed with the region's natives in which English manufactured goods were exchanged for animal skins and Indian slaves, which were then turned into needed capital and commodities to develop a plantation system. Thus, slavery lay at the heart of Carolina's economy, as captured Indians could be used either as laborers within the colony or as commodities to sell in order to acquire capital, or even more highly valued African chattel. Although Carolina's colonists, who included large numbers from Scotland, did not settle very far from the Atlantic Coast, by the 1690s the colony's Indian slave trade would affect, in various ways, native groups as far west as East Texas.

The region's Indians readily accepted the Carolinians' demands for indigenous slaves, as they all had traditionally taken captives from enemy tribes for numerous purposes. By returning to their villages with enemies taken alive, male warriors gained considerable status. Tribes usually tortured and killed male captives in a ritual ceremony that allowed the community to avenge the loss of kinsmen, while the group often adopted captive women and children in order to replace lost tribal members. Whereas English traders had little interest in male Indian captives, as they made troublesome slaves, the desire for trade goods and material gain gave indigenous raiders deep incentives to seize females and children in far greater numbers than they had prior to contact with the newcomers. Plus, there were strong incentives for Indian captors, as they were richly rewarded by their efforts in the slave raids. Manufactured woolen clothing and blankets replaced native-made buckskins and furs, while a variety of durable metal goods and weapons took the place of hard-to-fashion and easily breakable stone tools, knives, and arrowheads. Although guns, powder, and shot were not necessarily more effective than bows and arrows, firearms offered indigenous peoples an important labor-saving device. Nearly all Indians eagerly accepted the benefits provided by European manufactured goods not only for material reasons, but for political ones as well, as the trade allowed a wider array of the natives to acquire exotic goods, which consequently weakened chiefly authority.

The newly arrived Carolinians quickly became involved in the Indian slave trade through dealing with a tribe called the Westos, an Iroquoian-speaking group who had migrated from New Holland to the Savannah River in 1659. Using weapons provided by Virginia merchants, the armed Westos began attacking defenseless Muskogean towns located along the Oconee and Ocmulgee Rivers in present-day Georgia to obtain slaves for their trading partners in England's original colony. Seeking to redirect the commerce in Indian slaves toward Charleston, Henry Woodward, a representative of the Lords Proprietors, established a trading partnership with the Westos in 1674. As a result of the alliance with Carolina, over the next five years the Westos stepped up their raids on the region's Indians, extending their reach to the Muskogean villages on the Chattahoochee River as well as terrorizing the Spanish mission provinces of Timucua and Guale, the latter of which the Spaniards abandoned soon thereafter. In 1680, however, Carolinian independent traders wiped out the Westos in their successful bid to break the Proprietors' monopoly of the Indian slave trade. The traders then established a post on the north bank of the Savannah River across from present Augusta, Georgia. Various groups of Indians, such as the Yamasees, Yuchis, and Shawnees, who had previously been victims of Westo raids, now moved to the Savannah River to become agents of Carolina's growing slave trade empire.

The Westos' attacks led to great changes among the Muskogean villages along the Chattahoochee River, in what the Spaniards called Apalachicola province. In the 1670s Muskogeans from the Oconee and Ocmulgee Valleys took refuge with their kinsmen after fleeing westward to escape Westo raids, as did small groups of Timucuans and Guales from Spanish Florida. Although many of the Chattahoochee Valley residents had been victims of the Carolina slave trade, in 1677 the Muskogeans welcomed Woodward into their villages and established a truce in order to prevent further raiding and to establish trade. Within a few years the Indians of Apalachicola and the Carolinians were regularly engaging in commerce through the Savannah River middlemen, an exchange that included slaves obtained from tribes located farther south and west, many coming from the Christian Indians residing in the Spanish Franciscan mission province of Apalache.

The residents of Apalache boldly responded to the Carolinian-inspired threat. The Spaniards, who had maintained intermittent contact with the Muskogean towns along the Chattahoochee River since mid-century, gained direct influence in the interior in 1675 by establishing three missions among the Apalachicolas near the confluence of the Flint River. The following year the Apalaches conducted a retaliatory campaign against British-supplied Indians in the Chattahoochee Valley. Within Apalache the Franciscans established additional missions for various Indian groups, including a few Yamasees and Chacatos, who had fled to the region to escape Westo slave raiders. Officials also allowed civilians to settle in Apalache for the first time, and soon there were a number of Spanish ranches in the province. In 1677, to accommodate and protect the growing commerce of Apalache, the Spaniards fortified San Marcos de Apalache and placed the presidio at the confluence of the Wakulla and St. Marks Rivers.

Despite the Spanish attempt to gain control of Apalachicola and the Chattahoochee Valley, British commerce caused the region's Indians to turn against the Franciscans and toward their Carolina trading partners. In 1679 the Cowetas, whose close ties to the British traders had made them the leading town among the Chattahoochee River Indians, convinced the Apalachicolas to throw the missionaries out of their province and force them to return to Apalache. Two years later the Spaniards tried to reestablish the missions, only to have the Apalachicolas violently reject them once again. In 1685 the tensions in the region accelerated when Yamasee Indians conducted Woodward and a party of British traders to the Chattahoochee River, where the Indians allowed the Carolinians to erect two trading posts on the northern frontier of Apalachicola near the Coweta village. Threatened by the direct British intrusion into a province claimed by Spain, Lieutenant Antonio Matheos led expeditions to Apalachicola in September 1685 and January 1686 to capture the traders and restore the Indians to their proper "obedience." The Apalachicolas responded by fleeing their towns and hiding the traders from the Spanish troops. In retaliation, Matheos burned four villages, causing a generations-long breach between the Apalachicolas and Spain.

The Spaniards continued to act with impunity in the Chattahoochee Valley, driving the residents into an even closer alliance with their Carolina trading partners. In the fall of 1689 Spanish troops and their Apalache allies constructed a fort near the Coweta village to inhibit the British traders. The Cowetas and Cussitas responded the following spring by abandoning their towns and moving about one hundred miles eastward to the Ocmulgee River—what the British at the time called Ochese Creek—near present Macon, Georgia. Over the course of the following year, the other Apalachicola tribes also moved to Ochese Creek, as did a few Muskogeans from the Tallapoosa River. The new location gained the "Ocheses," or "Creeks," as the British came to call the various groups who inhabited the area, easier access to Carolina traders and their wares. From Ochese Creek, the Indians commenced a protracted war against Spanish Florida in order to acquire prisoners for the lucrative slave trade with Carolina. The Ocheses launched their first series of attacks just a few short months after the Coweta and Cussita exodus, when they joined the Yamasees and British in a raid on the Franciscan missions in Timucua province. In 1691 the Ocheses expanded their range to include the Christian Indians of Apalache. Although a force of four hundred Apalaches and a few Spanish soldiers directly attacked the Ochese Creek settlements in December 1694, it did nothing to stem the tide of their enemies' slave raids. The result was a severe depopulation of Timucua and Apalache, as many residents were killed, taken prisoner, or forced to take refuge in the woods.

With the collapse of the Ochese Creeks' relations with the Spaniards, Carolina expanded its commercial influence to the Abihkas, Tallapoosas, and Alabamas living along the Coosa and Tallapoosa Rivers. Since many of the area's native residents were related to the inhabitants of Ochese Creek, the British came to call them Creeks as well, and eventually "Upper Creeks" to distinguish them from the "Lower Creeks," who lived closer to Carolina. Through their ties with the Ocheses, Carolina traders steadily escalated their activities with the Upper Creeks in the 1690s by opening up a trade route that became known as the "Upper Path." Soon after the British began to trade directly with the Muskogean towns located near the Coosa and Tallapoosa Rivers, they also incorporated the Chickasaws into their network by extending the Upper Path to their villages on the Tombigbee River.

Throughout the final decade of the seventeenth century the well-armed Upper Creeks and Chickasaws conducted numerous slaving expeditions that laid waste to the many groups of Indians living along the major waterways to the south, from Mobile Bay to the Mississippi River near the Gulf Coast, as well as to the west, from the Pearl River all the way to the Neches in East Texas. In the quarter of a century following the British arrival on the South Atlantic coast in 1670, perhaps as many as twenty-five thousand Indians were captured from their villages and sold into slavery in Carolina. Aside from the sheer numbers taken, the slave trade added to the indigenous population loss by selectively removing women and children from their communities, thereby lessening reproductive rates and making it difficult to recover. Demographic losses were even more severe due to the violence and chaos associated with slaving activities. Countless men lost their lives defending their communities, while heightened warfare forced the residents to maintain compact settlements, leaving fields unplanted or their crops unharvested. Hunger increased, as men were more likely to stay at home to protect their communities rather than venture out into the dangerous hunting grounds. Already depleted and weakened, the Gulf South Indians were vulnerable to disease by the last decade of the seventeenth century, as the number of Europeans in the region only continued to increase.

Initial French Explorations

While the British traders made inroads into the Gulf South from the east, Frenchmen and Spaniards entered the region from the north and west. As with England, France did not begin to establish colonies in the Western Hemisphere until settling the problems caused by the Protestant Reformation. Following the accession of Henri IV to the French Crown in 1589, the Bourbon Huguenot converted to Catholicism and issued the Edict of Nantes in 1598, providing for religious toleration and ending the Wars of Religion in France. In 1603 the French Crown began to grant monopoly companies the right to settle in Acadia, along the Bay of Fundy, and in New France, along the St. Lawrence River. A few French families established farms and ranches in Acadia near Port Royal, and the entire population of the province stood at only about five hundred by the mid-seventeenth century. Samuel de Champlain founded the town of Quebec on the St. Lawrence River in 1608 and, for the first few decades of its existence, the Company of New France established commerce with the region's Algonquian and Iroquoian Indians, exchanging European finished goods for furs. In 1663 Louis XIV assumed control over all of France's overseas colonies and sent royal troops and families to Canada in order to develop the economy more fully. As a result, by 1670 about six thousand French people lived along the St. Lawrence, most residing near Quebec and Trois-Rivières, where the *habitants* established farms and raised livestock on their narrow, rectangular plots of land—called longlots—that fronted the river. Despite the development of agriculture, furs remained the most important and profitable feature of Canada's economy, and *voyageurs* and *coureurs de bois* continued to travel from Montreal to the Great Lakes to trade with the Indians. Like the English, during the middle third of the seventeenth century the French also established colonies in the Caribbean, the most important being Martinique, Guadeloupe, and Saint-Domingue. Whereas the early French settlers had engaged in raising tobacco and piracy, by the late 1600s they had shifted to the extremely profitable practice of cultivating sugar, using African slaves as laborers. By 1670 about thirty thousand people resided in the French Caribbean, half of whom were black slaves. As the French established their own slave trading stations along the west coast of Africa in the late seventeenth and early eighteenth centuries, the number of slaves sent to the West Indies rose dramatically. Although in 1669 Louis XIV created the Ministry of the Marine in part to deal with the development of the French overseas holdings, colonial administration remained vague throughout the seventeenth and eighteenth centuries. Louisiana, the colony that France would establish in the Gulf South during the same period, was a hybrid of both the Canadian and Caribbean strands of French colonial development, as the Indian trade and plantation agriculture—along with the use of African slave labor—would provide the basis of the colony's economy.

The French first approached Louisiana from Canada. In the late 1660s officials in New France began to send out parties westward from Montreal to explore the lands and to enter into commerce with the distant Algonquian nations. By 1670 French traders had traversed the vast Great Lakes region and established a post at Green Bay on Lake Michigan. From there, Frenchmen portaged across the watershed and entered streams that flowed southwestward toward a great river that the Indians called the Mississippi. When word of the river filtered back to Quebec, the recently appointed governor general, Louis de Baude, Comte de Frontenac, sent out an expedition in order to ascertain whether the Mississippi flowed south into the Gulf of Mexico as they hoped. If it did, the French would be able to hem in the English on the Atlantic Coast by building a chain of forts and trading posts along the Mississippi and the Great Lakes that would connect the St. Lawrence River to the Gulf of Mexico.

The French officials chose Louis Jolliet, a talented surveyor and cartographer, along with Jesuit priest Jacques Marquette, to lead the expedition. In May 1673 the two men embarked in canoes from the Straits of Mackinac along with five other Frenchmen. A month later the party entered the Mississippi River and headed downstream. In July, Marquette and Jolliet arrived at the four Quapaw villages near the mouth of the Arkansas River. The Quapaws, who had obtained a few French items through Indian intermediaries, greeted the group with great hospitality and performed the calumet ceremony, as they were extremely desirous of establishing a direct trading partnership with New France. After the Quapaws informed them that the river flowed southward to the Gulf of Mexico, Jolliet and Marquette decided to return to New France rather than continue downstream. Leaving the weakened Marquette at Green Bay, Jolliet arrived in Quebec in August 1674 and informed his superiors of their findings.

Although Jolliet requested permission to establish a settlement in the Mississippi Valley, Frontenac instead granted that privilege to a member of his coterie from Normandy, René-Robert Cavelier, sieur de La Salle. In preparation for his project, over the next few years La Salle established a chain of posts from Lake Ontario to the Mississippi River. Finally, in 1682 La Salle was ready to proceed down the Mississippi in search of the Gulf of Mexico. Leaving from the southern end of Lake Michigan in January, La Salle, along with twenty Frenchmen and thirty Algonquian-speaking Indians, crossed from the Chicago River to the Illinois and on to the Mississippi. Two months later, the party reached the Quapaw villages, the southernmost point of Jolliet's trip nine years before. The friendly Quapaws provided La Salle with guides, who led the party farther downstream in constant rain and fog, which hampered the Frenchman's understanding of his surroundings. After meeting with members of the Taensa and Natchez tribes, La Salle reached the Gulf of Mexico in early April and conducted a ceremony by which he claimed for Louis XIV possession of the country he called "Louisiana."

Although La Salle had determined conclusively that the Mississippi entered the Gulf of Mexico, he was extremely vague about where it did so. Not only did he calculate that the mouth of the river was more than one hundred miles south of its actual location, he did not understand the enormous delta at the river's mouth with its multiple passes projecting into the sea. As a result, he concluded that the Mississippi approached the coast in a southeastward direction, thus positioning it in western gulf waters. After returning to France in 1683, La Salle used inaccurate existing maps to reconcile the location of the Mississippi's mouth, accepting the idea that the river actually passed through a mythical large bay before making its final journey to the sea. La Salle's miscalculations would soon prove fatal to himself and hundreds of other Frenchmen.

The aggressive, expansion-minded Louis XIV accepted La Salle's proposal to establish a settlement upstream from the mouth of the Mississippi, and in the summer of 1684 the Frenchman left La Rochelle with one hundred soldiers and nearly three hundred colonists in four ships. The ill-fated expedition was plagued from the start, mainly as a result of La Salle's insecurity and paranoia, which caused him to quarrel incessantly with the expedition's naval commander, Taneguy Le Gallois Beaujeu, during the Atlantic crossing. When the flotilla reached the French island of Saint-Domingue in September, the leaders' disagreement allowed Spanish privateers to capture one ship and caused numerous other members of the expedition to desert. Continuing on with the remaining three ships, La Salle's misconceptions concerning the mouth of the Mississippi led the flotilla much farther south and west than the river's actual location. In early 1685, when the French ships arrived at Matagorda Bay, halfway down the Texas coast, La Salle believed he had found the bay through which the Mississippi entered the gulf. By the time La Salle finally accepted his error a few months later, the French party was stranded. Beaujeu had returned to France in the lead ship, and the other two vessels, filled with precious supplies, had run aground and sunk in Matagorda Bay.

After constructing a temporary site for the remaining colonists a few miles inland from the bay on Garcitas Creek, La Salle concluded that their only hope for survival lay in his ability to locate the actual Mississippi River and ascend it to the French post he and his lieutenant, Henri de Tonti, had founded on the Illinois River. In April 1686 the increasingly volatile La Salle set out to find the Mississippi along with about twenty men. A few months later the Hasinai Indians, eager for trade ties with Europeans, welcomed the French stragglers into their Neches River villages. The Hasinais agreed to lead the party eastward toward the Mississippi, but the mercurial La Salle became ill and the French group returned to the settlement on Garcitas Creek with the intention of returning to East Texas the following year.

Sickness, starvation, and attacks by the local Karankawa Indians reduced the Garcitas Creek outpost to fewer than fifty people by January 1687, when La Salle made another attempt to reach the Mississippi. Along with seventeen men La Salle left the coast and headed northeastward toward the Hasinais. Before reaching the tribe, however, quarreling broke out within the group, and La Salle and a few others were killed. The remnants of the French party continued on to the Hasinai villages. Half of them decided to remain in the villages, and the other half dozen continued on to the Mississippi. Hasinai guides took the French group to the Kadohadacho villages on the Red River, and from there they were led to the Arkansas Post, a small French trading facility that Tonti had recently established, with Quapaw permission, at the Osotouy village about thirty miles upstream from the mouth of the Arkansas. Ultimately, the French party ascended the Mississippi, made it to Canada, and returned safely to France.

Due, in part, to the outbreak of war with England, the French made no attempt to send a vessel for the two dozen colonists, who survived until early 1689, when Karankawa attackers killed all but a few children. Unaware of their fate, in January 1690 Tonti left the Arkansas Post and traveled among the Taensas, Natchitoches, Kadohadachos, and Hasinais before giving up the search and returning to the Quapaws. Within a few years Tonti and the few remaining traders abandoned the Arkansas Post and returned to Canada, thus ending the initial French attempt to settle in the Lower Mississippi Valley. Although the French effort in the late seventeenth century did not result in permanent settlement, the various travelers' positive encounters with the Caddo, Quapaw, and Taensa tribes did pave the way for the establishment of trading alliances and friendship when Frenchmen returned a few years later.

The Spanish Response to La Salle

The French intrusion into territory claimed by Spain forced the Spaniards to initiate a response that would ultimately lead to the occupation of East Texas and Pensacola Bay. Learning of the French incursion into Spanish waters from the captured Frenchmen who had deserted La Salle at Saint-Domingue, officials in New Spain undertook a large-scale search to find and destroy the intruders. Beginning in 1686 officials sent out five maritime expeditions and six overland parties seeking La Salle's outpost. Finally, in early 1689 an expedition led by Alonso de León left Mexico and discovered the ransacked French settlement on Garcitas Creek and a couple survivors, who informed the Spaniards that Karankawa Indians had killed most of the French colonists. After burying the remaining French cannons, de León and his Franciscan associate, Damián Massanet, encountered representatives from the Hasinai Indians, who, assuming that the Spaniards were French allies of La Salle, invited them to establish a trading post at their East Texas villages. The Spaniards, who had been hearing tales of the "great kingdom of the Tejas"—the Caddoan word for friend or ally—for nearly a quarter of a century, incorrectly thought that the Hasinais had asked them to establish missions in their midst. This misunderstanding would plague the Spanish effort among the Hasinais from the start.

Back in New Spain, de León and Massanet received permission to return to East Texas with one hundred soldiers and five Franciscan priests from the missionary College of Santa Cruz in Querétaro in order to bring Christianity to the Hasinais and to ensure there were no more Frenchmen in the area. Traveling first to Garcitas Creek to burn all remnants of La Salle's settlement, in May 1690 the Spaniards were greeted by the Nabedaches, the westernmost Hasinai group, at their village on the Neches River. Eager to cement an alliance with the visitors, the Nabedaches allowed the Franciscans to establish a mission near their town. To service other Hasinais, the Franciscans founded a second mission five miles to the east at the Neches Indian village. Finding no sign of the French, and misinformed about the Hasinais' desire for Christianity, de León returned to Mexico in late 1690, leaving only a small number of soldiers behind with the Franciscan priests.

Relations between the Franciscans and the Hasinais became tense soon after de León's departure. The Indians had invited the foreigners to their villages in order to acquire a military alliance as well as trade goods and weapons, only to watch the Spanish military contingent retire to Mexico and find that the Franciscans refused to provide them with guns or ammunition. Unlike the missionaries in Florida, the Franciscans among the Hasinais were isolated and had almost no support system on which to rely; thus the Indians had little respect for the priests and refused to succumb to their clumsy indoctrination efforts. Furthermore, the Franciscans alienated the Hasinais by ridiculing their religion—one missionary forced his way into the temple of the xinesí and threatened to burn the sacred objects, while another attempted to intervene in a native burial ritual. An epidemic, brought on by a Franciscan who died of smallpox, swept through the country in early 1691 and exacerbated the strained relations between the Hasinais and the priests. By the time the sickness had run its course in March, four hundred or so Hasinais and three thousand members of the other Caddo tribes had died.

Despite their unhappiness with the Franciscans, the Hasinais allowed a Spanish expedition of fifty soldiers and ten priests, led by Domingo Terán de los Ríos, to enter their villages in August 1691. Optimistic officials in New Spain had ordered Terán to accompany the Franciscans to East Texas in order to establish more missions among the Hasinais and their Kadohadacho allies. However, the Hasinais' sullen attitude toward the Spaniards during their five-month stay in Caddo country forced Terán to abandon attempts to construct new churches and caused all but three Franciscans—

along with a few lay brothers and soldiers—to accompany the troops when they headed back to Mexico in January 1692. The Hasinais' enmity for the Spaniards did not decrease following Terán's departure, as yet another epidemic swept through the country in the summer. The Hasinais tolerated the Franciscans' presence for another year, until October 1693, when the Nabedache caddí informed the priests that his people would kill them if they did not leave immediately. Choosing survival over martyrdom, the Franciscans buried the church ornaments, set fire to the missions, and headed to the presidio at Monclova, which they reached the following February. Thus, the flurry of activities that had occurred in Texas over the course of a decade came to an end. The Spanish attempt to win over the Hasinais by peaceful conversion to Christianity had failed, and the tribe's experience with the French had made the Indians more desirous of establishing a military and commercial partnership with the Gallic visitors.

At the same time a few Spaniards were failing at their initial efforts in East Texas, others who were searching for La Salle began steps that would lead to the rediscovery and occupation of Pensacola Bay. Juan Enríquez Barroto and Antonio Romero commanded the first Spanish maritime expedition to look for the French colony, which left from Havana in January 1686. Sailing north, Enríquez Barroto first sighted the Florida coast south of Tampa Bay and entered the port of San Marcos de Apalache two weeks later. Heading west, the Spanish ship entered a bay that the Indians called Pensacola, which one of the pilots, Juan Jordán de Reina, reported as being "the best bay I had ever seen." From Pensacola Bay—which the Spaniards had forgotten since abandoning Luna's colonization effort over a century before—the expedition moved on to Mobile Bay and to the mouth of the Mississippi, which they noted while failing to recognize its importance as the great river of the continent. Continuing westward, the Enríquez Barroto-Romero expedition reached Veracruz in March without finding any sign of the French settlement. A second sea expedition, piloted by Enríquez Barroto and Romero, but commanded by Martín de Rivas and Pedro de Iriarte, left Veracruz in December 1686. Traveling in two shallow-draft vessels that allowed them to remain close to the coast, the expedition inspected most of the bays and inlets from the Rio Grande to San Marcos de Apalache, providing the first detailed explorations of Galveston Bay and Sabine Pass, before returning to Mexico the following July. Three Spanish maritime expeditions followed up on these efforts in the next two years without adding much knowledge about the coast or noting anything that helped locate La Salle's colony.

While de León's discovery of the destroyed French settlement in April 1689 ended the need for further maritime searches, it did allow the Spaniards to direct their interest toward the reinvestigation of Pensacola Bay. Alerted to its importance by Jordán, Admiral Andrés de Pez petitioned the viceroy of New Spain, the Condé de Galve, for permission to explore the bay in June 1689. Although the viceroy gave his approval, bureaucratic intransigence delayed the expedition until March 1693, when Admiral Pez, accompanied by Mexico's leading scientist, Carlos de Sigüenza y Góngora, sailed from Veracruz with orders to explore and map Pensacola Bay. Arriving at the entrance to the bay in April, the Spaniards renamed it Bahía Santa María de Galve. During the expedition's eleven-day stay Sigüenza mapped most of the bay's features and landmarks. Upon his return to Mexico the scientist affirmed Jordán's opinion of Pensacola Bay by pronouncing it "the finest jewel possessed by his Majesty. . . not only here in America but in all his kingdom." This news, combined with the knowledge of the Carolinians' inroads in the area, convinced the Spanish Crown to endorse the settlement of Pensacola Bay in June 1694. Despite the royal directive, however, the Spaniards in Florida were preoccupied with other matters and made no immediate attempt to occupy Pensacola Bay.

The Great Southeastern Smallpox Epidemic

By the mid-1690s, then, two and a half decades of European activities in the Gulf South had connected native communities with each other and with the larger Atlantic world as they had never been before. British commerce, in particular, was affecting indigenous people all the way from the Atlantic Coast to East Texas. A high volume of people—traders, raiders, captives, and runaways—passed along this extensive trade network. While a few Indian communities had profited from the newly introduced system, others had been weakened or devastated by extensive slave raiding and disruption. The situation became even more deadly for the region's Indians in 1696, when ships loaded with African slaves brought smallpox to Virginia. After ravaging Virginia's British, African, and Indian populations, the smallpox virus arrived in Carolina early the following year and quickly traveled by way of the trading network to the Mississippi Valley and the Gulf Coast, decimating many of the Indian communities, particularly the weakened ones that had already been made susceptible by constant slave raiding. Before running its course in 1700, the Great Southeastern

Smallpox Epidemic caused an unparalleled and unprecedented population collapse, thus allowing the Europeans to make further inroads into the region over the course of the following century.

After arriving in Carolina in early 1697 and infecting the coastal tribes and those located along the Savannah River, the smallpox virus quickly traveled by way of the Upper Path to the Lower and Upper Creeks, as well as to the Chickasaws. Although they had benefited from the slave trade, the smallpox epidemic adversely affected the Indians of the Upper Path, causing a loss in population that forced them to abandon some villages and forge new communities. By 1700 the Creek population had been reduced by two-thirds, as only twenty-five hundred Muskogeans resided in the ten Lower Creek villages on Ochese Creek, while sixty-five hundred people lived in the forty Alabama, Abihka, and Tallapoosa towns of the Upper Creeks. The Chickasaws, who lived farthest from the British, declined at a lesser rate than the Creeks, as five thousand people—half as many as in 1670—resided in ten villages at the beginning of the eighteenth century. Although the smallpox epidemic caused the Creeks and Chickasaws to suffer devastating population losses, after the turn of the century their numbers would stabilize and actually increase during the 1700s.

In contrast, the tribes that had been victimized by the Carolina slave trade endured drastic population declines in the late 1600s, causing some groups to disappear as their numbers continued to drop precipitously in the early eighteenth century. The violence had forced these groups to live in compact and fortified villages where, because planting crops and engaging in long hunts was dangerous, the huddled residents suffered from hunger. When smallpox hit such communities, the mortality rates were catastrophic. The Indian tribes settled along the Lower Mississippi River and the Gulf of Mexico experienced the highest casualties, emptying the region on the eve of the second French colonization effort. In fact, as French explorers traveled throughout the region at the turn of the century, they encountered many deserted villages and found signs of epidemic sickness within the towns that were still occupied.

The Indian groups residing along the Gulf Coast from Mobile Bay to Lake Pontchartrain declined by half during the 1690s. By 1700 less than two thousand people remained among the five Mobilian and two Tohome villages located along the Mobile and Tensaw Rivers upstream from Mobile Bay. At the same time another fifteen hundred Pascagoulas, Moctobis, and Biloxis coalesced into proximate villages located on small bluffs overlooking the Pascagoula River. Weakened by the smallpox epidemic of the late seventeenth century, all of these groups would continue to suffer losses in the early decades of the 1700s.

The sickness also reduced the Indians living along the Lower Mississippi River, resulting in a similar pattern of village consolidation and intertribal assimilation. By 1700 less than one thousand Ouachas and Chaouachas lived in various small camps located along the Mississippi, about one hundred miles above its mouth. Farther upstream, disease and slave raiding forced the Quinipissas to join the Bayogoulas and form a single village, consisting of about one thousand residents, on the west bank of the Mississippi, just upstream from Bayou Lafourche. Slave raiders destroyed the smallpox-ravaged Acolapissa villages located near the mouth of the Pearl River, forcing the one thousand survivors to move west to establish settlements on the north shore of Lake Pontchartrain. Farther west, about two thousand Chitimachas resided between the Atchafalaya and the Mississippi. Another twelve hundred or so Houmas lived upstream from the Bayogoulas on the east bank of the Mississippi below its junction with the Red River. After suffering from the smallpox epidemic, in 1700 dysentery struck the weakened Houmas, reducing their numbers by half yet again.

The area along the Mississippi River between the Red and the Arkansas also underwent a long and severe process of depopulation during the late seventeenth century due to slave raiding and disease. By 1700 the Natchez Indians had lost half of their population, leaving three thousand or so people in five villages located on bluffs overlooking the east bank of the Mississippi. This group included some Tunicans who had taken refuge among the Natchez to escape Chickasaw slave raiders. The Taensas, who lived on the opposite bank of the river about thirty miles upstream from the Natchez near Lake St. Joseph, merged their villages into one concentrated town for defensive purposes in the 1690s. Less than one thousand Taensas remained by 1700, a large proportion of which were men (many of the women and children having been captured by slave raiders). In the wake of unprecedented sickness and death, lightning struck the sacred temple of the Taensas in March 1700, further demoralizing the declining tribe. Upstream on the east bank, sickness and violence forced about two thousand people from various groups to settle among the Tunica villages, located ten miles from the Mississippi on the Yazoo River. About thirty-five hundred Yazoos, Koroas, and Chachiumas coalesced into compact villages located farther up the Yazoo Valley. Near the mouth of the Arkansas River, the Quapaws also suffered large population losses in the late seventeenth century. By 1700 the Quapaws numbered only about two thousand people, representing a two-thirds decline. Soon thereafter, the decimated Tourimas and Tongingas joined together and established a village near the Kappas on the west bank of the Mississippi near the mouth of the White River.

The Carolina slave trade and the smallpox epidemic also affected the three Caddo groups, even though they were located several hundred miles west of the Mississippi River. The Hasinais of East Texas had already suffered from a European-introduced sickness when the smallpox virus entered their villages in the last few years of the seventeenth century. By 1700 the Hasinais had been reduced to ten principal villages, located along the upper reaches of the Neches, Angelina, and Sabine Rivers. Farther east on the Red River, the Natchitoches and the Kadohadachos bore the brunt of Chickasaw raiders, causing them to concentrate themselves into four towns apiece. By the beginning of the eighteenth century only ten thousand or so Caddos remained alive. The Caddoan-speaking Wichitas, who lived farther to the northwest along the Arkansas River, escaped the brunt of the slave raiding and disease, and maintained their population at about twenty thousand.

While sickness and violence caused many Gulf South Indians—particularly those located along major waterways—to die or be enslaved during the last decade of the eighteenth century, some natives fled and took refuge in the remote watersheds of the Pearl, Chickasawhay, and Tombigbee Rivers in present southeastern Mississippi. Very quickly, the people—most of them Muskogean speakers—conglomerated to form the group known as the Choctaws and divided themselves into three principal districts. The Western district was located along the tributaries of the Upper Pearl River and consisted of peoples who had recently migrated from farther up the river, as well as from the Upper Tombigbee River. The Eastern district straddled the headwaters of the Chickasawhay River and the western tributaries of the Tombigbee, and was made up of groups emerging from the Black Warrior River in northwest Alabama. People from various villages along the lower reaches of the Pearl, Pascagoula, and Mobile Rivers migrated north to form Sixtowns district, located along the middle reaches of the Chickasawhay. Although Creek and Chickasaw slave raiders, as well as the smallpox epidemic, were able to enter the region and inflict damage upon the emerging districts, the Choctaws were not as adversely affected as most of the other tribes. As a result, the Choctaws, who numbered at least fifteen thousand people, were the largest tribe in the region east of the Mississippi at the beginning of the eighteenth century. All in all, about eighty thousand Indians remained in the Gulf South—a decline of about one-third since 1670—just as new groups of Europeans began to arrive.

Initial French and Spanish Settlements

Following the conclusion of war with England in 1697, French Minister of the Marine Louis Phélypeaux, Comte de Pontchartrain, and his son, Jérome Phélypeaux de Maurepas—who would succeed his father as naval minister in 1699—decided that France should follow up on La Salle's plans to place a colony near the mouth of the Mississippi River. Hearing a rumor—which turned out to be true—that the British from Carolina were also planning to settle in the Mississippi Valley, Pontchartrain convinced Louis XIV to provide monetary support for an expedition to the Gulf of Mexico in early 1698. The king and his advisors chose Pierre Le Moyne, sieur d'Iberville, the third of eleven sons in a family noted for its contribution to the French conquest of Canada, to command the Louisiana enterprise. Iberville was the obvious choice, as he had recently emerged as a hero in the war that had just ended. As Frontenac's second in command in New France, the aggressive, cocksure Iberville not only helped defeat the English by land in a brutal massacre at Schenectady in 1690, he also engaged an English flotilla on Hudson Bay in 1697, sinking one ship and capturing another. During the summer of 1698, while Iberville organized his expedition in France, the Pontchartrains gathered all available knowledge of the Gulf of Mexico and the Mississippi River from existing maps and from survivors of La Salle's failed colony.

Meanwhile, in March 1698 Spanish officials learned of the French plan to occupy the Gulf Coast and ordered the viceroy of New Spain to take possession of Pensacola Bay before Iberville's arrival. By mid-November two expeditions, one from Veracruz commanded by Andrés de Arriola, and a second from Havana led by Juan Jordán de Reina, had arrived in Pensacola with four hundred men. The two commanders, along with Austrian military engineer Jaime Franck, selected the bluffs overlooking the entrance to the bay as the site for Presidio Santa María de Galve. While Franck laid out a fortification, the soldiers built palmetto-thatched huts. Within a week a gun battery was in position to challenge the French should they attempt to enter Pensacola Bay.

In October 1698 Iberville, along with his younger brother Jean-Baptiste Le Moyne, sieur de Bienville, gathered a fleet of four ships and four hun-

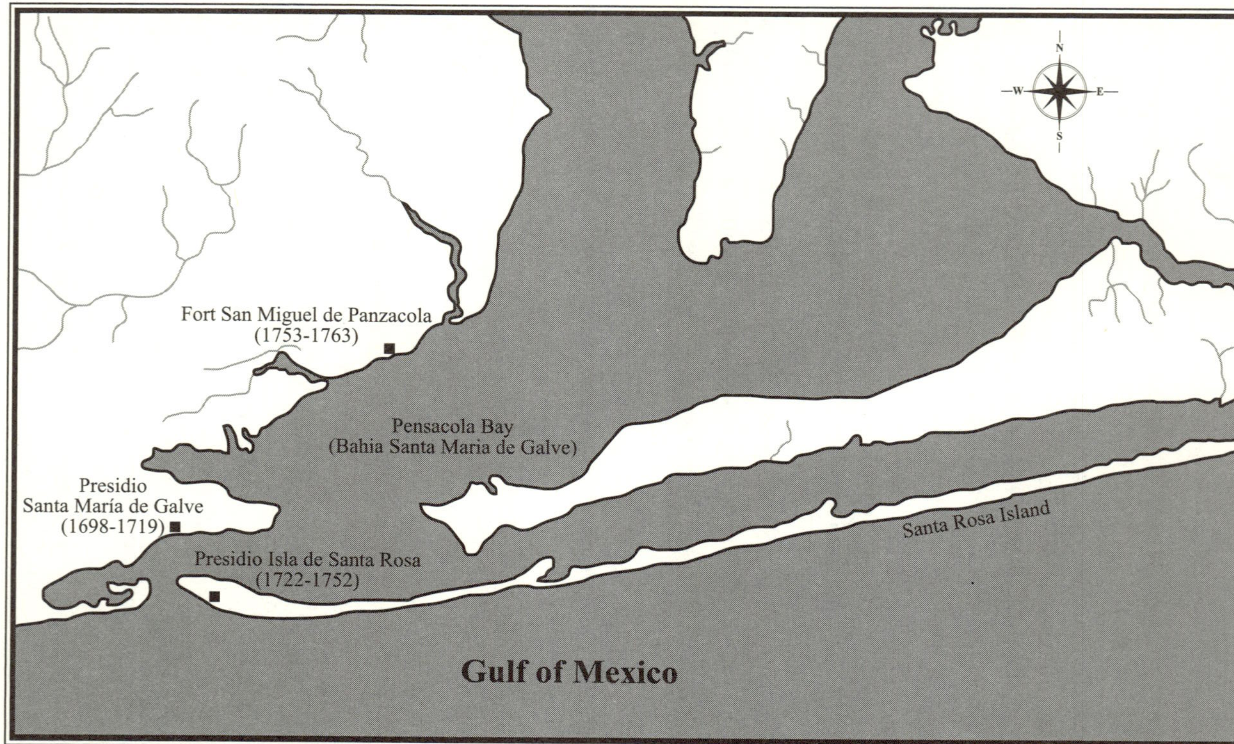

MAP 3. SPANISH SETTLEMENTS IN PENSACOLA BAY, 1698–1763

dred men, including a group of Canadian cohorts, and sailed from Brest. The operation was military in nature, as Iberville's title was commandant, an officer of the navy. In early December the French flotilla landed in Saint-Domingue and added a fifth ship as well as picking up a few pirates who professed knowledge of the Gulf Coast. The French fleet left Saint-Domingue on December 31 and arrived at Pensacola Bay in late January 1699. Arriola politely denied the French permission to enter the bay to take on wood and water, and Iberville, conceding that the Spaniards had established possession, continued westward. After stopping at Mobile Bay and Dauphin Island, Iberville set up a temporary base a few miles offshore on Ship Island in order to more fully investigate the mainland before establishing a permanent settlement.

Iberville then went ashore and established friendly relations with two Indian groups who were hunting on Biloxi Bay. The Biloxis, who lived on the Pascagoula River to the east, introduced Iberville to a party of Bayogoulas, who had come from their village on the Mississippi. After performing the calumet ceremony, during which the French distributed presents of "axes, knives, blankets, shirts, glass beads, and other things valued among" the Indians, Iberville and Bienville, along with forty Canadians and a few pirates, traveled west along the coast in two shallow boats and entered the Mississippi at its mouth. Heading upstream, the French party arrived at the Bayogoula village a few miles below the junction with Bayou Lafourche. Iberville distributed presents in the smallpox-ravaged town, surrounded by the "bodies of their dead on platforms . . . [that] stinks badly," for a few days before continuing up the river to the Houma village. The French party spent several days among the Houmas before deciding to return to Ship Island. On the way back, Bienville retraced the route down the river to the Gulf, while Iberville followed the Bayogoulas on a path that made it possible to avoid the long journey to the Mississippi's mouth. The Indians showed him a portage from the Mississippi to Bayou Manchac, a narrow stream that connected with the Gulf through Lakes Maurepas and Pontchartrain.

Iberville's expedition convinced him that the initial French settlement should be on the Gulf Coast rather than on the flood-susceptible lands along the Mississippi. Aided by his brother, Iberville conducted an additional survey of the shoreline before deciding on a site on the northeast side of Biloxi Bay, near present Ocean Springs, Mississippi. In early April 1699 the French began constructing Fort Maurepas, a small wooden structure defended by a dozen cannon and a garrison of eighty men. In May, soon after establishing the settlement on Biloxi Bay, Iberville returned to France in order to obtain supplies and enlist more colonists.

While Iberville was absent, various French groups explored the region and established alliances, based on trade and protection, with the local Indians. After first visiting an Acolapissa village near the mouth of the Pearl River in May, Bienville traveled up the Pascagoula River and met with the Biloxis, Moctobis, and Pascagoulas. Later in the summer, Bienville embarked with six men to seek the Mississippi via Lake Pontchartrain. Native guides led the French party along the south shore of the lake to the mouth of Bayou St. John, which they followed a few miles upstream to its source before taking a short portage to an abandoned Quinipissa village on the Mississippi River at the future site of New Orleans. Heading downstream, Bienville encountered an English ship that had been sent from Carolina to search for suitable settlement sites on the Mississippi. Bienville brazenly forced the English captain to abandon his plans and head out to sea by claiming he had a large body of French troops nearby. The encounter at English Turn—named for this incident—convinced the French that they should protect the mouth of the river, and by early 1700 Fort de la Boulaye had been constructed about fifty miles upstream from its Gulf of Mexico entrance.

While Bienville traveled among the Indians on the Gulf Coast and along the Lower Mississippi River, missionaries from Canada made contact with disease-ravaged tribes located farther upstream. In May 1698 the bishop of Quebec awarded the Seminary of Foreign Missions the right to bring Christianity to the Louisiana Indians. In the fall of 1698, at about the same time that Iberville was sailing from France on his first voyage to the Gulf, three missionaries descended the Mississippi along with a group of Canadian traders. During the next couple of years, these priests, along with three others who arrived a year later, visited the Quapaws, Chickasaws, Yazoos, Tunicas, Taensas, and Natchez. Although most of the tribes tolerated the missionaries' presence in their villages, the suffering Indians did not provide the men with food or shelter, nor did they show any inclination to be indoctrinated. By 1700 all of the missionaries except one had either abandoned their efforts or had died. Antoine Davion, however, did succeed in establishing a mission among the Tunica Indians on the Yazoo River. Although he was unable to convert the tribe to Catholicism, Davion's efforts forged an alliance between the Tunicans and the French that would last throughout the colonial period.

Iberville returned from France in January 1700 accompanied by a few more brothers as well as sixty Canadians commanded by Louis Juchereau de St. Denis, a relative by marriage. Iberville remained in Louisiana only until the end of May, but he made the most of his time, further exploring the region while continuing to engage with the Indians. In February he led a group of men through Lake Pontchartrain to the Houma villages and then on to the Grand Village of the Natchez, where he exchanged gifts with the Great Sun, who the Frenchman characterized as being "the most tyrannical Indian I have beheld." While Iberville returned to Biloxi Bay, Bienville and St. Denis went to the Taensa towns and then headed west to the Red River, where they rekindled the Caddo alliance, initiated by La Salle and Tonti, with Hasinai and Kadohadacho representatives at the Natchitoches villages. Although the visit went well, the Canadians were unable to ascertain whether or not the Spaniards had actually abandoned their missions among the Hasinais. As a result, following their return to the Gulf Coast, Iberville sent St. Denis back up the Red River to the Kadohadacho villages, where he finally was made to understand that the Franciscans had retreated to Mexico years before.

Upon leaving for France in May 1700, Iberville instructed Charles Levasseur to carry out the exploration of Mobile Bay and the rivers that fed into it, for he had come to understand that it provided access to the larger tribes in the interior, the Upper Creeks, Choctaws, and Chickasaws. Going up the Mobile River past the villages of the Mobilian Indians, Levasseur reached the town of the Little Tohome on the Lower Tombigbee River before returning to Fort Maurepas by way of the Tensaw River. In June 1701 the French on the Gulf Coast endured an epidemic in which sixty men died. Therefore, upon his return to Louisiana in December, Iberville ordered Bienville to reconnoiter the land upriver from Mobile Bay in order to move the colony promptly from the marshy lowlands of Biloxi Bay. Led by native guides, Bienville chose a site downstream from a Mobilian village on a bluff on the west side of the Mobile River, about fifty-five miles from the deepwater port the French had recently established on the eastern tip of Dauphin Island. In early 1702 construction began on Fort Louis, a four-hundred-foot-square wooden edifice that contained four groups of buildings placed around a drill ground. Streets were laid out in right angles to the north and west of the bluff on which the fort stood. In April Iberville distributed allotments along the streets in parcels of squares or rectangles. Leaving a few soldiers behind on Biloxi Bay, by June a little more than one hundred men and a few women had relocated to Fort Louis, which would continue to function as the French capital of Louisiana until 1711.

While Fort Louis was under construction, the French leaders attempted to initiate a trading relationship with the large Indian groups that lived in the interior. In March 1702 Iberville invited representatives of the enemy Choctaw and Chickasaw tribes to meet him in Mobile, where he admonished them for having been drawn into a costly war with one another by the Carolina traders. Providing each group with gifts of powder, arms, and finished goods, Iberville promised further trade if the Choctaws and Chickasaws would agree to live in peace. Two months later Bienville—who had assumed command of Fort Louis following Iberville's departure for France in April—met with a group of Alabama chiefs in Mobile and told them that the French would provide the Upper Creeks with all the items they desired if they would cut their ties with the British and refrain from taking slaves from the French-allied Mobilians and Tohomes. Although the representatives of all three visiting interior tribes politely agreed to these terms, the entire region soon fell into violence—exacerbated by the outbreak of war in Europe—that would bring even further death and destruction to many of its already suffering inhabitants.

War of the Spanish Succession

War, which had been brewing among the Europeans in the Gulf South for nearly three decades, seemed imminent after November 1700 when Louis XIV installed his Bourbon grandson on the Spanish throne, vacated by the death of the final Habsburg ruler. Fearing that the alliance between the French in Louisiana and the Spanish in Florida—sealed by Philip V's ascension as Spain's ruler—threatened the English position on the Atlantic Coast, in 1701 Carolinian emissaries began traveling from Charleston to the villages of the colony's Indian allies with large numbers of arms and ammunition to prepare them for the conflict that now seemed certain. At the same time the isolated Spaniards and French positioned at Pensacola and Mobile began to collaborate to defend themselves against the aggressive British and their native mercenaries. By the time the War of the Spanish Succession officially began in May 1702, when England and its allies declared war against France and Spain, the colonial Gulf South had already exploded in violence.

The Carolinians and their Creek allies struck first against feeble Spanish Florida, resulting in the destruction of the outlying Franciscan mission provinces and the death, enslavement, or scattering of the seven thousand or so remaining Apalaches. Full-blown war broke out in western Florida in May 1702 when a group of well-armed Apalachicolas attacked a Spanish garrison at Santa Fé in Timucua province. Although the Creeks destroyed the nearby Franciscan mission and killed thirteen Spaniards and Timucuans in the battle, Apalache auxiliaries stationed at Santa Fé killed two Apalachicolas during the fight. The Apalachicolas obtained vengeance a few months later by executing three Apalache men who had traveled to Ochese Creek to trade. Outraged, eight hundred Apalaches along with a dozen Spanish troops initiated a punitive expedition against the Apalachicolas in the fall of 1702. Word of the invasion reached the Ocheses and Carolinian traders, who hurried to a spot on the Flint River where they ambushed the Apalache-Spanish force, killing or enslaving nearly three-fourths of the invaders. The others returned to the missions thoroughly demoralized, with their province in an even weaker state than before.

In the meantime, Carolina governor James Moore attacked St. Augustine with a force of eight hundred British volunteers and Yamasee allies in November 1702. Unable to break through the shell-enforced walls of the Spanish fort, Moore retreated after besieging the Spaniards for nearly two months. Having failed to take St. Augustine, the Carolinians turned their attention westward as they discerned the vulnerability of Apalache province. In January 1704 Moore assembled a force of Carolinians and Ochese Creeks and launched a campaign that destroyed most of the missions and enslaved more than two thousand Apalaches. Another one thousand or so Apalaches, disillusioned with the Spaniards, agreed to accompany Moore when he withdrew after a few weeks of destruction and resettled among their attackers at Ochese Creek and on the Savannah River. In June 1704 the Ocheses acted on their own and attacked the few remaining missions in Apalache province, including San Luís de Talimali, killing and enslaving thousands of Indians. Realizing their inability to defend the province, Spanish authorities decided to abandon Apalache and ordered the troops to set fire to the few remaining edifices before retreating to St. Augustine. The surviving eight hundred or so Apalaches, along with two hundred Chacatos, also decided to leave their homeland. Half of the Apalaches headed east with the Spanish troops and attempted to take refuge in Timucua, but continued Creek raids forced the few remaining Spaniards and their Indian allies to abandon that province as well in late 1705. Resettling near St. Augustine, most of the remaining Apalaches were either killed or captured in yet another Yamasee slave raid the following year. The destruction of Apalache and Timucua reduced the once-impressive Spanish presence in Florida to the stronghold of St. Augustine and the isolated post at Pensacola.

The Chacatos and the other half of the Apalaches, most of whom were refugees from San Luís de Talimali, headed west to Pensacola before moving on to Mobile Bay, where they hoped for French protection. Bienville welcomed the Indians—who had brought their cattle along with them—when they arrived in August 1704 at his struggling settlement, and he assigned the Chacatos lands at the mouth of the Mobile River. The Apalaches, on the other hand, settled on the Mobile River about ten miles upstream from Fort Louis. The Apalaches, in particular, impressed the French with their industriousness and their insistence on being furnished with a priest to baptize their children. Both groups would remain allies of the French in the Mobile Bay area until the province was transferred to Great Britain in 1763.

Following the destruction of Apalache and Timucua provinces, the British and their Creek allies turned their attention toward the Spaniards at Pensacola and the French at Mobile. The Upper Creeks and the French had already clashed in 1703 when the Alabamas, prompted by Carolinian traders, killed three Canadians who had traveled from Mobile to their village in May. Early the following year Bienville led a reprisal force of Frenchmen to the Alabama towns, where they killed a few people and destroyed winter supplies. As a result, the Upper Creeks eagerly joined the Ocheses when, at the behest of the British, they began launching raids against the French and Spanish posts along the Gulf Coast. The first attacks commenced in the summer of 1706, when a band of Creeks assaulted Pensacola and captured several Spanish soldiers. The following May, Tallapoosas, Abihkas, and Alabamas waylaid a contingent of Spanish soldiers, killing one and capturing thirteen others. They then took their Spanish prisoners to Charleston for a monetary reward. Later that summer one thousand Creeks and a few Englishmen attacked the Spanish presidio at Pensacola and burned a few outlying buildings. The Creeks continued to attack the Spaniards until December 1707, when Bienville sent a contingent of Canadians and Indian allies from Mobile to help defend Pensacola from the enemy Indians. For the next few years small Creek war parties contented themselves by harassing the Spaniards outside the presidio's walls without making any direct assaults.

Having failed to force the Spaniards to abandon Pensacola, Carolina officials turned their attention toward the French in Mobile. In early 1708 the colonial assembly sent Thomas Nairne and Thomas Welch, veteran Indian traders, along the Upper Path to recruit Creek and Chickasaw warriors for an assault on Fort Louis. By this point, the Upper Creeks were beginning to view the French at Mobile as a possible counterweight to the increasingly demanding Carolinians, and therefore hesitated to accept the British proposal. It was not until May 1709 that an army of seven hundred Alabamas and Talapoosas launched an indirect assault on the French by attacking a Mobilian village upriver from Fort Louis, burning it to the ground and capturing nearly thirty women and children. When French and Tohome reinforcements arrived to confront the attackers, the Upper Creek war party immediately retreated without a fight. Although the Carolinians continued to use presents to convince the Creeks to assault Mobile, in 1711 the Indians instead chose to use the arms and ammunition to make a raid upon the Choctaws, killing eighty people and enslaving more than one hundred.

The Chickasaws also declined the Carolinians' offers to attack the French along the Gulf Coast, but tribal warriors continued to use British weapons to make devastating slave raids upon the Indians living along the Mississippi River, setting off costly intertribal conflicts that resulted in even more deaths and relocations. In the summer of 1706 the Chickasaw onslaught forced the Taensas to abandon their Lake St. Joseph village and take refuge with the Bayogoulas near the mouth of Bayou Lafourche. Soon thereafter the Taensas turned on their hosts, killing or enslaving most of the dwindling Bayogoulas. The Taensas then took a number of slaves from the nearby Chitimacha Indians before moving to various locations, ultimately landing on Mobile Bay, where they established a village a few miles downstream from Fort Louis. Assuming the French at Mobile had instigated the Taensas's attack, the Chitimachas killed a priest in November 1706. A group of Canadians, led by St. Denis, along with a force of Indian allies, obtained revenge the following year by destroying a Chitimacha village on Bayou Lafourche and taking a score of prisoners, who were sold as slaves to the French settlers at Fort Louis. French and allied Indian warfare against the Chitimachas continued for another decade, capturing many more women and children and making the decimated tribe the core of Louisiana's earliest slave population. The Tunicas, residing near the mouth of the Yazoo River, acted in a fashion similar to their Taensa neighbors. Fearing reprisals from the Chickasaws and Yazoos for capturing a Carolinian trader and handing him over to the French in Mobile, in October 1706 they fled from their towns and joined the Houmas. The Tunicas then drove the Houmas from their own village, killing at least half of them as they fled. Within a few years the remaining Houmas had settled downriver near where the Bayogoula village had once stood. Over the course of the second decade of the eighteenth century, all of these tribes would experience steep population declines from warfare and disease.

The fighting in the Gulf South ceased by late 1711, and the War of the Spanish Succession ended with the signing of the Treaty of Utrecht in April 1713. Although the Spanish and French posts along the Gulf Coast had survived the Carolinian-inspired Creek onslaught, the newly founded settlements at Pensacola and Mobile languished during the war, as officials in Spain and France ignored the relatively unimportant, isolated sites. By 1712 Spanish officers at Pensacola called for the abandonment of the post due to a variety of problems. Almost as soon as the Spaniards had established the garrison settlement at Pensacola in 1698, they were immediately confronted with the crucial problems of supplies and the maintenance and rehabilitation of the fortifications. At the root of many of the presidio's perennial problems were the climate, the configuration and infertility of the land, the quality of the personnel, and the delays in subsidy shipments. The fort was a constant source of worry, as the location of the presidio on top of a bluff overlooking the entrance to Pensacola Bay was subject to incessant winds that caused the sands to shift, with detriment to the fort's structure. While the fort was in constant need of repair, the other edifices, constructed mainly of dry palm thatch, caught fire at an alarming rate. One of the worst conflagrations took place in November 1704 when royal buildings, warehouses, bread ovens, and a guardhouse burned to the ground. Moreover, the wide mouth of Pensacola Bay posed a serious problem, as the Spaniards did not have powerful enough artillery to prevent enemy vessels from entering the port. One Spanish commander summed up the military situation at Pensacola by noting that the fort was hardly worth the name, as it consisted "solely of a quadrangle of logs which would serve only as a stopping-over place for the enemy."

The poor quality of the men employed at Presidio Santa María de Galve contributed to its uselessness, as the settlement ultimately functioned as both a military garrison and a penal colony. Spanish officials originally authorized over two hundred men to fill the garrison at the fort, but by 1708 only about one hundred, many of whom had inadequate equipment, remained at Pensacola. Constant sickness, malnutrition, enemy attacks, and desertion caused the decline in able-bodied men. Many of the surviving soldiers were convicts from New Spain, as it was impossible to recruit volunteers to man the forlorn post at Pensacola. The prisoners were a constant thorn in the side of the Spanish commanders at Pensacola; one complained that they often deserted and were not only a discredit to the military, they were also the greatest enemies of the Crown. The soldiers and convicts stationed at Pensacola, however, had ample reason to complain. The garrison was supplied almost entirely from New Spain, and shortages in provisions were frequent because of shipping delays. As a result, the struggling French settlement at Mobile often furnished the presidio with enough goods to hold the Spaniards over until the arrival of a subsidy ship. Although the soldiers at Pensacola attempted to grow their own food, the sterility of the sandy soil and the lack of a reliable supply of fresh water resulted in inadequate harvests. Due to these continuing problems, in 1712 Spanish commander Gregorio de Salinas Varona requested permission to move the presidio across the bay to Santa Rosa Island.

The French settlers and soldiers at Mobile, on the other hand, did relocate their fort before the end of the War of the Spanish Succession. As with the Spaniards at Pensacola, the lack of supplies and the inability of the settlers to raise crops near Fort Louis were chief among the reasons that the French moved downstream to the mouth of the Mobile River in 1711. During the first few years of the war France fairly regularly sent supply ships to Mobile. After the spring of 1706, however, no vessels landed at the deepwater port of Dauphin Island until February 1708. Another three years passed before the next ship resupplied the struggling colony in late 1711. As a result, the French colonists suffered through food shortages and were barely able to scrape by with what they raised in the paltry gardens they planted in the poor soil. However, in contrast to the Spaniards at Pensacola, the French at Mobile were able to call on the nearby Indian villages to supplement their meager diet with surplus corn and occasional meat. The natives also alleviated the French food shortages by taking in men from the garrison during the harsh winter months. Beginning in 1706 some French colonists moved downstream from the fort and settled at the mouth of Mobile Bay and on the eastern end of Dauphin Island in order to more easily obtain fish and raise cattle. In 1707 the French abandoned the isolated Fort de la Boulaye on the Mississippi River and transferred the few soldiers to Bayou St. John, where, along with a group of Mobile colonists who arrived the following spring, they raised a wheat crop for the starving settlers.

The breakdown of the French navy and the disruption of the nation's finances by the war were the main reasons that Mobile was left on its own for the better part of five years. However, the fraudulent actions of the founder of Louisiana also caused French officials to turn their backs on the infant colony. In January 1706, Iberville—who had left Mobile for Europe in the spring of 1702—was finally allowed to depart from France with orders to use his squadron of twelve ships to harass the English in the West Indies and Carolina. The Crown also provided Iberville with one huge ship, the *Coventry,* and purchased abundant goods that were intended to resupply Louisiana. However, following a successful attack on Nevis Island in which Iberville ransacked the island and forced the inhabitants to pay a ransom of three thousand slaves, he sent the *Coventry* to Veracruz and sold most of the cargo bound for Mobile, along with one-third of the captured slaves, to the Spaniards for indigo and silver. Iberville then dispatched a much smaller ship to Mobile that carried only a tiny part of the provisions and stores intended for the isolated colony, while he sailed with the main force to his two plantations on Saint-Domingue. Iberville sold the remaining confiscated slaves on the island for his own profit rather than for the French financiers who had invested in his expedition. Soon thereafter, however, the greedy Iberville died of yellow fever, just as the Minister of the Marine discovered his perfidy. As a result of Iberville's fraud, Pontchartrain no longer trusted any member of the Le Moyne family and lost interest in the Louisiana enterprise. The colony fell deeper into isolation as the Crown and other French merchants became uninterested in sending ships there.

Iberville's unsavory actions also called Pontchartrain's attention to the factional strife that had burdened the French settlement at Mobile since the governor's departure in 1702. On one side was the Bienville group, consisting largely of the Le Moyne brothers and most of the Canadians, along with a few Jesuit priests who had arrived soon after the move from Biloxi Bay to Mobile Bay. The king's commissary, Nicolas de La Salle, led the opposition party, which included the missionary priest Henri Roulleaux de La Vente, who arrived in 1704 as the pastor to the newly created parish of Mobile. La Salle, responsible for the maintenance of the king's merchandise and warehouse, joined La Vente in charging Bienville with incompetence and corruption, claiming that he was distributing the Crown's goods for his and his allies' own profit. After receiving these reports of malfeasance and learning of Iberville's questionable activities, in 1707 Pontchartrain tried to remove Bienville from his position as the leader of the colony, but his appointed replacement died en route to Mobile. However, a lesser official, Jean-Baptiste Martin Dartaguiette d'Iron, arrived from France with orders to investigate La Salle's charges against Bienville. Although the inquiry was indecisive, as both Bienville and La Salle maintained their official positions, Dartaguiette stayed in Mobile and served to calm the dispute between the two factions, which cooled following La Salle's death in early 1711 and La Vente's departure for France a few months later.

As a result of these difficulties, and Pontchartrain's indifference to Louisiana after 1706, the French population along Mobile Bay stagnated, as very few emigrants arrived in the colony. In 1703 just under two hundred French people resided in Louisiana, most being either soldiers or Canadian fur traders. The following year the Crown sent twenty-three French girls from Parisian convents and orphanages to Mobile, and marriages and pregnancies ensued soon thereafter. Although only a couple of French females arrived in Mobile over the course of the next seven years, a number of Canadian colonists took Chitimacha slave women as wives. By 1712 there were about thirty French families in the colony among the three hundred or so residents. In addition to the French population, about two hundred Indian slaves—most being captured Chitimachas—and ten African slaves toiled at Mobile.

By the spring of 1711 it had become evident that the French settlement at Fort Louis needed to be relocated. The fort itself, which had already been partially rebuilt in 1707, was once more in desperate need of repair. Plus, the post annually experienced long periods of flooding in winter and spring, forcing the inhabitants to leave their houses and move about in small boats. Many expressed their dissatisfaction with "living in a mud hole." The stagnant water, combined with the excessive heat and humidity of the region, caused an annual outbreak of fever and dysentery. In addition, Fort Louis was located too far up the river from the port at Dauphin Island. Thus, when the post suffered a succession of disastrous floods in 1710 and the following spring, Bienville and Dartaguiette agreed to abandon the site at the request of the population. The evacuation took place in June 1711, when most of the soldiers and settlers moved downstream to the mouth of the Mobile River to the site of the present city of Mobile.

While the soil was sandy and no more fertile than the land at Fort Louis, the plateau behind the riverbank was broad and drained well. Although the Chacato Indians already occupied the site, the French allies agreed to move a few miles downstream to settle on the banks of Dog River. A group of Apalaches also accepted Bienville's offer to settle just north of the town, while some Mobilians moved downstream to establish a village about seven miles above the French settlement. All three Indian groups helped the French build the second Fort Louis, which was completed by the end of the year and was surrounded by the colonists' houses and gardens. Soon thereafter, the French Crown turned the colony over to a series of private companies that would initiate the large-scale emigration of French settlers and African slaves, resulting in the province's main settlements being established to the west along the lower reaches of the Mississippi River, in the present state of Louisiana.

3

Establishing Louisiana, 1713–1731

The Gulf South continued to experience momentous changes during the second and third decades of the eighteenth century. Ironically, the Creeks—previously employed by the Carolinians to obtain captured indigenous slaves for the Atlantic Coast colony—led a pan-tribal rebellion against the British that, for the most part, brought the region's Indian slave trade to an end. At the same time France began to transport large numbers of African slaves, as well as Europeans, to Louisiana. As a result, by the end of the period the French had firmly established the colony—predominantly based upon the production of foodstuffs and cash crops by enslaved black laborers—along the lower reaches of the Mississippi Valley. The Spaniards, on the other hand, responded feebly to the French effort in Louisiana by reoccupying East Texas with a few priests and soldiers while barely maintaining a foothold on Pensacola Bay. Nonetheless, the French effort to develop Louisiana into a profitable endeavor on par with the West Indies was thwarted by an uprising of the Natchez Indians that destroyed one of the colony's most promising agricultural districts. This disaster suspended further growth in Louisiana, as it caused officials to neglect the colony for the following three decades that it remained in the possession of France.

The Crozat Monopoly

In September 1712 the financially troubled Louis XIV ceded the monopoly of Louisiana's failing commerce to Antoine Crozat, king's counselor and financial secretary, because of his wealth and numerous maritime and colonial operations. Attracted by the (false) promises of mineral riches,

Crozat assumed commercial control of the colony through a monopoly on imports and exports. He also held title to unoccupied land and the rights to supervise relations with the Indians, to exploit raw materials, and to choose governing officials. Preferring to remain in Paris, Crozat appointed Antoine de la Mothe, sieur de Cadillac, as governor with the explicit goal of making Louisiana more economically productive. Cadillac, who had helped found Detroit the previous decade, arrived at Mobile in May 1713 and assumed command of Louisiana, with Bienville remaining in charge of the small contingent of French soldiers stationed in the colony.

Cadillac's direction of Louisiana, however, was hampered by the appointment of Jean-Baptiste du Bois Duclos as *commissaire-ordonnateur,* or finance officer, responsible for the administration of the royal funds and the commerce of the colony. Although Pontchartrain attempted to define their respective prerogatives clearly, there were overlapping areas of jurisdiction that created conflict between the two men that was exacerbated by their intense mutual antipathy. In order to provide Louisiana with the civil administration it had lacked during the first decade of military rule, the Crown created the Superior Council, composed of the governor, the finance officer, the king's leading military officer, two councilors, an attorney general, and a registrar. According to the instructions, the governor was subordinate on the Superior Council to the finance officer, who held the position of First Councilor, or chief judicial officer of the colony. This duality of powers, which had been a source of constant conflict between Bienville and La Salle, led to the same quarrels under the government of Cadillac and Duclos, and would persist throughout the entire era of French control. By March 1716 the situation between the two men became untenable, and Jean Michiele, sieur de Lépinay, replaced Cadillac as governor. Marc-Antoine Hubert took over the position of finance officer from Duclos soon thereafter.

In the meantime Cadillac realized soon after assuming the governorship that, because neither Crozat nor the king was willing to provide funds to populate Louisiana with French settlers or African slaves, trade with the natives and with the Spaniards in New Spain would be the only possible ways to make the colony profitable. Mexican officials at Veracruz, however, rebuffed Cadillac's first attempt to establish a commercial relationship with New Spain by turning away the ship he sent in the fall of 1713. Refusing to yield to Spanish mercantile policy, Cadillac decided to initiate trade with New Spain, as well as with the Indian tribes on Louisiana's western flank, through the reestablishment of the Spanish missions among the

Hasinais of East Texas. The French governor seized upon this strategy after receiving a letter from a Spanish Franciscan, Father Francisco Hidalgo, who had worked at the failed Hasinai missions in the 1690s. Hidalgo addressed Cadillac as a fellow Catholic, asking him to help save Hasinai souls either directly through the establishment of French missions or indirectly by inspiring Spanish officials to rebuild their stations to prevent Gallic occupation. Interpreting the Franciscan's religious invitation as an opening to create a market for French goods in East Texas, Cadillac ordered St. Denis, who had recently become the commandant at Biloxi, to establish a trading post on the western boundary of Louisiana along the Red River.

St. Denis eagerly responded and immediately dispatched a messenger to the Natchitoches Indians, who had recently moved to Lake Pontchartrain in order to escape Chickasaw slave raiders. He proposed that they return to their former village site and help the French construct a fort in exchange for a steady supply of Gallic goods, weapons, and protection from their enemies. The Natchitoches group readily embraced the offer, and in late 1713 they accompanied St. Denis, twenty-four Frenchmen—most of them from Canada—and five boatloads of merchandise up the Red River. When the party reached the old Natchitoches home site in early 1714, St. Denis convinced the tribal members who had remained in the area to rejoin their kinsmen and resume the planting of agricultural fields. The natives assisted St. Denis in constructing living quarters for the Frenchmen and two warehouses for the safekeeping of merchandise on an island in the middle of the Red River. This fort and the nearby Indian settlements together formed the rudimentary beginnings of the French village called Natchitoches.

Having laid the town's foundations, St. Denis used it as a center from which to develop commerce with the Hasinais and with the Spaniards in Mexico. St. Denis traveled to East Texas, distributed presents to the Hasinais, and managed to persuade the tribal leaders to ask for the return of Spanish missionaries. He explained that, because Spain and France had recently become allies, the French now recognized the Spanish claim to the Hasinai territory and therefore, despite the wishes of the tribe, his people could not settle there. The Canadian convinced the Hasinais that having the Spaniards as well as the French nearby would be advantageous as the tribe would share in the profitable trade that promised to develop. To convince the Spaniards to return, however, the Hasinais had to once again play upon the Franciscans' desire to convert the natives to Christianity. Therefore, the Nabedache caddí agreed to accompany St. Denis and three Frenchmen to the nearest Spanish establishment at Presidio San Juan Bautista, located several hundred miles away near the Rio Grande.

Upon their arrival at the presidio in July 1714, St. Denis explained to the commandant, Diego Ramón, that he was responding to Father Hidalgo's letter and only sought to assist the Spaniards in rebuilding missions among the Hasinais. Ramón placed St. Denis and his party under house arrest while awaiting instructions from the viceroy in Mexico City. In the interim the forty-year-old St. Denis opportunistically courted Ramón's seventeen-year-old step-granddaughter, Manuela Sánchez Navarro, whom he married soon thereafter. In early 1715 Spanish officials sent St. Denis to Mexico City for interrogation. Following months of consideration the Spanish bureaucrats answered Hidalgo's prayers by deciding to reoccupy East Texas in order to resume the conversion efforts among the Hasinais, but they thwarted St. Denis's commercial schemes by continuing to declare French trade with Mexico illegal.

St. Denis, realizing that the Franciscans and soldiers in East Texas would most likely be dependent on French merchandise in spite of the law, agreed to assist the Spaniards in reestablishing missions among the Hasinais. In April 1716 the Canadian led Captain Domingo Ramón (Diego's son), twenty-five Spanish soldiers, and two groups of Franciscan missionaries—one from the Colegio de la Santa Cruz de Querétaro and the other from the Colegio de Nuestra Señora de Guadalupe de Zacatecas—back to the Hasinai country. When they entered East Texas in late June, the Hasinais, in conformity with St. Denis's desires, allowed the Spaniards to establish four missions near the Nabedache, Hainai, Nacogdoches, and Nadaco villages and an accompanying presidio. In order to halt the French at the Red River, Ramón also established a mission approximately fifteen miles west of Natchitoches at the Adaes Indian village. The Franciscans founded another mission at the Ais Indian village, just west of the Sabine River. All in all, Spaniards placed six missions—split equally between the Franciscans from Querétaro and Zacatecas—in an attempt to instruct the natives in Christianity and Hispanic civilization while securing the frontier from the French. Although the Spanish presence in East Texas checked the establishment of legal trade with New Spain, the few Frenchmen in Natchitoches were still able to employ their new post as a center from which to develop small-scale illegal trade with the ill-equipped Spaniards, as well as commerce with all three Caddo groups. In the fall of 1716 St. Denis formed a commercial partnership with six other Frenchmen and acquired a large cargo of trade goods at Mobile, which he transported to the French post at Natchitoches. During the next couple of years the French strengthened ties with the Caddos by exchanging these European-manufactured wares for furs, horses, and Indian slaves captured in Texas.

Whereas the Caddos, located too far west to have trade ties with the Carolinians, eagerly accepted a commercial alliance with the French in Louisiana, Cadillac's attempt to bring the Natchez Indians into the Gallic network was fraught with difficulties due to the tribe's interaction with British traders. Although the French had established an association with the Natchez through the Great Sun and his brother, the Tattooed Serpent, both of whom resided at the ceremonial center at the Grand Village in the Flour district, the outlying villages of White Apple, Jenzenaque, and Grigra had allowed Carolinians into their towns during the early eighteenth century. By gaining direct access to Carolina trade goods, the three eastern settlement areas obtained a degree of freedom from the Grand Village. Therefore, in order to obtain French goods and counteract the British influence, in 1714 the Great Sun allowed two of Crozat's handpicked employees to build a small trading post near the Grand Village. However, Cadillac, who did not yet understand the Natchez's strategic importance in Louisiana, provoked tribal wrath in late 1715 by passing through their territory without stopping to celebrate the calumet or to distribute presents. Interpreting this negligence as a sign of hostility, a Natchez war party killed five French traders and pillaged Crozat's trading facility in retribution.

Bienville refused to be cowed by the Natchez act of aggression and, along with thirty-five Frenchmen, headed up the Mississippi seeking vengeance and the right to reestablish a trading relationship with the tribe the following spring. In May 1716 the French party met with the Great Sun and the Tattooed Serpent, along with Natchez leaders from each of the five native settlement areas, on an island in the river just downstream from the Grand Village. When the Natchez leaders hesitated in the face of Bienville's demand that they provide him with five heads in reparation for the murdered Frenchmen, the commander boldly took them all hostage. After weeks of negotiations the Natchez finally delivered the heads of three assassins; plus the Great Sun gave Bienville permission to execute the pro-British chiefs of the Grigra and Jenzenaque villages. In addition, the Great Sun and the Tattooed Serpent allowed the French to construct Fort Rosalie on a bluff overlooking the Mississippi about three miles from the Grand Village. By late 1716 a small contingent of French soldiers was stationed at the fort, which had a trading post and warehouse located nearby.

Although the presence of British traders complicated the French effort among the Natchez, Carolinian abuses in the commerce caused the Creeks to seek an accommodation with their erstwhile Gallic enemies in Louisiana and Spanish foes in Florida. By the end of the first decade of the eighteenth century the Creeks and many other regional tribes had become severely indebted to the Carolinian traders, who provided them with European manufactured goods, including alcohol, on credit. When the Spanish missions in Florida—the principal source for Indian slaves—collapsed around 1706, the Creeks were forced to search for new sources of human chattel, as well as increasingly turning toward providing the Carolinians with deerskins as payment. Nonetheless, by 1711 the Lower Creeks were collectively in debt for one hundred thousand deerskins—about 250 skins (several years' work) per man. In addition to being trapped in an oppressive spiral of warfare and debt, the Creeks and their allies were enraged by English traders who publicly beat and whipped indebted men and molested native women.

In the spring of 1715 an angry Chief Brims, mico of the Lower Creek town of Coweta, organized an insurrection of the Carolina-allied Indians. Although the Lower Creeks planned the uprising, the so-called Yamasee War began in April 1715 when warriors from that tribe tortured and executed visiting Carolina officials and several resident traders. Within a few days other tribes located on the Savannah River, as well as the Muskogeans on Ochese Creek, killed the English traders who resided in their towns. The Yamasees and warriors from other groups then conducted raids against outlying Carolina settlements, forcing the survivors to flee to Charleston for safety. Soon thereafter the Upper Creeks and Chickasaws rose up and either killed or ejected the Carolinian trade workers among them. Less than a month after the Yamasee War began, Carolina's native slave trade was in ruins and the colony itself was threatened with destruction. However, the British were saved when the powerful Cherokee tribe decided to join with Carolina in an alliance against the attackers. By the end of 1715 the Carolinians and the Cherokees had destroyed the rebellious Indian towns on the Savannah River, dispersing the survivors, some of whom joined the Lower Creeks while others relocated to St. Augustine, where they received the support and protection of the Spanish.

In early 1716 the well-armed Cherokees focused their wrath on both Creek groups, forcing the Lower Creeks to abandon their villages on Ochese Creek and return to their former homes on the Chattahoochee River. Chief Brims, understanding that the British could not be driven from Carolina, then led the Creeks to alter their former pro-English policy in favor of a neutral stance in which they would play the three European powers off one another. Therefore, in the summer of 1716 Lower Creek diplomats traveled to St. Augustine and initiated friendly relations with the Spaniards that resulted in an officer visiting the Chattahoochee River villages in September 1717 to distribute presents. The Lower Creeks also made peaceful overtures to the Carolinians, in April 1717 returning two English captives to the newly established Savannah Fort, which led to the celebration of a peace treaty in Charleston in November. Although the Creeks allowed the Carolinians to send traders to their towns, as well as to the Chickasaw villages located along the Upper Path, they firmly prohibited the British from establishing any settlements south of the Savannah River.

While the Lower Creeks negotiated agreements with the British in Carolina and the Spaniards in Florida, the Upper Creeks initiated relations with the French in Louisiana. Seeking to counterbalance the trade with Carolina, Alabama leaders traveled to Mobile in September 1715, offered to make peace with Governor Cadillac, and invited the French to establish a trading post among the Upper Creeks. Although the Louisiana commander hesitated to build a fort among the Alabamas out of fear of British reprisals, French trading boats from Mobile began to land among the Upper Creek towns before the end of the year. Finally, in the summer of 1717 a French detachment of twenty soldiers constructed Fort Toulouse on the east bank of the Coosa River, just above its confluence with the Tallapoosa. Significantly, the Alabamas persuaded the French to construct the fort on an ancient mound located next to their principal town of Pakana.

Although the Alabamas allowed the French to establish a trading post in their midst, the Upper Creeks joined their brethren in following a policy of neutrality, as the Tallapoosas welcomed Carolinian traders into their villages only a month later. In fact, British and French representatives met and exchanged guarded greetings under watchful Tallapoosa eyes at the village of Tukabatchee in August 1717. Seven months later, in March 1718, leaders from all the major Creek groups met at Coweta and officially agreed to Chief Brims's plan to avoid European entanglements and to harmonize the factional interests within the Creek nation. As a result, for the next century or so the Creeks would be a major force in the diplomacy of the Gulf South. In addition, the Creek stance helped put an end to the large-scale trafficking in Indian slaves that had decimated the region for the past four decades. Disease and depopulation had already undermined the economic basis of Carolina's relations with its indigenous partners, and diplomatic considerations tempered the British desires to profit from a continued slave trade. Although the French in Louisiana had already developed commerce with the Indians in Texas that provided them with a few native slaves obtained through warfare, they would soon follow the Carolinians' lead in turning toward the importation of large numbers of Africans to meet their labor needs.

The expansion of French trade with the interior tribes was the only successful economic activity that occurred under Crozat's proprietorship. No mines were discovered, and staple-crop agriculture failed to develop because of the lack of emigration from France or importation of African slave laborers. Only a little over two hundred civilians and soldiers arrived in Louisiana during Crozat's regime, increasing the French population to around five hundred people by 1717. Most of them settled near Mobile, where they survived by establishing small gardens and raising livestock. In January 1717 the disillusioned Crozat, realizing that Louisiana would not turn a profit without further large-scale investment on his part, received permission to be relieved of responsibility for the stagnating colony.

The Company of the Indies

Soon thereafter, France began taking major steps to develop Louisiana in accordance with the expansionist policies implemented by the Ministry of the Marine, which had assumed further control of all French colonies following the death of Louis XIV in September 1715. His successor, Louis XV, ascended to the throne as a small child, so a Regency Council, headed by the duke of Orleans, conducted affairs of state. The Comte de Toulouse, vice-admiral of France and a reputed expert in colonial affairs, dominated the Ministry of the Marine, which determined to bolster colonial defenses in the aftermath of the War of the Spanish Succession through the expansion of colonial populations and garrisons. The effort to increase Louisiana's military capabilities, however, was overshadowed by an even more extensive effort to build its civilian population. The massive civilian influx, in turn, was shaped by the Regency's efforts to deal with the nation's financial troubles, particularly the massive debt inherited from Louis XIV's reign.

In response to the financial crisis, the Ministry of the Marine awarded the Louisiana proprietorship to the Company of the West, a joint stock company guided by a financial dreamer named John Law, a French subject of Scottish origin. Having fled from Scotland as a young man after getting in trouble with the authorities, Law had gambled his way through Europe before taking up the study of banking in Holland and then moving on to France. While in Paris, Law amassed a great fortune based on speculation and, in the meantime, befriended the duke of Orleans. Enamored with his radical economic schemes, in 1716 the Regent allowed Law to organize a national bank created on the model of the English and Dutch state banks. The following year Law convinced Orleans to grant monopoly control of Louisiana to his Company of the West—soon to be renamed the Company of the Indies after absorbing a few other royal monopolies, including a slave trading company operating out of West Africa—based on a far-reaching scheme that the Scot promised would solve France's economic difficulties and save the indebted country from bankruptcy.

Law's plan called for the full-scale development of Louisiana's agricultural potential in which capital raised from stock sales would finance the Company of the Indies' settlement of the colony. Envisioning success comparable to the French Caribbean, Law proposed granting land to wealthy concessionaires, who would develop their grants through the labor of indentured servants working alongside African slaves provided by the Company. The endeavor would enrich the state through trade and the retiring of the public debt. Depending on settlers and investors to make his scheme work, Law and his associates orchestrated a fantastic promotional campaign that stressed the bounteous nature of Louisiana and its limitless potential for wealth. This strategy worked to overcome French aristocratic prejudices against commercial investment, and greedy upperclass gamblers entered into a frenzy of speculation that drove the price of the Company's stock to heights that would have been impossible to sustain even if Louisiana had immediately been profitable. By early 1720, however, it was apparent that the Company of the Indies would not be paying out dividends anytime soon, and the "Mississippi Bubble" of investment soon burst. Rumors of the company's insolvency flew throughout Paris, precipitating a run on the national bank, which ultimately failed. In the ensuing crisis, stock in the Company of the Indies became worthless and Law was forced to flee the country. Although the government reorganized the Company of the Indies by making it a public stock venture and appointing a commission to oversee its operation, Louisiana, for a variety of reasons, had already acquired a terrible reputation in the minds of most French citizens.

Whereas Law's efforts to attract investors worked all too well, the Company was less successful in populating Louisiana, as few French men and women were willing to settle voluntarily in a distant colony already known for its hardships, despite the extravagant promotional literature. Nonetheless, between October 1717 and May 1721, the Company of the Indies transported about 350 employees and 2,500 indentured servants, along with 1,700 or so wives and children to the Gulf Coast. Most servants, or *engagés,* had been contracted to serve the 119 recipients of land concessions for an average term of three years. In addition, about 1,100 soldiers were assigned duty at various posts in the colony. Although most of these people were natives of France, nearly 1,300 of them had been recruited from various parts of Germany and Switzerland.

In addition to these 5,700 colonists, the Company also transported about 1,300 criminals to the Gulf Coast, a move that reinforced the negative popular image of Louisiana, resulting in a virtual halt to French emigration after 1721. Lack of response to the propaganda campaign caused the Regency and the Company of the Indies, in their mutual desire to make Louisiana profitable as quickly and cheaply as possible, to implement the disastrous policy of forced emigration. As early as fall 1717 Law accepted a plan to transport salt smugglers to Louisiana. The government soon added army deserters to the list of exiles and, in a further demonstration of the close working relationship between the Regency and Law, the Company agreed to bear all costs for transporting convicts to Louisiana. It was only a short administrative step from exiling deserters to ridding the country of vagabonds, prostitutes, beggars, indigents, and other social outcasts. Therefore, between February 1718 and April 1720, the government issued a series of ordinances calling for the rounding up of criminals and the transportation of them to Louisiana. The first ship carrying salt smugglers to the Gulf Coast left La Rochelle in March 1719. Shipments of other criminals and undesirables began in earnest later that summer. In early 1720 the campaign to empty the jails and fill the colony expanded as the Company sent press gangs to scour the countryside to find its settlers. The wholesale arrests caused the general French populace to rebel, and a series of riots against the system forced the government to issue an order banning any further deportations to Louisiana in May 1720. Despite the edict, a few more ships left France loaded with exiles, the final one landing at Dauphin Island in January 1721. Although only about sixty of the deportees remained alive by November 1721, most people in France came to regard Louisiana as a penal colony, unfit for settlement by respectable citizens. Abbé Antoine-François Prevost summed up and reinforced the French view of Louisiana in his popular 1731 novel, *Manon Lescault,* stating that the colony was full of "wretched exiles," who resided in "mere assemblage[s] of poor cabins . . . made of planks and mud" surrounded by "unknown reaches, deserted or inhabited by wild beasts and savages equally barbarous."

Louisiana's unsavory reputation was reinforced by the actual hardships the settlers faced once they landed on the Gulf Coast, and negative reports about the colony began to filter back across the Atlantic soon after the arrival of the first ships. Although the Company of the Indies transported flour, cattle, and other supplies aboard its ships and even purchased large quantities of corn and meat from Indian villages, the continual flow of people from the vessels through the coastal ports and toward their concessions created a persistent food shortage. The immigrants stranded at the coastal ports lacked the knowledge or energy to gather fish or other available food sources; one colonist claimed that more than five hundred people died of hunger at Biloxi in the winter of 1718–1719. Settlers who survived long enough to move beyond the coast often succumbed to malaria and other sicknesses, or to the unaccustomed oppressive heat and humidity, or just to general weakness caused by their stressful travel and lack of decent nutrition. By 1731 only about two thousand French and German settlers remained in Louisiana, most of the other five thousand having died in the colony, while a few lucky ones had returned across the Atlantic.

The incredibly high death toll of the Europeans only reinforced the decision to transport African slaves to Louisiana. The Company of the Indies maintained several trading posts on the west coast of Africa, including Fort St. Louis and Gorée near the mouth of the Senegal River, as well as one farther south at Juda in the Bight of Benin. The first slave ship, *l'Aurore,* arrived in Louisiana in the spring of 1719 carrying a cargo of two hundred slaves who had been obtained at Juda. Over the course of the next four years, nine ships transported another nineteen hundred slaves to the Gulf Coast: eleven hundred from Juda, five hundred from Senegambia, and three hundred who had been obtained at Cabinda in Portuguese-controlled Angola. The slaves who landed on the Gulf Coast formed a heterogeneous group, coming from three different African regions and a wide variety of nations. The slaves shipped from Fort St. Louis and Gorée—where ultimately about two-thirds of the slaves transported to Louisiana would originate—had been obtained in the Senegambia region of West Africa, an area containing many ethnic groups that the colony's officials often misidentified as Bambaras. Language, war, and religion divided the slaves, even though most Africans sent to Louisiana were brought up in agricultural communities involved in crop raising and animal husbandry. Various language groups dominated each of the three African regions, where different dialects were spoken. Often, warfare—exacerbated by the slave trade—broke out between the regional ethnic groups. Muslims constituted a small number of the slaves shipped to Louisiana, but the majority of West Africans were polytheistic, with varied religious practices.

Despite their disparity, the Africans who landed in Louisiana in this period had a much higher survival rate than the Europeans. By 1726, fifteen hundred slaves, nearly three-fourths of the twenty-one hundred transported between 1719 and 1723, were still alive. Slaves fared better than their European counterparts for a variety of reasons. The Company showed great concern about its highly prized cargo and took steps to avoid high mortality at sea, such as preventing overcrowding, providing adequate food, maintaining cleanliness, and avoiding long stays in port. As a result, the slave trade voyages to Louisiana through 1723 had a loss in transit of less than 4 percent. Therefore, the Africans generally disembarked on the Gulf Coast in better condition than the Europeans. Most importantly, the Africans were resistant to malaria and were more used to the hot and humid climate than the French and German settlers. Most were also skilled at feeding themselves by hunting, fishing, and cultivating rice, corn, melons, and other food crops.

After a lull in the slave-trading voyages after 1723, the transportation of Africans to Louisiana picked up once more in 1726, when two ships brought five hundred captives from Senegambia. The trade increased greatly the following year, due to treaties arranged between the Company of the Indies and the Dutch and the English that recognized the French company's exclusive trade monopoly over most of the Senegambia region. As a result, between 1727 and 1731 nine ships brought twenty-seven hundred slaves from Senegambia to the Gulf Coast, while only one ship carrying 450 Africans arrived from the Bight of Benin. Whereas few slaves had died crossing the Atlantic during the first years of the trade, during the latter period more than 8 percent died while in transit, the result of poor conditions while waiting to embark. A steady stream of captives filled the West African trading posts while the Company of the Indies struggled to refit its ships in France and send them back quickly to Senegal to load them. As a result, the slaves died en masse in the posts, and the survivors were so weakened that many of them perished aboard ship. For example, *La Galathée* left Gorée in October 1728 with four hundred slaves and arrived at the mouth of the Mississippi three months later with only 260 survivors. Many of the Africans, as well as some crewmen, had died of scurvy. Nonetheless, by 1731 about four thousand of the nearly six thousand Africans brought to the Lower Mississippi Valley by the Company of the Indies remained alive.

As the number of slaves in Louisiana rose in the 1720s, rules were needed to regulate their conduct. In March 1724 the French government issued the *Code Noir,* or Black Code, for the colony, based on a similar set of rules laid down in 1685 for the French West Indies. The code's goal in defining the parameters of slave treatment was to bring order by modifying the behavior of brutal masters and encouraging the indulgent ones to be more strict. To be sure, the regulations contained a few features designed to protect the slaves, such as one article requiring that all slaves be converted to Catholicism and another permitting slaves the rite of Christian marriage. However, in practice, all protective clauses were interpreted to the slaveowners' advantage. The code stipulated severe punishment, even mutilation, for runaway slaves. It permitted the authorities to remove the ears and brand a fleur-de-lis on the shoulder of any slave who absconded for a month; for a second offense, the punishment was hamstringing (cutting the slave's hamstring tendons, rendering him or her lame) and branding on the other shoulder; the death penalty was decreed for a third offense. Thus, the Code Noir gave slaves little genuine protection, while it decreed harsh punishment.

Settlement in Louisiana

While the French had concentrated their efforts on Mobile Bay and the Gulf Coast for the first twenty years of Louisiana's existence, the Company of the Indies focused on developing the Mississippi River Valley during its proprietorship. Therefore, most of the European and African immigrants were sent to the river that drained the heart of the continent, resulting in the establishment of a wide variety of settlements by 1731, the most important being New Orleans. In 1717 the Company ordered that a principal town should be built on the Mississippi River site recommended by Bienville the previous decade. The following year Company directors gave instructions for the design, envisioning a fortified city surrounded by cultivated lands.

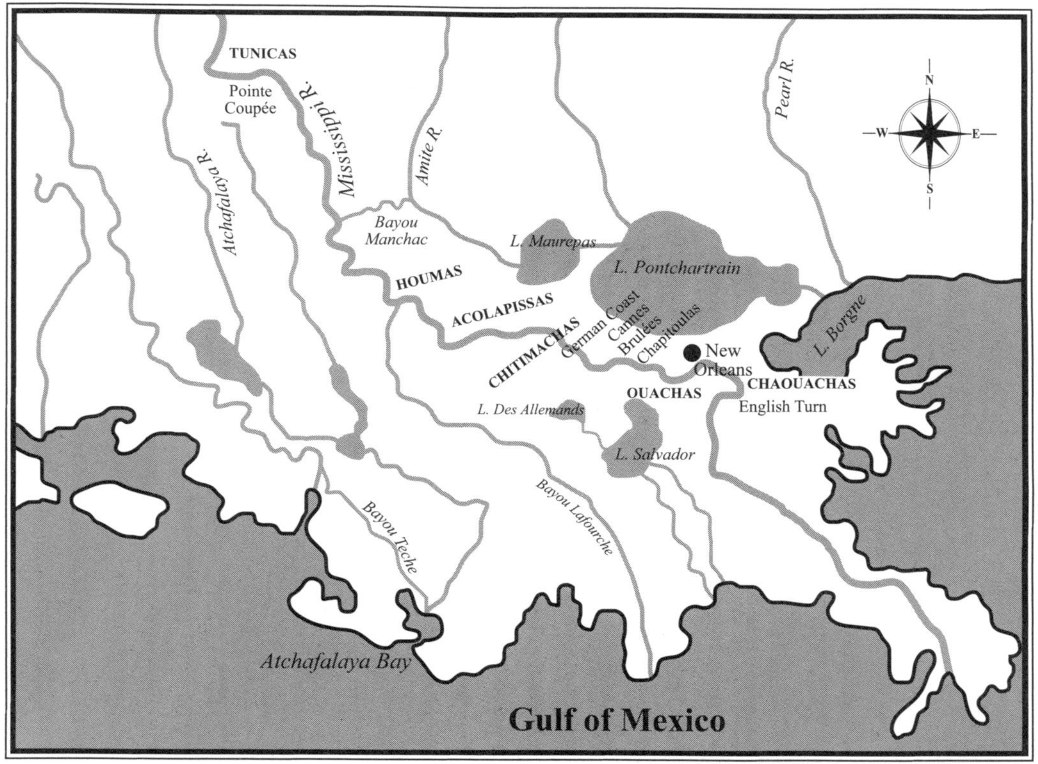

MAP 4. THE LOWER MISSISSIPPI, CA. 1725

In response to these directives, in March 1718 Bienville ceremonially cut the first cane at the chosen site for the town named New Orleans, after the Regent. Within a year a handful of impermanent structures had been erected, most constructed of cypress posts and boards with roofs of palmetto thatch. Although each year's spring flooding hampered settlement, by December 1721, when New Orleans was officially designated as the capital, the population—within the limits of what is now known as the Vieux Carré—stood at nearly 250 Europeans and 100 African and Indian slaves.

While the first settlers at New Orleans had arranged their houses in a haphazard manner, French officials, inspired by Enlightenment ideas concerning urban planning, sought to construct Louisiana's capital based on a rational scheme, expressed through a regular geometric design that separated and ordered the city's many functions—military, commercial, trade, political, and residential. Therefore, the Company of the Indies commissioned Adrien de Pauger, a French military engineer and disciple of Sébastien Le Prestre de Vauban, France's foremost urban planner, to lay out a town design and then oversee its execution. Pauger arrived at New Orleans in the summer of 1721 and, after observing the situation, drew a plan that called for a city enclosed by walls on three sides in which the streets would form a simple grid with rows of square blocks extending on either side of a central plaza that contained the official government buildings and a church. Ultimately, Pauger's dream for New Orleans was only partially fulfilled and was barely under way by the time he died of fever in 1726. In September 1722 a hurricane destroyed most of the initial ramshackle edifices, aiding construction efforts by clearing the way for the construction of Pauger's gridiron of streets and the establishment of the main plaza. Permanent whitewashed wooden structures, some of them two or three stories high, began to take the place of the earlier crude cabins. Work also began on an extensive levee system designed to hold back the river. On the other hand, the wall that Pauger had envisioned enclosing the city never materialized, and the government buildings on the main plaza maintained an air of impermanence. Military barracks took up much of the public space.

The semiorderly construction of the city, combined with the transfer of official French power to the Mississippi River, caused the population of New Orleans to expand almost three-fold during the 1720s, reaching over 600 Europeans and 250 slaves—almost all of them Africans—by 1731. More than a hundred soldiers and officials also quartered in the town. Although many people maintained gardens, and livestock roamed around the margins of the town, New Orleans emerged soon after its founding as an urban place characterized by a wide variety of nonagricultural activities and professions. About one-third of the three hundred or so household heads were skilled artisans, such as carpenters, blacksmiths, coopers, candlemakers, and tailors. Other people worked unloading ships and as unskilled laborers. Unlike most of the rest of Louisiana, New Orleans concentrated the colony's poor freemen, whose trades benefited from an urban setting or who simply lacked the skills and resources to live off the land.

Whereas New Orleans quickly became a city populated predominantly by French people, plantations with numerous African slaves surrounded the town up and down the Mississippi River for about twenty miles in each direction. Forty or so concessions, each laid out in a longlot fashion similar to the model established in New France along the St. Lawrence River, were situated on both sides of the Mississippi from just below the town to English Turn. Each parcel included a river frontage of two to four arpents—one arpent measuring just under two hundred feet—and stretched back from the Mississippi toward the cypress swamps in a rectangular fashion for nearly a mile. Just upstream from New Orleans, in the area that is now Uptown, lay huge concessions belonging to Bienville and the priests of the Jesuit order. Another forty plantations, laid out in a similar method to those situated below New Orleans, stretched upstream on both sides of the river, through the plantations at the Chapitoulas settlement, before concluding at Cannes Brulées on the east bank. A few other concessions were just north of New Orleans on Bayou St. John and in Gentilly.

Unlike in New Orleans, where more than two-thirds of the residents were free Europeans by 1731, along the upper and lower coasts of the Mississippi River the thirty-one hundred or so slaves—less than forty of whom were Indians—greatly outnumbered the seven hundred French settlers. These toiling bondsmen represented over four-fifths of the plantations' inhabitants. During the period of the Company of the Indies' proprietorship, the small slaveowning elite that would come to dominate Louisiana economics and politics throughout the eighteenth century began to emerge from among the concessions of the Lower Mississippi Valley. The most successful plantations were found at Chapitoulas, where five concessionaires owned 450 slaves, all but six coming from Africa. The concessionaires used their numerous slaves in a variety of ways. After constructing levees and drainage canals, the slaves planted fields containing cash crops, such as tobacco and indigo, in addition to cultivating rice, felling cypress trees, and herding cattle, sheep, pigs, and horses. Including the city of New Orleans, most of Louisiana's wealth and about four-fifths of the colony's European and African residents were concentrated along the Mississippi River downstream from Cannes Brulées.

In response to the influx of Europeans and Africans to the Lower Mississippi Valley, some of the Indian tribes in the region—who still numbered about three thousand in the mid-1720s despite continual outbreaks of disease—moved closer to New Orleans in order to sell meat and vegetables to the new arrivals. In 1718 the Chitimachas, who had previously been attacked by the French in order to obtain slaves, moved their village from Bayou Lafourche to the Mississippi River among the incipient plantations. From the backcountry south of town, the Chaouchas settled within several miles of New Orleans on the east bank of the Mississippi, while the Ouachas moved about twenty miles above the town on the opposite bank. The Acolapissas relocated from the north shore of Lake Pontchartrain to the east bank of the river upstream from the Ouachas, not too far from the Houma village near Bayou Lafourche. One Frenchman noted that "all these nations are highly industrious and all are quite helpful in furnishing food to the French, to the troops as well as to the people on the concessions." In addition to providing much-needed food, the men of the various tribes also worked as packhorsemen accompanying traders and as crewmen on boats. French officials likewise paid bounties to Indians who captured and returned runaway slaves and soldiers. For most of the first half of the eighteenth century, the French at all the Louisiana settlements made sure there were Indian tribes located nearby in order to provide the newcomers with important goods and services.

The Company of the Indies also established or expanded various posts located in Louisiana's interior. The organization of these posts stood in direct contrast to that of the African-dominated plantation district downriver. The German Coast, or *Côte des Allemands,* was situated only about ten miles upstream from Cannes Brulées. Following Law's fall from grace in late 1720, most of the few German emigrants remaining in the colony demanded to return to Europe. Bienville, however, convinced them to stay in Louisiana by granting the Germans concessions on empty lands already cleared by Ouacha Indians on the west bank of the river, about thirty miles upstream from New Orleans. In the summer of 1721, under the direction of a former Swedish army officer named Karl Friederick, Chevalier D'Arensbourg, the German settlers—mainly from Alsace and other states located along the Rhine River—began to settle on their concessions.

By November 1724 about sixty German families had established small farms that fronted the Mississippi. During the second wave of African immigration to Louisiana about half of the German households obtained slaves, and by the end of the proprietorship 120 bondsmen lived among three hundred or so Europeans. Unlike the plantations along the Lower Mississippi River surrounding New Orleans, the German Coast consisted of small family farms that raised subsistence food crops and cattle. The farms also differed from the French-owned plantation district in that the overwhelming majority of the slaveholding German households contained less than four African laborers.

The Company of the Indies also granted a few concessions in the region located between forty and eighty miles upriver from the German settlements. The first concession in this region, and the one located farthest upstream, was established in 1717 at Pointe Coupée on the west bank of the Mississippi near the Tunica Indian village. Over the course of the following decade French and African immigrants settled at a few other isolated concessions downstream from Pointe Coupée, as 125 Europeans lived among twenty African and Indian slaves in 1726. Over the course of the next five years the French settlers obtained a large number of slaves, and by 1731 the 200-plus Africans outnumbered the 150 Europeans. Although the Pointe Coupée region was not as prosperous as the plantation district near New Orleans, almost all of the households owned slaves and used them primarily to cultivate tobacco, in addition to raising corn and beans and tending livestock. During the period of the Company of the Indies proprietorship, the settlers at Pointe Coupée laid the foundation for the plantations that would thrive later in the century.

About twenty miles upstream from Pointe Coupée, the Red River entered the Mississippi from the west. The small trading post of Natchitoches, established in 1714 on the Red about one hundred miles above its mouth, grew into a settled community during the years of the Company's proprietorship, despite its isolation relative to the rest of the French establishments. Immediately after Law gained control of Louisiana, steps were taken to expand the Indian trade that had already taken root at Natchitoches. In 1718 the Brossaut brothers, merchants from Lyon, obtained a trading concession at Natchitoches, and the volume of commerce exchanged with the Natchitoches and Hasinai Indians expanded greatly. The following year Bénard de la Harpe received a concession for the Kadohadacho village upstream from Natchitoches, and it was through him that the third Caddo group also established a full trading partnership with the French. With the tribe's permission, La Harpe erected the Nassonite Post (officially known as St. Louis de Cadodaquious) at the bend of the Red River in the summer of 1719. From the Nassonite Post, French traders began to obtain furs, horses, and Indian slaves from the three main Wichita groups—the Kichais, Tawakonis, and Taovayas—who lived in sedentary, agricultural villages north of the Red River in present Oklahoma. During the 1720s a Natchitoches Indian tribe called the Yatasis allowed the French to establish a third trading post among the Caddos near their village on Bayou Pierre, opening up further trade with the Indians of East Texas. Soon thereafter the concessions lapsed and Commandant St. Denis assumed control of the commerce with the Indians, employing a few French traders in the process.

The Company of the Indies also sent French soldiers, settlers, engagés, and a few Africans to Natchitoches, causing the population to increase to 160 by 1726. As commandant of Fort St. Jean Baptiste des Natchitoches, St. Denis had fifty soldiers under his command early in the decade, including five officers, a storekeeper, and six troops stationed upstream at the Nassonite Post. The French men and women who arrived at the post established small farms and ranches along the east bank of the Red River, just upstream from the Natchitoches Indian village. As a result, the civilian population grew to just over one hundred people in 1726, many of whom were retired soldiers and their families. Only a couple of Natchitoches settlers obtained African slaves at this time, and only thirty or so toiled in the region by the end of the decade. A few French colonists also obtained Indian slaves through native suppliers and raids, but most were sold downstream at the capital.

Although a few Natchitoches inhabitants successfully raised tobacco early in the 1720s, Louisiana officials judged it to be of lesser quality than that produced elsewhere in the colony. In response, the settlers obtained corn and beans from the Natchitoches Indians and began to raise large amounts for their own consumption and to sell to the Spanish soldiers and priests in East Texas. In exchange for the agricultural produce, the Spaniards provided the French with cattle, and the settlers established *vacheries* (ranches) on islands in the Red River, using the natural flow of the water to contain the animals and to prevent them from damaging their crops. The French also obtained horses and mules from the mount-rich Hasinai Indians. As a result of these efforts, the French settlers at Natchitoches successfully prepared the way for their community to profit from Indian trade, agriculture, and ranching in the future.

In contrast to Natchitoches, the French post at Natchez minimized the importance of commerce with the Indians in favor of staple crop agriculture during the period of the Company's proprietorship. French settlers at Fort Rosalie had already realized that their tobacco was of an excellent quality, causing the Company to pay particular attention to the crop's development. In 1720 the Company established two concessions, St. Catherine's and White Earth, on either side of the Natchez Grand Village, and by 1726 more than two hundred French settlers and African slaves resided there. Although they concentrated on cultivating tobacco, the settlers also raised subsistence crops and tended horses, cattle, and pigs. Another thirty-five French soldiers were stationed at Fort Rosalie, located halfway between the concessions and the Mississippi. Inspired by the successful production of tobacco at the two concessions, Company officials sent more French settlers and African slaves to Natchez over the course of the next three years. By 1729 the number of French settlers had risen to 430, while the number of African slaves had increased to 280. Unlike most of the Indian tribes that lived in close proximity to French settlements in the Lower Mississippi Valley, the fifteen hundred or so Natchez Indians were uncomfortable with the sudden European and African presence in their midst. The disgruntled Natchez still had the means to respond violently to their declining situation and would ultimately disrupt the Company of the Indies' plans for the colony. The Company also established a small trading post and fort, called St. Pierre, on the Yazoo River in order to prevent Carolinian traders from winning over the Indians of the region. Throughout the 1720s a garrison of ten or so French soldiers manned the small fort, and only a few civilians settled nearby. By 1725 the Chachiumas, living on the Upper Yazoo, numbered about one thousand people, while six hundred Yazoos resided in a single village farther downstream near Fort St. Pierre.

Among the French settlers at Natchez was Antoine-Simon Le Page du Pratz, a young man who arrived there along with his Chitimacha female slave in 1720. After establishing his own tobacco plantation between Fort Rosalie and the Grand Village, du Pratz learned the Natchez language and befriended the local native leaders, including the Tattooed Serpent. Du Pratz became an ardent champion of the Natchez Indians, documenting in considerable detail the tribe's relationship with the French during the fateful third decade of the eighteenth century. Following his return to France in 1734, du Pratz began to write memoirs of his colonial experience, culminating in the 1758 publication of *Histoire de la Louisiane,* which included the most favorable descriptions of the Natchez tribe penned by any European observer.

Whereas Natchez developed from an Indian trading post to a cash crop producer in the 1720s, the French settlement on the Arkansas River moved in the opposite direction. The Company of the Indies granted one of the largest concessions, located on the Arkansas about twenty miles above its mouth, to John Law himself, and he soon made arrangements to establish a settlement near the site that Tonti's trading post had occupied in the late seventeenth century. In August 1721 about one hundred French indentured servants and African slaves arrived at the Arkansas to prepare the way for the concessionaires to whom Law had granted the land. Soon thereafter a troop of about twenty soldiers established a small post (with Quapaw permission) about ten miles up the Arkansas River from Law's concession, near the Osotouy village. Although Law's agent, Bertrand Dufresne, assumed control of the concession in March 1722, it soon became apparent that because of the proprietor's downfall no concessionaires would join him. Therefore, the Company moved most of the slaves to concessions nearer New Orleans and freed a number of the French servants from their indentures. Only a few remained to take the place of the concessionaires, raising subsistence crops to sell to the French soldiers. Because these settlers found the virgin land difficult to cultivate, the Quapaws invited them to farm fields previously worked by native women near Osotouy. Even so, within a year only twenty Frenchmen and six slaves remained at Law's concession, while about thirty French settlers lived at Osotouy. Although they were farming successfully, the Company frustrated their hopes in 1724 by withdrawing the garrison from the Arkansas Post in order to cut costs. With no market for their goods and no soldiers to protect them, more settlers abandoned the area, leaving only about thirty French men, women, and children behind. Most of those who stayed gave up farming and became full-time hunters, increasingly depending on the fifteen hundred or so remaining Quapaws for protection and agricultural produce. Declining population and Chickasaw raids over the course of the decade caused the Kappas and Tourimas to move their village from the Mississippi River to the south bank of the Arkansas, where they established separate towns about ten miles upstream from their Osotouy kinsmen.

A few hundred miles upstream from the Arkansas Post lay the Illinois country, which fell under the jurisdiction of Louisiana when the colony was awarded to the Company of the Indies. By 1718 less than one hundred French settlers, traders, and missionaries resided at the posts of Cahokia and Kaskaskia on the east bank of the Mississippi. In early 1719 a Canadian, Pierre Dugué, sieur de Boisbriant, commanded a convoy containing settlers and soldiers up the river to establish the Company presence in Illinois. Later that summer Boisbriant established Fort Chartres, between Cahokia and Kaskaskia, near the Michigamea Indian village. Over the course of the next decade the Company sent French settlers and African slaves to Illinois, and by the end of the proprietorship the total population of the region stood at about five hundred, one-third of whom were black slaves. The rich soil and temperate climate allowed the inhabitants to raise Old World cereal crops, most importantly wheat, which they milled into flour and sent downstream to the residents of the Lower Mississippi Valley, who were desperate for French-style bread. Although distant from New Orleans, the Illinois country would play an important role in Louisiana's internal economy throughout the French period.

Despite the removal of the capital to New Orleans and the resulting focus on the Mississippi River Valley, French immigrants and African slaves continued to settle along the Gulf Coast. By 1726 Mobile's population had risen to over 500 people, including 250 French civilians and 150 African slaves. Reflecting the continued importance of the Indian trade with the Choctaws and the Creeks, among others, fifty Native American slaves also resided in Mobile. Although the soil was too sandy to raise a cash crop, about one-third of the one hundred households in Mobile owned slaves, most of whom worked in small gardens raising food to sell to the one hundred or so French soldiers stationed at the newly established Fort Condé and to the isolated Spanish troops at Pensacola. Another one hundred French settlers and African and Indian slaves resided on farms and ranches located outside of Mobile at Dauphin Island, Pascagoula, and Biloxi, which had been relocated from its original site to the west side of Biloxi Bay. Despite the small-scale farming carried out at the various French settlements, all of them depended on the nearby seventeen hundred Indians—Mobilians, Tohomes, Pascagoulas, Biloxis, Apalaches, Chacatos, and Taensas—for venison, corn, and other necessities.

Spanish Posts in West Florida and East Texas

The French settlement and development of the Mississippi Valley dramatically impacted the Spanish possessions in West Florida and East Texas when war broke out between the two countries soon after the Company of the Indies assumed the Louisiana proprietorship. Spain, unhappy with 1713 Treaty of Utrecht and the loss of its Italian possessions, carried out an ill-advised invasion of Sicily in 1717 and Sardinia the following year. In response, Great Britain, France, Holland, and Austria declared war on Spain in January 1719. As with previous conflicts, the War of the Quadruple Alliance spread from Europe to North America, inspiring the French in Louisiana to attack the feeble Spanish posts on the colony's eastern and western flanks. Soon after learning of the declarations of war, Company of the Indies officials at Mobile launched the first French assault on Spanish possessions by attacking Pensacola in May 1719. Bienville and two of his brothers, accompanied by a force of about three hundred Frenchmen and four hundred Choctaw Indians, surprised the Spanish garrison at Pensacola and forced the governor to surrender after a three-hour bombardment. The 250 captured Spanish troops were sent to Havana, and Antoine Le Moyne, sieur de Châteaugué, took possession of the fort with his ragtag army of French troops, indentured servants, and Choctaws. The following month Spanish officials in Cuba ordered don Alfonso Carrascosa de la Torre, in command of twelve ships and eighteen hundred men, to retake Pensacola. The Spanish expedition arrived at Pensacola Bay in August and forced the overwhelmed Châteaugué to surrender rather hastily after ninety Frenchmen deserted to join the invaders. The Spaniards, however, held Pensacola for only one month before a French squadron commanded by Admiral Desnos de Champmeslin retook the post in September 1719. Once again the Spanish troops were forced to abandon Pensacola, and a small French garrison remained in possession of the fort.

In March 1721, despite the French desire to retain Pensacola and keep the Spaniards out of the northern Gulf of Mexico, a peace treaty was concluded that called for the return of all possessions taken during the conflict. It took until November 1722, however, for the new Spanish governor, Lieutenant Colonel Alejandro Wauchope, a Scotsman who had served in Spain's Irish Brigade, to arrive at Pensacola with three ships of troops and workmen from Mexico. Although little remained of the presidio, Wauchope had already received instructions to build a new fort on Santa Rosa Island. The Spaniards chose a spot about one mile east of Point Sigüenza on the north side of the island to construct the new presidio and built within a few months a church, a warehouse, officers' quarters, barracks, powder magazines, a cook oven, and small houses for civilians. In February 1723 Wauchope turned over command to Captain Pedro Primo de Rivera and left for Veracruz. Despite orders forbidding trade with the French at Mobile, the one hundred or so Spanish soldiers and workers who remained at Pensacola continued to depend on their Gallic neighbors for food and other supplies for the remaining three decades of the post's existence. The Spanish also reestablished the small post at San Marcos de Apalache during this period, manning it with about fifty soldiers.

Similar events occurred on the western flank of Louisiana in East Texas. In June 1719 a small French force from Natchitoches attacked the nearby Spanish mission at the Adaes Indian village. Fearful of an uprising of the French-allied Hasinai Indians, Captain Domingo Ramón abandoned the region, ending the second effort at establishing Spanish settlements in East Texas. Although officials in Spain and Mexico City soon thereafter decided to reoccupy the region, it was not until after peace had been signed in March 1721 that the marqués de San Miguel de Aguayo, a wealthy resident of Coahuila, crossed the Rio Grande at the head of an expedition that included five hundred men and enormous herds of horses, cattle, sheep, and goats. After reinforcing the small Spanish outpost of San Antonio de Béxar, a mission-presidial complex established in 1718 to support the Franciscan effort in East Texas, Aguayo began to take steps to reestablish and secure the six abandoned missions among the Caddos. In August the huge expedition arrived at the Neches River, where Aguayo easily convinced St. Denis to recall his small French contingent back to Natchitoches. Without hope of French support, the Hasinais reluctantly allowed the Spaniards to rebuild the presidio and the four Franciscan missions that had been established in their midst five years before. Aguayo continued eastward and restored the mission at the Ais town, as well as adding a presidio to the mission at the newly named Los Adaes, which would remain the official capital of Spanish Texas for the next half century. Leaving 125 soldiers in East Texas, Aguayo headed south and initiated construction of a new fortification, called Nuestra Señora de la Bahía del Espíritu Santo, to guard the Texas coast at Matagorda Bay. By the time he returned to Coahuila in May 1722, Aguayo had successfully anchored Spanish Texas at three vital points—Los Adaes, La Bahía, and San Antonio. For the time being, French provocation had resulted in strengthening rather than weakening Spanish Texas.

Within a decade, however, the Spanish presence on the Louisiana border had diminished greatly, making San Antonio the main focus of Texas. Although Aguayo had placed the Franciscans in East Texas, the Hasinais remained aloof from the priests' conversion efforts. Brigadier General Pedro de Rivera y Villalón visited the Hasinai country in 1727 while conducting an inspection tour of northern Mexico and found that the Indians had not gathered at any of the four missions. Rivera was even more disturbed by the close ties the Hasinais maintained with the French at Natchitoches. Fifty mounted Nabedache warriors "armed with French guns, with flasks of powder and bags of bullets, [looking] like the most expert troops" met the inspector general upon his arrival in East Texas. Rivera realized that the Hasinais had embraced the French influence, and he recognized the futility of maintaining two presidios in East Texas. He recommended the abandonment of the presidio among the Hasinais and suggested that sixty troops would be sufficient at Los Adaes, since 125 was already insufficient in the event of war. In 1729 the viceroy of New Spain issued a decree calling for the implementation of Rivera's ideas. In 1731 the Querétaran missionaries, who had been left unprotected by the military withdrawal, abandoned their three missions among the Hasinais and retreated to San Antonio. Only the mission run by the Franciscan fathers of Zacatecas, located near the Nacogdoches village, remained among the Hasinais, along with the two missions for the Ais and the Adaes. As with the Spaniards at Pensacola, the isolated soldiers and priests in East Texas maintained illegal ties with the nearby French settlers in Louisiana in order to obtain the basic necessities for survival. Most importantly, the feeble Spanish presence in East Texas would allow French traders from Natchitoches the freedom to develop strong commercial ties with the region's Indian tribes for the following thirty years.

Internal Dissension among the French

Despite the French successes at the expense of the Spaniards on the boundaries of Louisiana, internal dissensions continued to plague the colony throughout the period of the Company of the Indies' control. In the area of religion, the Jesuits' conflict with the missionaries that had divided the French settlement at Mobile during the first decade of the eighteenth century was replaced by a jurisdictional dispute with the Capuchin Order in the 1720s. In 1723 the Company granted the Capuchins the right to minister to French settlements and Indian tribes located south of the Yazoo River, while the Jesuits gained control of the region to the north. The Capuchins, led by Father Raphaël de Luxembourg, however, did not have the manpower or funds to effectively move beyond New Orleans and Mobile. Therefore, in 1726 the wealthier, enterprising Jesuits, headed by

Father Ignace de Beaubois, won responsibility for all the native missions in the colony. Not only did this anger the Capuchins, they were also threatened by the Jesuits' acquisition of land just upstream from New Orleans and the fact that Beaubois established his headquarters in the capital. While this petty conflict exacerbated divisions among the French officials in Louisiana, it had little effect on the evangelization of the Indians, as the Jesuits made little progress among the tribes, and only the Apalaches near Mobile continued to accept the ministrations of a Catholic priest.

The arrival of the Ursuline Sisters—a teaching order of nuns, whose introduction into the colony resulted from an initiative of Father Beaubois—complicated the tensions between the Capuchins and the Jesuits. Realizing the need for nurses and a hospital in New Orleans, the Jesuit Beaubois negotiated a contract for the founding of a convent in the city with a small contingent of Ursuline nuns from Rouen on behalf of the Company of the Indies. The Ursulines were charged with directing a hospital and establishing a program for the education of French, Indian, and African females. The first contingent of twelve nuns, led by Marie Tranchepain, arrived in New Orleans in August 1727 and soon thereafter began to minister to the needs of local girls in a rented house. Although the Ursulines had reluctantly agreed to take on the nursing role as part of their official duties in Louisiana, they reneged on their hospital responsibilities by arguing that the Company had not built them a convent. The Ursulines also exacerbated the conflict between the Capuchins and the Jesuits by choosing Beaubois as their spiritual director, despite Father Raphaël's jurisdiction in New Orleans. In fact, the Ursulines skillfully exploited the quarrel to establish a degree of independence that allowed them to expand even further their teachings among the town's young women, free and slave alike.

The Company of the Indies' attempts to build a new administrative system on the foundations of the extant institutions in Louisiana accelerated the tensions that already divided the French settlement on the Gulf Coast. A new Superior Council, consisting of all the Company's local directors, replaced the one that had been created during the Crozat regime. Company officials in France suspended the position of governor of the colony, but allowed Bienville, the commandant-general of the military, and Commissary Hubert to occupy the chief positions on the Superior Council. Following the collapse of the Mississippi Bubble and Law's downfall, French officials sent two commissioners to Louisiana to investigate local conditions and to reorganize the government. One of the royal commissioners died soon after arriving in New Orleans in April 1723, leaving Jacques de la Chaise as the sole representative of the king. La Chaise formed a new Superior Council, with Commandant-General Bienville and his lieutenant, Louis-Pierre Leblond de La Tour, serving as chairman and deputy chairman. Five other men, each assigned specific administrative functions, comprised the rest of the Superior Council.

With the new government established, La Chaise then ruthlessly went about the business of investigating the administration of the colony, correcting abuses in spending, charging many clerks with malfeasance, and generally alienating most of the important citizens of Louisiana. Most seriously, La Chaise assumed a position that was systematically hostile to Bienville, turning most of the military, the Jesuits, and the original Canadian settlers against the newcomer. The other members of the Superior Council joined the Bienvillists' opposition to La Chaise in August 1724 when the Crown, prompted by Company officials in France, appointed the newcomer to the key position of senior councilor. Although La Chaise had few supporters within the colony—mainly just the Capuchins—he triumphed over his detractors when the Company recalled Bienville and his brothers to France in January 1725. Moreover, four months later the Company appointed La Chaise as intendant with the sovereign power to decide all matters relating to police, commerce, and finances. The new commandant-general, Étienne Périer, arrived in Louisiana in March 1727 and immediately began to support La Chaise in his unrelenting campaign against the Bienvillist opposition. The military was purged of the leading Bienville supporters—including his nephews, the Noyan brothers—and two new members were appointed to the Superior Council.

Indian Affairs and the Natchez War

Whereas Périer's arrival helped silence the outspoken opposition to La Chaise, it left responsibility for the management of the colony's complex Indian affairs in the hands of a man with no experience in Louisiana, nor with Native Americans. Upon his arrival in the colony, Périer's most important task was to maintain the loyalty of the numerous Choctaws, whose territory provided a buffer for French Louisiana from the aggressive British in Carolina. Bienville, understanding the necessity of maintaining a strong alliance with the Choctaws, had plied the tribe with gifts and trade, in addition to encouraging them to pursue constant warfare against the Carolinian-supported Chickasaws. In the early 1720s Bienville had funneled gifts to the tribe through the office of the Great Chief of the Choctaws, a French-created position awarded to the chief of Couechitto, a town in the Eastern district. As a means of influencing the Choctaws, however, the position of the Great Chief was inadequate, as the office was largely just an honorific title with little power to force the subordination of other tribal leaders. As a result of the Great Chief's impotence, the French found it necessary to make direct payments to Choctaw warriors—in the form of separate bounties for scalps and slaves—in order to encourage them to continue the hostilities against the Chickasaws. These methods were costly, and the French soon ran out of supplies, spurring the Choctaws to accept a truce with the Chickasaws in December 1724. Over the course of the next few years, Choctaw headmen—particularly in the Eastern district, located near the Upper Path—welcomed Carolinian traders into their villages and maintained the peace with the Chickasaws. Nonetheless, the Choctaws in the Western district and in Sixtowns, who lived closer to Mobile than their Eastern district brethren, continued to have friendly relations with the French, particularly once Périer increased the amount of trade goods and gifts destined for those villages.

While Périer was scarcely able to maintain the alliance with the Choctaws, the inexperienced commandant-general failed to contain the dangerous situation with the Natchez Indians that he inherited from Bienville. As a result, the Natchez rose up against the French in 1729, ultimately bringing an end to the Company of the Indies' control of Louisiana. Violence had first erupted between the French and the Natchez tribe in October 1722 when soldiers stationed at Fort Rosalie clashed with Indians over a corn payment. The hostilities then spread to the White Apple settlement district, a hotbed of pro-English/Chickasaw sympathy, when tribesmen from that village began sniping at the St. Catherine's concession from concealed positions. Other Natchez parties roamed at night, shooting livestock and burning French houses. Before matters escalated, however, the pro-French Tattooed Serpent intervened and negotiated a peaceful agreement between the colonists and the White Apple villagers. Despite the settlement, resentments continued to mount over the following year as the plantation managers at the St. Catherine's concession failed to promote peace with the residents of the nearby White Apple, Jenzenaque, and Grigra settlements, all of whom maintained ties with Carolinian traders and the Chickasaws. The Indians often killed cattle and horses that strayed from the concession into their fields, leading the St. Catherine's directors to whip the culprits and put them in chains.

In September 1723 Bienville overreacted to the tense situation by aggressively taking up arms against the Natchez. Along with four boatloads of Frenchmen from New Orleans and Tunica and Choctaw warriors from the Sixtowns district, Bienville traveled to Natchez and met with the Tattooed Serpent, who assured the commandant-general that the outlying villages were responsible for the hostilities. Gathering a mob of about seven hundred French soldiers, settlers, and Indian allies, Bienville burned the White Apple, Jenzenaque, and Grigra villages and temples to the ground, destroyed their granaries, and killed numerous tribespeople. Bienville and his army then returned to the Grand Village and threatened to destroy it as well for allegedly harboring refugees from the torched towns. As before, the Tattooed Serpent convinced the French commander to spare his home district and ceremonial center by providing Bienville with the heads of six enemy leaders. At the conclusion of the hostilities many homeless Natchez Indians took refuge among their kinsmen near the Grand Village in the Flour district or left the area and settled with the Chickasaws. Within a few years, however, the Natchez reestablished the White Apple settlement at its former location.

Unsurprisingly, Natchez resentment continued to fester against the French settlers, whose numbers, when combined with their African slaves, increased to more than seven hundred during the 1720s. In June 1725 the French lost their most important Natchez ally when the Tattooed Serpent suddenly passed away. Even before he died, the Tattooed Serpent began to question the French alliance, asking du Pratz, "What need did we have of the French? Before them . . . we lived like men who knew how to do with what they have, whereas today we walk like slaves who do not know what they wish." Three years later the Great Sun and the Flour chief, the last advocates of the French alliance among the Natchez, also died. When the high chief's office devolved upon a new Great Sun who was immature and ineffectual in tribal politics, anti-French leaders at White Apple and Flour took up the reins of power among the Natchez. At the same time Commandant-General Périer egregiously appointed Sieur de Chépart, a known drunkard and bully, to the position of commandant at Fort Rosalie. Seeking to make a profit for himself, in the fall of 1729 Chépart brashly ordered the people at the reconstituted White Apple district to vacate their lands so that he could establish a tobacco plantation. The insulted Natchez leaders decided that they had borne the burden of the French long enough, but pretended to acquiesce to Chépart's demand while they planned a preemptive strike. To buy themselves additional time, the Indians pleaded that they needed to harvest their fall crops. Although rumors of attack spread among the French settlers, Chépart confidently disregarded all warnings. As a result, well-prepared Natchez warriors easily overwhelmed the French colonists on the morning of November 28. Within a few hours the Indians killed 250 French settlers and captured nearly three hundred black slaves in addition to some fifty French women and children. A few weeks later Natchez warriors assisted the Yazoos in destroying Fort St. Pierre and killing the small contingent of French soldiers and the Jesuit priest who were stationed there.

Twenty or so French survivors of the Natchez attack straggled into New Orleans in early December, causing a wave of panic to spread throughout Louisiana. Fearing a general Indian uprising that might be made worse by an alliance with the numerous Africans on the Lower Mississippi plantations, Périer divided the two groups by dispatching a band of slaves downriver from New Orleans to destroy the Chaouchas village of about 150 tribespeople. Périer felt that this murderous campaign served to keep "the other little nations up the river in a respectful attitude." About three hundred warriors from the small tribes located along the Mississippi then joined two hundred French soldiers and settlers, under the command of Henri de Louboey, at the Tunica village near Pointe Coupée in preparation for making a retaliatory strike against the Natchez. At the same time Charles Le Sueur convinced about five hundred Choctaws, led by Alibamon Mingo, the mico of the Sixtowns village of Chickasawhay, to join him in attacking the Natchez. Learning of the two approaching forces, the Natchez gathered in two forts near the Grand Village. Le Sueur's Choctaw army arrived first and hastily assaulted the Natchez on January 27, 1730, killing nearly one hundred warriors while recovering most of the French hostages and about one hundred slaves. Louboey and his group moved upriver a week or so later and began a protracted bombardment of the Natchez forts with cannons. After two weeks under siege at the Grand Village, the Natchez agreed to release the remaining hostages in return for the French withdrawal. Within a few days, however, the Natchez slipped by the French force and crossed the Mississippi, ultimately establishing a hastily constructed settlement on a ridge along the Tensas River. The Choctaws, disgusted by Louboey's inability to destroy the Natchez, ransomed the French hostages and headed back to their villages with most of the black slaves.

During the summer of 1730, while the French were mobilizing several regiments upriver against the Natchez, a group of African slaves near

New Orleans took advantage of the confusion to plan an uprising. The French uncovered the plot before it could get under way, however, and several male conspirators were broken on the wheel, while a woman was hanged before their eyes. With the colony seemingly teetering in the balance, in December 1730 Commandant-General Périer finally set out from New Orleans with a contingent of French soldiers and Tunica warriors. A month later Périer surrounded the Natchez village on the Tensas and forced nearly four hundred Indians to surrender. The hostages, who included the young Great Sun and a few family members, were taken to New Orleans and then herded onto a ship and transported to the French island of Saint-Domingue, where they were sold into slavery. Another forty or so Natchez families eluded the French and took refuge among the Chickasaws. The anti-French Flour chief also remained at large in command of a Natchez force of about 150 warriors. They sought revenge on the French-allied Indians and attacked the Tunicas in June 1731 before heading west to assault the Natchitoches post. The overwhelmed St. Denis was forced to call upon his Caddo Indian allies, as well as Spanish soldiers from nearby Los Adaes, to defeat the Natchez attackers, who lost over half of their force. Over the course of the next few years, Natchez stragglers joined their brethren on the Tombigbee River, where about three hundred refugees eventually formed their own independent town near the Chickasaw villages. A few remaining Yazoo Indians also joined the refugees after the French-allied Quapaws destroyed their villages in the wake of the Natchez uprising.

Although the French soon reconstructed Fort Rosalie, they were never able to rebuild their colonial settlement at that promising location. Following the Natchez disaster the Company of the Indies decided that it no longer could maintain such a vast unprofitable colony that was also militarily vulnerable. By a decree dated January 23, 1731, the Company officially relinquished control of Louisiana to King Louis XV of France, thus ending more than a decade of activity in which the Lower Mississippi Valley was colonized by huge numbers of French settlers and African slaves. Although Crown control of the colony would, to some extent, stifle the future economic progress of Louisiana, it would serve to stabilize the Gulf South for most of the region's inhabitants over the course of the following three decades.

4

Stability and Maturation of the Gulf South, 1732–1763

In contrast to the first thirty years of the eighteenth century, the European colonies in the Gulf South stabilized during the following three decades. Despite French and African immigration to Louisiana slowing significantly during the period, the colony's population grew through natural increase, and the people in the various settlements established productive plantations and farms on which they raised staple crops for export and enough foodstuffs to be self-sufficient. At the same time the Spaniards in East Texas and West Florida maintained their minimal posts and missions, while British traders continued to deal with the Indian tribes of the interior. Whereas the French successfully expanded their commercial and military alliances with the Indians west of Louisiana, their efforts east of the Mississippi resulted in two disastrous campaigns against the Chickasaws and the outbreak of civil conflict among the Choctaws. The Creeks, on the other hand, were able to maintain their neutral stance despite British attempts to engage them in battles against the French and Spanish during two European wars, the latter of which resulted in France abandoning North America altogether, Spain possessing Louisiana, and Great Britain being rewarded with Florida.

Louisiana under Crown Control

The administration of French Louisiana, which had been plagued by jurisdictional confusion, factionalism, and petty jealousies during the early part of the eighteenth century, was marked by stability during the period of royal control. Understanding the colony's dire circumstances following the Natchez uprising, Louis XV appointed Bienville, the most knowledgeable person in France regarding Louisiana, to the post of royal governor. Bienville arrived in the colony in March 1733 and quickly developed a cooperative relationship with the finance officer, Edmé Gatien Salmon, who had assumed his position two years earlier. Both men worked harmoniously with the Superior Council, which gradually assumed the function of a de facto local legislature, despite not having received official Crown authority. Bienville retired in 1743, and another Canadian, Pierre François de Rigaud, Marquis de Vaudreuil, son of the governor-general of New France, took his place. Although Vaudreuil lacked his predecessor's understanding of the colony, the governor's background and strong, yet diplomatic, personality allowed him to avoid conflict with the series of finance officers who succeeded Salmon after 1744. Vaudreuil's elite status and service in Louisiana pleased French officials so much that they rewarded him with a promotion to the position his father had held in Canada. In February 1753 Louis Billouart, Chevalier de Kerlérec, a veteran French soldier from Brittany, arrived in Louisiana as Vaudreuil's replacement. Although Kerlérec clashed with Vincent Gaspard Pierre de Rochemore, who became finance officer in 1758 and used his position for personal profit, the dispute did not affect the colony's administrative steadiness. The outbreak of the Seven Years' War in 1756, however, caused France to neglect Louisiana during most of Kerlérec's term, which ended with his recall in June 1763. The metropole's lack of direction permitted the attorney general and the Superior Council—now dominated by creole elite planters—to increase their influence over Louisiana's administrative system at the end of the era of French Crown rule.

Just as the governance of Louisiana stabilized during the period, so did the colony's economy. By mid-century Louisiana officials and planters had determined the best crop possibilities for each region as well as the number of laborers necessary for their success. Although Louisiana never came close to developing the great wealth produced in the French West Indies, with their exorbitantly profitable sugar and coffee plantations, the colony generated a modest income for its citizenry and France through a mixed economy based on raising foodstuffs for domestic use, planting the moderately lucrative cash crops of tobacco and indigo (used to dye cloth), and exporting lumber products and furs. Vegetables and meat were the most important items raised by Louisiana agriculturalists, as the colony became fully self-sufficient in food during the period. Rice was the colony's staple grain, and most planters with slaves raised the crop

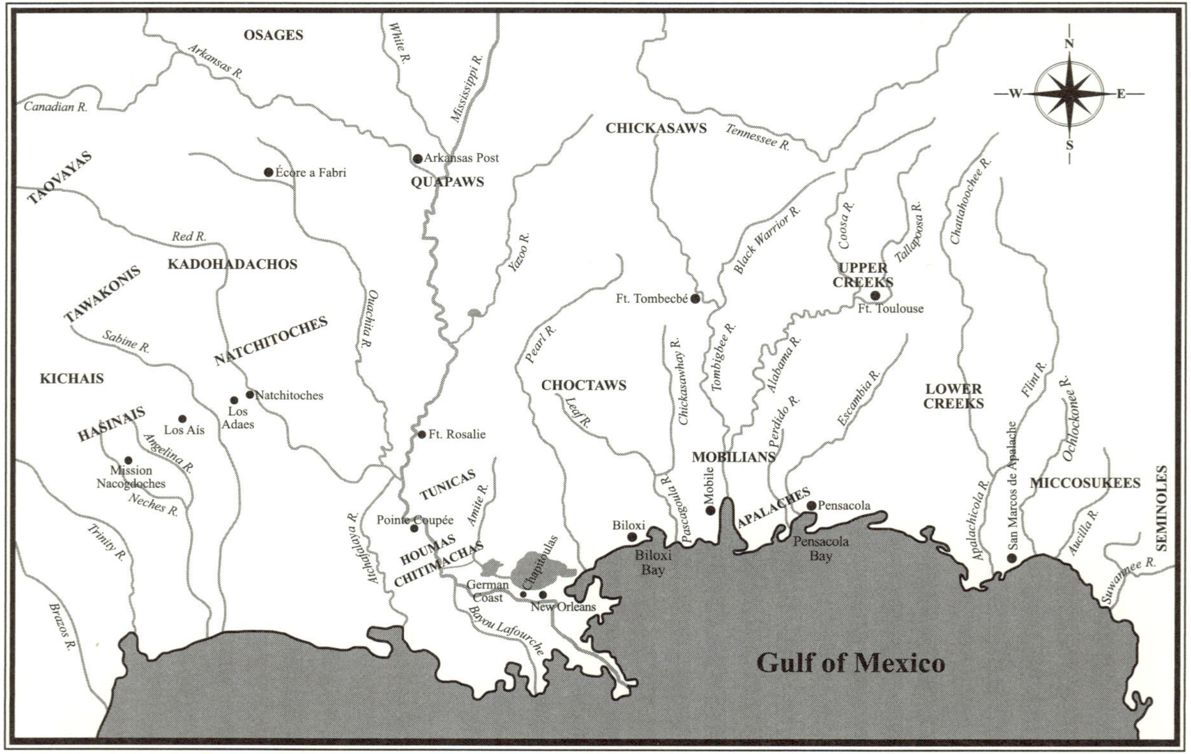

MAP 5. THE GULF SOUTH, CA. 1750

for their own subsistence, as well as marketing surpluses in New Orleans. Small amounts of rice were also exported to the French West Indies, which, located only two weeks' sail away from New Orleans, became Louisiana's second most important trading partner after the metropole during the era. Most small farmers, as well as large planters, also raised corn and beans for food. Cattle and sheep were numerous in the colony, and most French Louisiana residents no longer had to depend on allied Indians to supply them with venison, as they had during the period of Company control. By 1763 Louisiana contained nearly seven thousand cattle and forty-five hundred sheep.

Although Louisiana planters experimented with cotton and sugar during the first half of the eighteenth century, indigo and tobacco became the colony's staple cash crops by the 1740s. The Company of the Indies had concentrated on tobacco cultivation during the 1720s and, accordingly, most of the plantations located along the Mississippi River initially raised the leaf, which required only a minimal amount of investment and labor. During the 1730s, however, prices in France rose for indigo, and most of the large slaveholders located near New Orleans began to raise the crop in earnest, as only they had the capital, labor, and hot and humid climate sufficient for its success. Indigo required a large field labor force, certain skilled workers familiar with the dye-making process, buildings and machinery for the *indigoterie* (indigo works), and sufficient acreage in cultivation to make the investment worthwhile. By 1754, fifty of Louisiana's wealthiest planters, located mainly on the Mississippi River surrounding New Orleans, produced 82,000 pounds of indigo, worth 410,000 livres. Six years later indigo production had tripled to more than 270,000 pounds, worth 1,350,000 livres. One observer noted that Louisiana indigo was "much esteemed for its beautiful color and good quality."

Tobacco cultivation took place on smaller farms and plantations located farther up the Mississippi and on the Red River. In 1754 Louisiana planters raised 160,000 pounds of tobacco, worth 300,000 livres; by 1760 this figure had increased to just over 250,000 pounds, worth 480,000 livres. Lumber products, mainly derived from the cypress trees that abounded in the swamps behind the plantations located along the Mississippi, provided Louisiana with a staple to trade with the French West Indies. In 1754 the colony's lumber output was worth 180,000 livres. The French Crown subsidized pitch and tar, necessary for shipbuilding, by allowing it free passage on the king's ships. As a result, a few tarworks were established in the pine forests located north of Lake Pontchartrain and along the Gulf Coast around Mobile, supplying naval yards in France. Finally, furs obtained from indigenous allies, mainly through Natchitoches and Mobile, brought another 250,000 livres to the colony's coffers by the end of the French era. In 1762 Louisiana exported more than 6 million livres' worth of goods. The colony's output, however, paled in comparison to the French West Indies. Saint-Domingue alone exported over 60,000 tons of sugar per year in the 1760s, worth about 40 million livres.

As a result of the increasingly dependable food supply, the population residing in the French settlements of lower Louisiana grew during the period by 50 percent, from six thousand in 1731 to nine thousand in 1763. The population increase was mainly from reproduction, as European and African immigration to French Louisiana diminished greatly during the period of royal control. The white population remained stable at about two thousand people until about 1740, after which it began to increase due to a relatively equal number of males and females. During the following two decades the white population in lower Louisiana nearly doubled to reach thirty-eight hundred people in 1763, most of them being creoles, the term used for people of either European or African descent who had been born and raised in the colony. Except for about one hundred Alsatian immigrants, the only people who arrived from France during the period were soldiers and administrators. Generally, there were about one thousand marines stationed in lower Louisiana, with nearly half of them located around New Orleans. Although the black slave population in Louisiana initially declined from three thousand people in the 1730s, their numbers grew during the latter period of Crown rule, also through natural increase. Officially, only one ship from Africa—carrying 190 slaves from Senegambia—arrived in New Orleans during the period. A few hundred other slaves, however, were probably smuggled into the colony by way of the French Caribbean. Nonetheless, by 1763 most of the fifty-one hundred black slaves (and about one hundred free people of color) residing in lower Louisiana were creoles, like their white counterparts. Another one hundred or so Indian slaves were found among the various French settlements. As with wealth, Louisiana lagged far behind the French Caribbean in population, as almost half a million whites, free people of color, and slaves resided in Martinique, Guadeloupe, and Saint-Domingue by mid-century.

Despite being in the minority, the French settlers of Louisiana—along the Lower Mississippi as well as in far-flung outposts in the interior—established hegemony over the numerous black slaves during the period of Crown control. Aware of their precarious situation, the French maintained the integrity of their culture as a bulwark against the possibility of hostilities by disgruntled slaves or Indians. The settlers shared a number of factors: a common language, as even the Germans at Des Allemands spoke French, an economy based in agriculture, the Catholic Church, a hierarchical social system, an allegiance to France, and patrilineal and patriarchal family forms. Although there were class differences in colonial Louisiana, particularly between the poor, single residents of New Orleans and the wealthy planters who lived nearby, the fact that they shared a culture and resided in a slave society tended to enforce unity among the free people. Plus, because so few immigrants arrived after 1731, the colony's white population intermarried across barriers of social status (particularly before 1750, after which mobility into the upper ranks became circumscribed), thus making it fairly common for Louisiana's free citizens to enter the slaveholding ranks. The rules of inheritance that divided estates reinforced this tendency by reapportioning the slave population among a large number of slaveholders. By the end of the era nearly two-thirds of Louisiana's free households contained slaves. The nonslaveholders, however, understood the dangerous racial situation that existed in French Louisiana and, sharing a similar background with their wealthier brethren, were compelled to form a bond with their fellow free residents to keep the black slave majority in a subordinate position. The Catholic Church also helped unify the colony's Euroamerican population during the period. The jurisdictional disputes of the early era diminished, and by the 1740s each French settlement was centered around a church, usually manned by a Capuchin priest who held weekly mass in addition to performing baptisms, marriages, and funerals, all of which reinforced a shared sense of community.

Despite being subordinate to the free Euroamerican minority, during the first half of the eighteenth century the slaves in Louisiana were able to create a creole community that combined various African and French elements within the loose confines of the paternalistic colonial slave system. The ability to establish families was the most important factor in the formation of colonial Louisiana's black slave community. In contrast to the French West Indian colonies—and keeping in common with the slave regimes of British North America—Louisiana's slave population increased naturally rather than through constant importation. The relatively benign nature of the colony's tobacco and indigo culture, coupled with ample land to raise food and livestock, proved much healthier than the debilitating work involved in the sugar cultivation that dominated the small French

Caribbean islands, which had little room to spare for vegetable crops or cattle grazing. As a result, the initial male-dominated group of slaves who arrived in Louisiana was able to raise a new creole generation. The creolization of the slave population, combined with the decline in imported slaves, resulted in an evening out of the sexes among Louisiana's bondspeople, and the relative balance between male and female slaves permitted them to form families of their own. Moreover, Louisiana officials and colonists encouraged family formation among bondspeople in the not unreasonable belief that slave unions yielded more children and helped stabilize life on the plantations by giving slaves less incentive to flee or cause trouble.

Because two-thirds of the slaves brought to Louisiana came from the Senegambia region of West Africa, many of the original group who landed on the Gulf Coast shared a similar culture based on religion, crop raising, and animal husbandry. Although many West African traditions were maintained in Louisiana, the creolization of the bondspeople led to the development of a distinctive French-speaking, nominally Catholic, creole slave community by the middle of the eighteenth century. The wide variety of languages spoken among the slaves who arrived in Louisiana, coupled with the hegemony of the colony's homogenous Gallic community, forced the newly arrived Africans in Louisiana to adopt French as their common tongue. Article Two of the Code Noir, implemented in Louisiana in 1724, required that slaves be converted to Catholicism. As a result, priests baptized most slave children, who quickly outnumbered their African-born parents. The black creoles grew up in relatively close proximity to their owners, hearing a French *patois* from birth, and were familiar with Christian teachings and practices throughout their lives.

Louisiana slaves' relatively light workload, combined with the large amount of unoccupied (albeit swampy) land, allowed the bondspeople a degree of freedom, especially compared to their less fortunate brethren in the French West Indies. In addition to working in the fields, many slaves tended livestock and developed a wide range of skills, including blacksmithing, woodworking, shipbuilding, and sailing. The bondspeople's various jobs led to the creation of an internal slave economy, particularly in New Orleans and its outskirts, in which creole blacks grew their own crops, worked for wages, marketed, and acted as consumers. In time, the slave economy expanded so much that white merchants, eager for new customers, willingly catered to bondspeople. Many masters allowed slaves to have guns and ammunition in order to hunt for the plantation community's meat, some of which was sold by enslaved hunters in various markets. The freedom of movement in Louisiana allowed some slaves, as individuals or groups, to commit *petit marronage,* or running away, and live in the swamps near the plantations for a short period of time. Although slave runaways were a common occurrence in French Louisiana, there was no *grand marronage*—where large groups of slaves took permanent refuge in the hinterland, forming self-sufficient communities beyond the authorities' control—as was common on the larger islands in the Caribbean and in Brazil. The planters, supported by the Superior Council and the entire free community, policed runaways extensively and developed arrangements for allied Indians to return fugitive slaves for a reward. Despite the limited degree of freedom the Louisiana slaves had during the era of Crown rule, the French maintained control over their bondspeople through the threat and actual practice of brute force. The Code Noir gave masters the right to flog or brand their slaves with a fleur-de-lis for minor crimes such as stealing livestock or food, while authorities could impose the death penalty upon slaves for major thefts or striking any free person. Although the law contained safeguards against the extreme brutalization of slaves—for example, overzealous whipping and ear cropping were forbidden—the French officials who administered Louisiana rarely enforced these edicts.

The Lower Mississippi Valley

The major portion of Louisiana's free and slave population continued to reside along the Lower Mississippi River during the period of royal control. Over two-thirds of the colony's residents—about sixty-three hundred men, women, and children—lived between English Turn and Cannes Brulées by the end of the French regime. Just under four in ten of the region's residents, or about twenty-four hundred people, lived within the confines of New Orleans, while the other inhabitants resided on the plantations that stretched along the river for twenty miles on either side of the city. During this era New Orleans matured from a shantytown to a cosmopolitan harbor that was similar to other ports located throughout the Gulf of Mexico and the Caribbean. Along with the government buildings, military barracks, and the church, most of the houses within the well-laid out streets of the Vieux Carré were free-standing with a small yard for a garden. Many were built of brick and lumber, consisting of one floor with galleries on the outside around them, raised eight feet above the ground to avoid floodwaters. One observer noted that the "back and sides of the town are mostly laid out in gardens . . . [with] orange trees . . . [that] in the spring afford an agreeable smell."

Whereas the plantation district surrounding New Orleans contained a large slave population and only a small number of wealthy planters and their families, the city itself consisted of a slight majority of whites of all classes, including a large number of skilled artisans, unskilled laborers, itinerant sailors, and French and Swiss soldiers. Nearly half of the city's households contained no slaves, and three of four slaveholding residences had less than five bondspeople. Although most of the colony's elites—particularly the planters who maintained farms near New Orleans—kept a townhouse in the city, these people made up less than a quarter of the port's free population. Most of the city's slaves resided as servants for the upper class, whose houses were located along the main plaza and on the streets nearest the river. The Ursuline convent, established just downstream from the main plaza in 1734, provided Louisiana's elite girls, as well as some less privileged women—in addition to a few Indians and blacks—with an educational opportunity. As a result, female literacy in colonial Louisiana was relatively high. Meanwhile, there were no educational institutions available for men in New Orleans during the period and most lower-class males were illiterate.

The majority of the city's lower-class whites, along with a few slaves and free people of color, lived in the area farthest from the river. This rowdy group—many of whom were poor, single men—contained the first in a long line of inhabitants that helped solidify the Crescent City's reputation as a chaotic, disorderly town wracked by vice, corruption, and violence. Cabarets and taverns abounded in the back section of town, where fraternization across class and race lines frequently took place. The bars confounded the colonial elite, who believed that the public houses not only had a corrupting influence on morals, but that they also encouraged criminal activity. One colonial official complained that "the rear of the City is infested with numbers of men without occupation . . . they adulterate the liquors they sell . . . [and] incite [the slaves] to pilfer and steal from the houses of their masters." Despite the Superior Council's continued attempts to reduce the number of taverns in order to discourage the mixing of slaves, soldiers, and free people, these lower-strata meeting places showed no signs of disappearing by the end of the French era.

Despite the infamous chicanery that dominated the rear of the French Quarter, it hardly threatened the wealth and power of colonial Louisiana that was concentrated in the plantation district that surrounded New Orleans upstream and downriver. The large slave population located there provided the basis for the great prosperity that propelled many creole planters to high positions of colonial authority. Of the thirty-nine hundred people living in the plantation district by the end of the era, three thousand or so were slaves. They made up an overwhelming percentage of the population, with more than three-fourths of the people being bound laborers, nearly all of them creoles of African descent. Most of the slaves were concentrated on the large holdings, and over two-thirds of them resided on the fifty-one plantations that contained twenty or more bondspeople. By 1763 eighteen planters around New Orleans owned more than fifty slaves each. At the same time few free people without slaves resided in the plantation district; only nineteen households—most of them being among a group of free people of color who lived near English Turn—contained no slaves, while thirty-three farms held between one and nine. The great planters used their numerous slaves to generate most of the colony's wealth. Most plantations had indigo works and lumber mills, and the blue dye and cypress planks were the most important items exported from the region. The slaves not only raised staple crops, but also tended livestock and grew rice, so that the plantations were self-sufficient in food. In addition, the planters employed their slaves in the building of levees to protect their land from floods and in the maintaining of paths to New Orleans along the large earthen mounds.

Although there were very affluent planters situated downstream from New Orleans, the largest concentration of wealth, power, and influence was located at Chapitoulas, upriver from the capital. Three Chauvin brothers (Sieurs de Léry, de Lafrénière, and de Beaulieu), Canadian associates of Iberville and Bienville, established concessions at Chapitoulas before the founding of New Orleans. They were joined soon thereafter by Joseph de Villars Dubreuil, a Frenchman who turned his Chapitoulas concession into the most productive plantation in the colony. In addition to raising rice and indigo, he also engaged in a remarkable variety of economic pursuits. Dubreuil constructed some of New Orleans's major buildings, imported slaves (he brought the final shipment of bondspeople from Senegambia in 1743), invented an early cotton gin, and promoted sugarcane cultivation on a limited scale. By 1746 Dubreuil was the wealthiest man in Louisiana, owning over five hundred slaves on several plantations. He died in 1757, and his wealth was disbursed among his descendants. As a result, the largest slaveholder at Chapitoulas in 1763 was Jean Baptiste Payen, sieur de Noyan, Bienville's grand-nephew, with seventy-nine slaves. Another nine hundred or so bondspeople resided at Chapitoulas, more than two-thirds belonging to the other twelve planters (mainly descendants of Dubreuil and the Chauvin brothers) who owned thirty or more slaves. The Chapitoulas planters—who, with their families, made up only one-thirtieth of Louisiana's free population—owned one-sixth of the colony's slaves, one-fourth of its cattle, four-fifths of its horses, and one-third of its sheep.

The power and influence that the Chapitoulas planters accrued was just as important as their wealth. The first-generation creoles enhanced their position in the 1730s by marrying officials sent from France. For instance, Dubreuil's son married the daughter of the commissary, Jacques de la Chaise, while Bienville's nephews wed the daughters of a wealthy concession manager. By the 1740s the rich creoles were marrying each other, consolidating ties among most elite families. For example, Lafrénière's son, Nicolas, married the daughter of a fellow Chapitoulas planter, Jacques Hubert de Bellair. Their daughter then wed the wealthy Sieur de Noyan. Following his wife's death, Nicolas Lafrénière married La Chaise's granddaughter, who was also the grandchild of D'Arensbourg, the German Coast commandant. Lafrénière's cousin, François de Léry, married her sister. Another La Chaise descendant wed Joseph Roy de Villeré, a planter and militia captain at Des Allemands who was also the grandson of Sieur de Léry. By the late 1740s these entwined elite families used their standing to obtain seats on the Superior Council. Nicolas Lafrénière became a member of the Superior Council in 1749 and assumed the position of attorney general in 1763, at which time he and his relatives—either by blood or by marriage—held seven of the body's twelve seats. The Superior Council, dominated by the local creole elite, then used its power to enhance the interests of the wealthy planters and merchants instead of the metropole. In addition to granting the planters great liberty to govern their own slaves, the Superior Council tended to neglect mercantilist trade regulations, allowing the planters and merchants to engage in smuggling with Spanish, British, and French ports throughout the Caribbean.

Most of the interior posts of French Louisiana also grew into mature, established communities during the period of Crown control. The population at the German Coast rose from about four hundred people in 1731 to seven hundred or so by 1763. In contrast to the rest of lower Louisiana, immigrants augmented the free population at Des Allemands, as three groups of Alsatians—totaling about one hundred men, women, and children—arrived in the colony during the 1750s and established farms among the German community. Like most of the other four hundred Euroamerican settlers on the German Coast—which by the end of the French era existed on both banks of the Mississippi—the newcomers raised corn, rice, and beans, along with cattle and sheep, which they sold in the markets of New Orleans. Although about two hundred slaves lived in the region—twice as many as thirty years prior—they continued to be disbursed relatively equally among the farms of the original German Coast settlers, and no great planters emerged at Des Allemands as they had farther downstream at Chapitoulas. In fact, almost two-thirds of the German Coast households contained no slaves, and one-fifth owned between one and four bondspeople. Only four German families had more than twenty slaves, including the Chevalier D'Arensbourg, who maintained command of the German Coast throughout the entire period.

Although Pointe Coupée was situated some eighty miles upriver from the German Coast, the settlement actually had more in common with the plantation districts that surrounded New Orleans than with Des Allemands. First, a majority of the people at Pointe Coupée were enslaved, as the six hundred or so bondsmen accounted for just under 60 percent of the population. Second, over two-thirds of the Pointe Coupée households contained slaves, with one-fourth of the families owning more than ten bondspeople each. Although the plantations were not as large as those farther downriver—only two cultivators had a force of over thirty slaves—most of the Pointe Coupée residents also focused on raising a cash crop for export. Having fewer slaves at their disposal and residing on land that was higher and drier than farther downriver, the Pointe Coupée planters continued to raise tobacco, because the crop was less labor intensive than indigo and the soil was more suitable. By 1735 Pointe Coupée already dominated the colony's tobacco production, as almost all of Louisiana's 100,000 pounds of the crop was raised there. By the end of the era of French Crown rule, Louisiana produced nearly 250,000 pounds of tobacco for export, most of it from Pointe Coupée.

The increasing number of European and African creoles living along the Mississippi from English Turn to Pointe Coupée—along with the establishment of levees that limited the amount of floodplains and wetlands—caused a sharp decline among the region's Native American groups, as the Indian population shrank from three thousand in 1731 to only seven hundred in 1763. The tribes nearest New Orleans suffered the most; the Ouachas and Acolapissas disappeared altogether, while the Chaouacha tribe, living about ten miles upstream from the capital, dwindled to only forty people. About three hundred Chitimachas resided on the west bank of the Mississippi upstream from the German Coast, while just under two hundred Houmas lived near the mouth of Bayou Lafourche. The Tunicas, who maintained their village just above Pointe Coupée, had about the same number as the Houmas. Whereas the Indians had previously worked hard to sell meat and vegetables to the residents of New Orleans, the French failure to regulate the sale of alcohol to the tribespeople caused many to become "very lazy and debased," in the words of Governor Kerlérec. Nonetheless, the French continued to value the four tribes as military allies who served "as an advance post and barrier against the incursions" of enemy Indians.

The Louisiana-Texas Frontier

Despite being located far up the Red River on the distant western edge of Louisiana, the French settlement at Natchitoches grew in the same manner as most of the rest of the colony. The population rose to nearly six hundred inhabitants by the end of the era, with the free residents maintaining a slight majority of the community. Despite composing less than half the population, the black slave numbers at Natchitoches actually grew at a higher rate than that of the French, from around thirty in 1726 to just under 250 four decades later. The growth in the slave population was enhanced by the fact that Natchitoches residents did not produce an export staple crop for most of the period, instead choosing to concentrate on raising livestock and grain. As a result, the bondspeople were not overworked and were relatively well fed, allowing the creole slave population to grow accordingly. Not until the 1760s, when the price of tobacco rose in France, did Natchitoches planters begin to concentrate on the cash crop, raising eighty thousand pounds of the leaf by the end of Crown control. As with most of Louisiana's other agricultural districts, a majority of the Natchitoches households contained slaves; nearly six in ten owned bondspeople, but only one in eight families owned more than ten slaves.

In contrast to most of the other French Louisiana settlements, however, the Natchitoches economy also depended heavily on trade with Native Americans, many of whom resided in Spanish Texas. From the trading posts at Natchitoches, Bayou Pierre, and at the Kadohadacho villages, the town's residents exchanged European manufactured goods—which arrived in New Orleans annually in the spring and then were transported up the Red River and distributed to the tribes following their winter hunt—with various Indian groups in return for furs, bear oil, horses, and a few enslaved women and children taken from enemy tribes. Although many Natchitoches men were involved in the commerce as low-level traders, workers, and crewmen, St. Denis, the founder and commandant of the post, used his position to consolidate his family's control of the Indian trade. Even after his death in 1744, St. Denis's family continued to dominate the commerce and the post through the strategic marriages of the commandant's daughters. In 1746 Athanase de Mézières, a newly arrived high-ranking officer from France, married a St. Denis daughter, as did Cesaire de Blanc four years later, soon after he became the post's commandant. Although the Spaniards in Texas considered French trade with their colony's Indians illegal, the St. Denis cartel easily circumvented the law by allowing the Spanish governors who resided at nearby Los Adaes—and who were powerless to halt the exchanges in any case—to profit from the commerce. In 1754 the cartel ensured continued Spanish cooperation when yet another St. Denis daughter married a Los Adaes officer named Manuel Bermúdez de Soto. Throughout the rest of the century these three men and their descendants would continue to play important roles in the Indian trade and in the administration of the Natchitoches post.

The Natchitoches commerce with the Indians of Texas profoundly impacted the Native Americans living to the west of French Louisiana. Although the French trade enriched the Caddos, living in close proximity to the Euroamericans caused their population to decline by at least one-third from the ten thousand people who had lived in the three groups in 1700. By mid-century the Kadohadacho confederacy had been reduced from four villages to two, the Hasinais dropped from ten to four, and only the Yatasis and Natchitoches remained of the third group. Population loss, combined with the increase in economic activities designed to attain French goods, also caused the Caddos to do away with the religious position of the xinesí.

The twenty thousand or so Wichitas, on the other hand, moved southward in order to gain greater access to their French trading partners from Natchitoches. By the 1750s the Tawakonis had moved from the Arkansas Valley to form villages near the Kichais in the area between the Sabine and Red Rivers in East Texas. The Taovayas established the most important

Wichita settlement at a place that became one of the landmark villages on the southern Plains for the next half century. The excellent site they chose was on the Red River just west of the thin sliver of forest known as the Western Cross Timbers. On the north bank of the river, in present Jefferson County, Oklahoma, the Taovayas constructed an impressive fort with a twelve-foot-high stockade, surrounded by a deep trench. French traders traveled to the village (which was the farthest point upstream that could be reached by boat) to exchange goods with the tribe, who they referred to as the *Panis Piques,* or Pricked Pawnees, because of their tattoos. The Taovayas also cemented a very profitable alliance with the nomadic, equestrian Comanches, who lived to the west, establishing themselves as middlemen in the lucrative trade between the powerful Comanches and the French. Comanches provided the Taovayas with horses and buffalo skins in return for a portion of the French goods the Wichitas were receiving, as well as the agricultural produce the Panis Piques raised in the fields surrounding their fort. The Comanches not only became trading partners of the Wichitas, the two tribes also formed a military alliance aimed at the Lipan Apaches of Central Texas, who increasingly found themselves outgunned by their French-supplied enemies. The two tribes constantly targeted the Apaches for slaves, selling mainly women and children to French traders, who distributed them throughout Louisiana and the West Indies. Although Frenchmen developed liaisons with Indian women when they visited the Caddo and Wichita villages to trade, most men maintained French creole wives in Natchitoches. However, a few traders did take Apache slave women as wives or concubines.

By 1749 incessant Comanche and Wichita slave raiding—made much more effective by the increased availability of French firearms—forced the beleaguered Apaches to negotiate a peace treaty with the Spaniards at San Antonio. However, the slaving expeditions increased in the 1750s as the Caddos joined with the Comanches and Wichitas to plunder the Lipans. The raids induced the Apaches to ask their ally to establish a mission and presidio in their country in hope of gaining protection from their enemies, whom the Spaniards grouped together under the name of *Norteños.* The Spaniards responded by constructing a mission-presidial complex for the Apaches on the San Saba River northwest of San Antonio in 1757.

Although the Lipans desired Spanish military protection, they had no intention of being reduced to mission life or accepting Christianity. A few Apaches visited the mission as they passed through the area on the way north to hunt buffalo, but none agreed to give up their nomadic lifestyle and settle down. The Norteños, meanwhile, believed that the mission would provide the Lipans with a safe refuge from which to make retaliatory attacks. Therefore, in March 1758 two thousand Norteño warriors, half of whom were carrying French weapons, gathered near the mission on the San Saba. They planned to kill any Lipan they encountered and to frighten the rest of the tribe from ever returning. The Norteños, led by a well-armed Comanche chief dressed in a French military officer's uniform, surrounded the mission and forced the priests to let them inside the walls. When the native army found there were no Apaches present, they turned on the Spaniards, killing eight (including two priests, one of whom they decapitated) and setting fire to the mission. The brutal attack caused the Spaniards to seek retribution against the Norteños. In August 1759, Colonel Diego Ortiz Parrilla led an expedition consisting of 360 Spanish troops and about 200 Indian allies, mainly Lipan Apaches, from the San Saba River. Two months later Ortiz Parrilla's troops attacked the Norteños at the Taovaya village on the Red River. The well-armed natives outnumbered the Spanish-Indian force, however, and Ortiz Parrilla's men could not penetrate the Taovaya village, over which flew a French flag. The stunned Spanish colonel was forced to retreat to the San Saba River after suffering fifty or so casualties. Spanish officials in Mexico, as well as the Franciscan missionaries, blamed the entire affair on the French traders from Natchitoches, a situation that would cause a great deal of problems in the future, after Spain assumed control of Louisiana following the Seven Years' War.

In addition to the Indian trade, French merchants in Natchitoches developed an exchange system with the isolated Spaniards at Los Adaes and East Texas, who were utterly dependent on the Louisiana settlement for supplies. Although the number of Spanish troops in East Texas had been reduced in 1729, by mid-century about four hundred citizens of New Spain—many of whom were former soldiers and their families—had established farms and ranches among the three Franciscan missions and the presidio. Spanish officials frequently had to permit the soldiers and priests to purchase foodstuffs and manufactured goods from the French despite occasional efforts on the part of their superiors to end the practice. A brisk trade in corn, beans, and other vegetables in exchange for horses and cattle formed out of necessity between Natchitoches and Los Adaes. Other French goods were smuggled from Natchitoches to the Spanish ranching families in East Texas through one ranch in particular, called El Lobanillo de Gil, located about fifteen miles west of Mission Los Aís. During the first half of the eighteenth century the ranch became an important site of illegal trade with members of the important Gil Ibarvo family. Certainly, by the end of the era the Spanish settlers in East Texas depended on support from nearby French Louisiana far more than from distant Mexico.

Arkansas

The French settlement on the Arkansas River continued to stand in sharp contrast to the other Louisiana communities during the period. The population remained small, hovering around only fifty Gallic people, in addition to about twenty slaves of African descent. Staple agriculture did not develop at Arkansas, and the ten or so households raised a few cattle and pigs, in addition to establishing small gardens of tobacco and vegetables for their own consumption. Religion played little role, as no church was constructed. A series of Jesuit priests came and went in the 1740s, but none stayed. In 1750 Louis Carette arrived to minister to the Quapaws, but the Jesuit abandoned the Arkansas Post eight years later, unable to convert the Indians or even to command the respect of his French congregation. After Father Carette's departure, the Arkansas Valley had no resident priest for the next forty years.

Although the Crown reestablished the French military presence at Arkansas during the period, the post did not provide much stability or protection for the civilian residents or for the nearby allied Quapaws. In 1732 French troops built a fort on the north bank of the Arkansas River opposite the Osotouy village, about thirty miles from the Mississippi. In the 1740s flooding and Chickasaw attacks caused the Osotouys to move their village ten miles upstream to a place the French called *Écores Rouges* (Red Bluffs), on the edge of a fertile prairie near the Kappa and Tourima towns. In May 1749 the Chickasaws attacked the now isolated Arkansas Post, killing six Frenchmen and capturing eight women and children. As a result, the French relocated the fort to Écores Rouges to join the Quapaws for protection. Although the new site was free from floods, it proved unsatisfactory from a strategic standpoint because its distance from the Mississippi made it inconvenient for boats traveling between New Orleans and Illinois. Therefore, in 1756 the French moved the fort yet again, this time to a swampy spot only about ten miles above the mouth of the Arkansas, at a site subject to annual inundation. Throughout the period only about twenty soldiers were stationed at Arkansas Post, few of whom remained at the isolated community following their discharge. The post's instability was further exacerbated by the constant turnover of commandants, as ten officers were assigned to direct the garrison during its thirty-four-year existence under French Crown rule. As a result, no one man or family came to dominate the post, as St. Denis did at Natchitoches.

With little military or religious authority present to regulate their actions, most of the French male residents at Arkansas chose to engage in commercial hunting for deer, buffalo, and bear rather than settling down to raise crops and a family. In fact, military deserters and poor laborers from Louisiana took refuge at Arkansas Post throughout the eighteenth century, attracted by a self-sufficient life relatively free from mistreatment and martial discipline. Although Quapaw men also hunted in order to obtain European metal goods and cloth, their close ties to the French and their declining numbers (disease reduced the population of the three villages to less than one thousand people by 1763) encouraged the tribe to permit Gallic men to hunt in the forested, hilly regions of the Arkansas, White, and St. Francis River Valleys. Despite the commandant's efforts to control the trade by issuing permits and ordering the men to return to the post following their annual winter hunts, as time went on an increasing number of hunters formed permanent camps, at places such as Little Rock and Cadron, hundreds of miles up the Arkansas River.

The French hunters generally circumvented the post commandant's directives, but in doing so they hazarded clashes with the Osage Indians, the Dhegiha Siouan-speaking tribe that sought to establish control over the Arkansas Valley hunting grounds. A majority of the ten thousand or so tribespeople lived among the Big Osages, on the prairies near the headwaters of the Osage River in present southwestern Missouri, while the smaller Little Osages resided farther north near the junction of the Osage and the Missouri. Armed with weapons obtained from French traders in Illinois, in the 1730s Osage warriors aggressively pushed farther south into the Arkansas Valley in search of game. They occasionally clashed with French hunters from Arkansas Post, but more often waged war upon the Caddos and Wichitas—obtaining slaves for their French commercial partners in Illinois—who also hunted in the region. As a result of Osage pressure, in the 1740s a few French hunters moved from the Arkansas southward to the Ouachita River, where they established a semipermanent settlement at *Écore a Fabri* (Fabry's Bluff), in present Camden, Arkansas.

Gulf Coast Settlements

The French and Spanish posts located east of the Mississippi River along the Gulf Coast developed slowly throughout the period. The French population between Mobile Bay and Biloxi increased by one-third to about 500 people by mid-century, while the number of black slaves more than doubled, reaching 350 or so. Whereas about half of the 140 French households in the region contained slaves—a small number were Native American—only a few residences had sufficient bondsmen to be considered plantations. For example, by the end of French rule Chevalier Montault de Montberaut maintained a ranch south of Mobile on which twenty-six slaves managed cattle, horses, sheep, and pigs. Most French settlers, however, were farmers or herders who hunted, gathered, and fished with the assistance of a few slaves, selling their surpluses to the one hundred or so French soldiers stationed at Fort Condé as well as to the Spaniards at Pensacola. One observer complained that Mobile's location, "at the place where the fresh and salt waters mix . . . render[s] the air putrid." Whereas the French and African creole population grew between 1731 and 1763, the numbers of Indians residing near Mobile declined from disease by one-third, to about one thousand. The indigenous groups coalesced during the period, as most of the Indians lived among the Mobile, Biloxi, Pascagoula, Taensa, and Apalache villages. The five groups maintained close ties to the French settlement, continuing to provide venison and corn in addition to performing such wage-earning services as rowing pirogues, carrying trade merchandise, and delivering messages between posts. The Apalaches, having moved to the east shore of Mobile Bay, remained dedicated to Catholicism and regularly had their children baptized by the Capuchin priest from Notre Dame de la Mobile.

Like the presidio at Los Adaes in Texas, the isolated Spanish post on Pensacola Bay continued to depend on trade with the French at Mobile throughout the period. The settlement on Santa Rosa Island was typical of a Spanish frontier presidio, consisting of a fort, church, and village. The fort, which by 1750 had fallen into disrepair, occupied the east side of the settlement, while a village of forty or so houses was located to the west near Point Sigüenza. About sixty soldiers and two hundred civilians resided at the presidio by mid-century. In the mid-1740s the Spaniards built a small blockhouse, called San Miguel, on the mainland in the downtown area of present-day Pensacola. This post proved its worth in November 1752 when a hurricane destroyed the settlement on Santa

Rosa Island, forcing the survivors to take refuge at San Miguel. Although Spanish troops returned to the island soon thereafter and reconstructed the fort, in early 1757 Colonel Miguel Román de Castilla y Lugo arrived in Pensacola with orders to build a new post, named Presidio San Miguel, on the mainland at the site of the small blockhouse. By 1760 the post had a stockade that contained a government house, a church, warehouses, and barracks for the two hundred soldiers. Despite the presidio's newness, one observer complained that all of the buildings were constructed of "bark . . . and most of them without floors; so that in the summer they were as hot as stoves, and the land engendered all sorts of vermin." About four hundred Spanish civilians resided in "miserable huts" near the presidio. Although the Spanish Crown authorized the construction of a stone fort at San Marcos de Apalache in the 1750s, the edifice was never completed, as a powerful hurricane struck the coast in 1758 and drowned forty men.

Choctaws and Chickasaws

As with Natchitoches on the western edge of French Louisiana, Mobile on the eastern flank was the center of the Indian trade with the natives of the Southeast. However, in contrast to the Indians of Texas, who depended solely on Natchitoches traders to provide them with European manufactured goods, the French in Mobile had to compete with the British from South Carolina and Georgia, after the latter's establishment in 1733, for the southeastern tribes' commerce and, more importantly, military assistance. The Choctaws, as the military bulwark to Louisiana's security and its most populous trade partner, held the most powerful position in relation to the French. Despite constant warfare with the Chickasaws and a deadly civil war in the late 1740s, the population among the Eastern, Western, and Sixtowns Choctaws remained stable throughout the period at about fourteen thousand people. In order to maintain the essential Choctaw alliance, the French at Mobile annually distributed 50,000 livres' worth of presents to visiting leaders from each district, in addition to sending traders to their villages to purchase furs, mainly deerskins. Although British traders had made inroads into Eastern villages in the 1720s, the French increased their efforts among the Choctaws in the early 1730s and won the support of the important Sixtowns chief, Alibamon Mingo. As a result of the Chickasawhay town mico's influence, Eastern leaders maintained their ties to the Louisiana French throughout the decade.

The French needed the Choctaw alliance because, during the years immediately following Louis XV's resumption of control over Louisiana, officials foolishly insisted on seeking vengeance against the three thousand Chickasaws and the several hundred Natchez refugees whom the former had welcomed into their Tombigbee River villages. Both groups continued to receive goods from Carolina traders along the Upper Path and used the British weapons to make raids upon the Choctaws and the outlying French posts along the Mississippi. Louisiana officials initially hoped to avoid a costly full-scale Indian war, and accordingly, Governor Bienville paid the Choctaws to send a continual stream of war parties into the Chickasaw villages. Chickasaw and Natchez warriors responded through guerrilla actions aimed at the French settlements upstream from New Orleans, in addition to attacking the annual convoy of boats that traveled between Illinois and the capital. Unhappy that the slight French effort had failed to yield tangible results, officials in France ordered Bienville to assemble soldiers and supplies for a major military campaign into Chickasaw country. As a result, in early 1736 the Louisiana governor organized a two-pronged assault, one from Illinois and the other from Mobile, upon the Chickasaw and Natchez towns. As with the Spanish attack on the Taovaya village on the Red River two decades later, both French campaigns into the heart of Indian country failed miserably.

In February 1736 Pierre d'Artaguiette left Illinois with a force of over 150 French soldiers and 300 Indian allies, including a number of Quapaws. Upon arriving at the Chickasaw Bluffs near present Memphis, Tennessee, d'Artaguiette constructed a fort and, leaving a small garrison behind, headed east toward the Chickasaw towns hoping to coordinate his attack with Bienville, who was assembling his troops at Mobile. Well into his march, however, d'Artaguiette learned that there had been major delays on the southern end of the planned campaign. Short on provisions, d'Artaguiette decided to push on and attacked the easternmost Chickasaw village of Ogoula Tchetoka on March 25. Although the French and Indian force initially advanced into the town, a few hundred Chickasaw and Natchez warriors from nearby villages arrived in time to force the attackers to flee in retreat. In the ensuing panic most of the Indian allies made their escape while about fifty Frenchmen were killed. The Chickasaws captured another twenty French soldiers, including the wounded d'Artaguiette, and burned them alive later that day.

In the meantime Bienville had gathered about six hundred men at Mobile, including a small company of black slaves with free people of color as officers. In early April the force moved northward and encamped at Fort Tombecbé, where an advance company of soldiers had constructed a rudimentary outpost in the heart of Choctaw territory. Bienville met with Choctaw leaders Red Shoes of the Western Division and Alibamon Mingo at the newly constructed fort—which fulfilled a decade-long promise by the French to establish a post near their villages—and agreed to pay them with munitions and other goods if they would join the attack. The two men agreed to provide a force of another six hundred warriors, and the Choctaws met the French troops just south of the Chickasaw and Natchez villages in late May. Although Bienville wanted to destroy the Natchez towns, Red Shoes insisted that the French-Choctaw force attack the first Chickasaw villages they reached, the tightly clustered hamlets of Ackia, Apeony, and Tchoukafala. Bienville relented, and the French and Choctaw forces began to march against the fortified town of Ackia on the afternoon of May 26. Well armed with English weapons, the Chickasaws responded to the assault with a deadly hail of musket balls that immediately killed about seventy Frenchmen and twenty Choctaws. The Chickasaws, who held the higher ground, then forced the attackers to withdraw in humiliation. Insult was added to injury in early June when Bienville reached Mobile and learned that d'Artaguiette had also suffered a terrible defeat.

Despite the wasted expenses and loss of manpower in the failed assault upon the Chickasaws, Bienville began almost immediately to plan a second campaign. In the meantime he encouraged the Choctaws to wage guerrilla warfare against the Chickasaws, having the attackers destroy the enemy cornfields and paying them one gun, one pound of powder, and two pounds of bullets for each scalp. Although the Chickasaws suffered greatly from the Choctaw raids, the French were unable to follow up on their ally's successes, due to flooding and sickness. Finally, in early 1739 Bienville established a depot called Fort Assumption near the Chickasaw Bluffs, where the French collected a large cache of munitions and supplies over the course of the next few months. By November the Louisiana governor had gathered nearly two thousand troops at Fort Assumption, including three hundred sent directly from France, along with five hundred Native American allies and three hundred black slaves. At Alibamon Mingo's Chickasawhay village another one thousand Choctaws assembled, waiting for orders to march from the south to prevent the Chickasaws from escaping in that direction.

Despite the extensive preparations, bad weather, sickness, and desertion thwarted Bienville's plans and the force became bogged down at

Fort Assumption. The Chickasaws, however, upon learning of the large assemblage on the Mississippi and unaware of the army's inability to mobilize, immediately began negotiating for peace. After only a few skirmishes, seven Chickasaw leaders met with the Louisiana governor at Fort Assumption in February 1740 and offered to return the handful of Natchez refugees that remained among them—most had already fled to live among the Creeks—if Bienville would cancel the French invasion. Bienville, realizing his second Chickasaw campaign had already been too costly and was in total disarray, disappointedly agreed to the terms, then dismantled Fort Assumption and returned to New Orleans in disgrace. Soon thereafter the dejected Bienville asked to be relieved of his position as Louisiana's governor. He was replaced in 1743 and retired to France, where he died in 1767. The Chickasaws, on the other hand, remained strong in their villages, having weathered two French invasions in half a decade. Soon after making peace with Bienville the Chickasaws resumed their attacks against the French convoys and settlements. Nonetheless, disease and warfare caused the Chickasaw population to plummet over the following two decades, falling below two thousand people by 1763.

In response to the Chickasaw attacks, the French continued to rely on the Choctaws to carry out intimidating raids, hoping to weaken their enemy and drive out the British traders. Warfare against the Chickasaws, however, soon took its toll on Choctaw society and strained the tribe's political order, eventually leading to the outbreak of civil war. Western Choctaw groups had begun to tire of Louisiana's insistence that they perpetuate hostility against the Chickasaws, particularly when British traders began to infiltrate their own villages in the late 1730s and offered merchandise at cheaper prices than the French. In fact, Western war chief Red Shoes had traveled to South Carolina in 1738 and had concluded a commercial treaty with the English governor before switching sides and joining the French the following year during the second Chickasaw campaign. Distrustful of Red Shoes, Bienville reproached the Choctaw leader and withheld his annual gifts in 1740. Governor Vaudreuil, Bienville's successor, continued to ostracize Red Shoes, causing him to seek an exclusive alliance with the Chickasaws and the British traders, especially after the French raised the price of European-manufactured merchandise in 1745 and cut back on the number of annual gifts distributed to Indian allies. Although Red Shoes attempted to enlist the Eastern and Sixtowns leaders in his pro-British campaign, Alibamon Mingo and the other chiefs chose to maintain the French alliance, in part because they resented Red Shoes' threat to their power.

The tension within the Choctaw nation soon led to civil war. In 1746 Red Shoes concluded a peace treaty between the Western Choctaws and the Chickasaws. Eastern chiefs responded by attacking the Chickasaw villages and killing the diplomat who had arranged the accord. Enraged Western Choctaw leaders killed three Frenchmen and drove all other Louisiana traders from their district. Soon thereafter the Western chiefs traveled to South Carolina to renew the treaty Red Shoes had previously arranged, and British trading parties immediately set out from Charleston for the Choctaw towns. In retaliation for the murders of the Frenchmen, Governor Vaudreuil demanded the heads of three Western chiefs and ordered Alibamon Mingo to kill Red Shoes. Although the Sixtowns leader refused to murder his Western counterpart, a young Choctaw, encouraged by the French offer of a bounty for the head of the rebel chief, assassinated Red Shoes in June 1747 while he was escorting a group of South Carolina traders to his home village of Conchitto.

The ensuing revolt of Western Choctaw villages spiraled violently into intratribal warfare and quickly spread to French Louisiana, as rebel warriors made raids on Mobile, Pointe Coupée, and the German Coast. Governor Vaudreuil responded by ordering the destruction of all the Western Choctaw villages and tripled the bounty offered for enemy scalps. In 1749 Alibamon Mingo presented Vaudreuil with the scalps of one hundred Western warriors as well as the skulls of three of their most prominent chiefs. The following year the governor received another 130 Choctaw scalps and the heads of three English traders. At this point the Western towns were suffering tremendously, as the Carolina traders proved unable to provide them with enough weapons to carry out their rebellion. As a result, by the summer of 1750 only two Western villages remained pro-British, and they were defeated later that year by nine hundred Eastern Choctaw warriors, in conjunction with troops from the French garrison at Fort Tombecbé. The Choctaw civil war came to an end in November 1750 when the last few weakened Western warriors agreed to lay down their weapons. Although peace had come to the Choctaws, none of the three divisions was prepared to forsake its autonomy and unite with the others against the Europeans. Instead, the Eastern and Sixtowns chiefs reaffirmed their relationship with the French, and the defeated Western leaders continued to deal with the British among the Chickasaws, while at the same time allowing traders from Mobile to reenter their villages.

Creeks and Seminoles

In the meantime the Creeks were dealing with three European powers. The Upper Creeks exchanged goods with British and French traders in their Alabama, Abihka, and Tallapoosa villages, while the Lower Creeks had relations with the British as well as with the Spaniards in Florida. In contrast to the Choctaws and Chickasaws, however, both Creek groups maintained their neutral stance and avoided major warfare during the period. As a result, their population rebounded to about five thousand people in the Lower towns along the Chattahoochee River and eight thousand residents in the Upper villages located on the Coosa, Tallapoosa, and Alabama Rivers. Although the Upper Creeks had allowed the French to build Fort Toulouse among the Alabamas in 1716, in the 1730s they decided to permit British traders to establish a trading post in their midst in order to gain more leverage in their dealings with the Europeans. In 1735 the Abihkas authorized Georgia traders to construct a post at Ocfuskee, a town on the Tallapoosa River. At the same time Lower Creek leaders entered into an agreement with Georgia as well, and traders from Savannah entered their villages. However, Coweta and Apalachicola chiefs traveled to the presidio at San Marcos de Apalache and renewed ties with the Spaniards, who responded by sending ships from Havana loaded with presents for their Lower Creek friends. The Creek diplomatic maneuvers paid off when Great Britain declared war on Spain in October 1739. During the so-called War of Jenkins' Ear, Georgia governor James Oglethorpe lowered the price for trade goods by one-third in an attempt to maintain peace with both Creek groups. He also hoped to enlist the Lower Creeks in a campaign against the Spanish fortress at St. Augustine. Although a few Indians joined the Georgia force, the number of Creek warriors who actually fought for Oglethorpe, whose two attacks against St. Augustine both failed, fell far short of the fifteen hundred the Cowetas promised him in return for the price reduction. Both Creek groups also remained neutral when France and Great Britain were at odds during the War of Austrian Succession (1743–1748). The Lower Creeks refused to let the South Carolinians build a trading post among their villages, while the Upper Creeks thwarted British plans for attacking Fort Toulouse. As a result of the Creeks' neutral stance, little action took place in the region during the war.

By mid-century, however, the lure of trade with the British began to draw a large number of young, male Creeks from their towns, and away from their leaders' control. Many traveled to Augusta, Charleston, and

Savannah to trade with the locals or to solicit gifts from colonial officials. Other groups of people, mainly from the Lower Creek towns, permanently abandoned their villages and established small encampments in Spanish Florida. One group, led by Cowkeeper, a mico from the Oconee village on the Chattahoochee River, settled in the Alachua region of north-central Florida—near present Gainesville—on lands that at one time had harbored Timucuan settlements and a large Spanish cattle ranch. They attached themselves to Georgia traders and made intermittent raids on St. Augustine. The Spaniards began using the term *cimarrones* (wild ones) to distinguish the people at Alachua from the main group of Lower Creeks, who called them *ishti semoli* (wild men). Eventually the name would be Anglicized, and the Creek migrants in Florida became known as the "Seminoles." At about the same time a different group of Lower Creeks, led by Secoffee, moved south to settle in the territory formerly controlled by the Apalaches. Unlike Cowkeeper, Secoffee considered the Spaniards to be allies and encouraged other Creek bands to establish villages between his towns and San Marcos de Apalache. By the latter half of the eighteenth century this group, known as the Miccosukees, came to be considered Seminoles as well.

The Seven Years' War

During the first half of the eighteenth century the Choctaws and Creeks played the various European groups off of one another to each tribe's advantage. However, British successes in the Seven Years' War (1756–1763) left Louisiana isolated from France and tilted the balance of power dramatically in favor of the Georgians and South Carolinians. By 1759, when British troops defeated the French forces in Canada, Louisiana was four years behind on its annual payment of presents and trade goods to the Choctaws and Upper Creeks. The Choctaws responded by attacking French settlements throughout the colony for refusing to pay them tribute. Leaders from all three Choctaw divisions also met with British officials to request trade. In July 1759 three hundred Choctaws complained to traders at the Upper Creek village of Waulyhatchey that the French could no longer supply their needs and invited the British to build posts in their towns. A few months later another group of Choctaw leaders made a similar request of English traders at Ocfuskee. Although the British were unable to establish posts among the three districts due to continued hostilities with the French and Spanish (the latter declared war on Great Britain in 1762 in support of France), most of the Choctaws agreed to abandon their former allies in Louisiana by the end of the war.

Although French trade with the Creeks also dried up during the war, the Upper and Lower villages responded to British dominance in a variety of ways, most of them seeking to maintain the neutrality that had served them so well over the past four decades. France's closest Creek ally, the Alabamas, found themselves in a particularly difficult position during the hostilities. In 1758 British officials drew up plans for a coordinated land and naval attack on the French posts at Mobile and Fort Toulouse. Edmund Atkin, a South Carolinian recently appointed to the newly created post of Superintendent of Indian Affairs for the Southern district, was charged with the task of enlisting Creek support for the attack on Fort Toulouse. In the fall of 1759 Atkin met with Upper Creek leaders at the Tuckebatchee village and coerced the Alabamas, already suffering from lack of trade from Louisiana, into signing an agreement in which they denounced their French allies and acknowledged their dependence on British commerce. Nonetheless, the Alabamas refused to authorize a British attack on Fort Toulouse. In fact, one group of Alabamas, led by a war chief known as the Mortar, defied the agreement and killed eleven British traders in June 1760. The Mortar's faction then joined with the Cherokees to attack outlying settlements in South Carolina. Other Upper Creek leaders, however, maintained their neutral stance, protected the British traders in their villages, and refused to join the Mortar's band. Whereas most of the other Creeks successfully stayed out of the fray, Cowkeeper's Alachua bands escalated their attacks on St. Augustine, while a few Lower Creek warriors chose to defend South Carolina and fought against the Cherokees. Ultimately, the Alabamas' antagonistic stance forced the British to cancel their planned campaign against French Louisiana. British diplomatic heavy-handedness caused the Alabamas to remain opposed to the Georgians and Carolinians when the Treaty of Paris brought the war to an end in February 1763.

Although no major battles took place in the Gulf South during the conflict between Great Britain, France, and Spain, the treaty negotiations impacted the region dramatically, as French Louisiana and Spanish Florida changed hands at the war's conclusion. In November 1762, three months before the final treaty officially ended the conflict, France ceded Louisiana west of the Mississippi, as well as the so-called *Isle d'Orléans*—located on the east bank from Bayou Manchac to the river's mouth—to Spain in the secret Treaty of Fontainebleau. Louis XV gave the colony to his Bourbon cousin, Carlos III, to compensate Spain for losses incurred during the war and because Louisiana had always been considered an economic drain on French coffers. Although the Spaniards understood that the colony was a financial sinkhole, Carlos III and his ministers reluctantly accepted Louisiana to ensure that it did not fall into the aggressive hands of the British, who might then push into Texas and Mexico. In February 1763 both France and Spain relinquished other North American colonial liabilities in exchange for profitable Caribbean islands they had lost to the British during the war. France ceded Canada to the British in order to recover the sugar islands of Guadeloupe and Martinique. Spain handed over Florida, extending westward from Pensacola all the way to the Mississippi River, in exchange for Cuba, which the British had conquered in the summer of 1762. Thus, the French abandonment of Canada and Louisiana left Great Britain and Spain as the only remaining European rivals of consequence on the North American mainland.

The Gulf South had been spared the ravages of war between 1756 and 1763 mainly because France, Spain, and Great Britain viewed the region as a backwater, unworthy of any costly attention. Over the course of the following twenty years, however, British dominion over Florida, coupled with Spanish rule of Louisiana, would transform the Gulf South into a dynamic and economically vital area, as fully involved in the Atlantic World as their holdings in the West Indies. As a result, when conflict broke out in 1778 between Great Britain and Spain because of the War for American Independence, the two European powers would stage major military campaigns in the Gulf South in order to maintain control of the emerging, valuable region.

5

Transformation of the Gulf South 1763–1783

Whereas the European powers basically neglected the Gulf South during the middle third of the eighteenth century, following the end of the Seven Years' War Great Britain and Spain took active measures to increase the number of people—white and black—living in West Florida and Louisiana in addition to taking steps to stimulate the economy of each colony. As a result of these initiatives, the Gulf South entered the increasingly active Atlantic World over the course of the following two decades, causing the two powers to compete militarily for control of the region during the War for American Independence. Although reforms implemented throughout the Spanish empire positively affected the newly acquired colony of Louisiana (following a delay in taking possession), the same modifications caused the Spaniards to neglect even more their already isolated settlements in East Texas. Whereas the Gulf South's Europeans and Africans came to outnumber the region's native inhabitants for the first time during this period, the Indian tribes successfully adapted to the situation and remained in control of the interior areas while continuing to play an important role in the area's diplomacy.

British West Florida

The British aggressively moved to take possession of Florida, which they divided into two colonies separated at the Apalachicola River. They designated Pensacola as the capital of West Florida, which stretched westward to the Mississippi River, with the 31st Parallel as the original northern boundary. Ultimately, however, in order to encourage settlement farther upstream, the northern border of West Florida was redrawn eastward from the mouth of the Yazoo River at 32 degrees, 28 minutes. The British formally took possession of the colony in August 1763 when Lieutenant Colonel Augustin Prevost sailed into Pensacola Bay from Cuba with the 3rd Battalion of the Royal Regiment. One month later Pensacola's six hundred Spanish subjects—including soldiers, civilians, convicts, and Christian Yamasee Indians—evacuated the town, boarding eight ships and sailing for Veracruz. In October Major Robert Farmar of the 34th Regiment of Foot arrived at Mobile from Havana and received the post from the French commandant, who subsequently relocated to New Orleans with 350 troops from forts Condé, Toulouse, and Tombecbé. In contrast to Pensacola, most of the five hundred French settlers in and around Mobile remained at their residences and swore oaths of allegiance to the British Crown. Although the British forces did not immediately occupy Fort Toulouse out of respect for the Upper Creeks' wishes, Major Farmar sent thirty British troops to the Tombigbee River post, now called Fort York.

As most of the one thousand or so British soldiers in West Florida set about repairing the dilapidated bastions at Pensacola and Mobile, rechristened Forts George and Charlotte, respectively, a few others moved west to take possession of the Mississippi River. Hoping to avoid New Orleans and gain access to the Mississippi via Bayou Manchac—the boundary between British West Florida and Spanish Louisiana—a small contingent of British soldiers attempted to clear the streambed of debris in late 1763. Although the effort failed due to the spring flooding that caused a logjam of trees and driftwood, in early 1765 the British constructed Fort Bute on the north bank of Bayou Manchac near the Mississippi River and stationed one hundred soldiers there. In May 1765 Major Farmar, along with Lieutenant Philip Pittman, who kept a journal of the expedition, departed from Mobile with two hundred British soldiers bound for Illinois. With the permission of French officials who were still in possession of Louisiana, Farmar passed through New Orleans and headed upstream to Bayou Manchac and into British territory. The force stopped for a few days at Natchez, taking note of Fort Rosalie's poor condition, before continuing on to Illinois. The following year the British sent a contingent of fifty soldiers from Pensacola to Natchez, where the troops rehabilitated the post, now called Fort Panmure.

Civilian settlement of West Florida began in earnest following Governor George Johnstone's arrival at Pensacola in October 1764. The Scottish ex-naval officer energetically tackled his duties, first establishing a twelve-

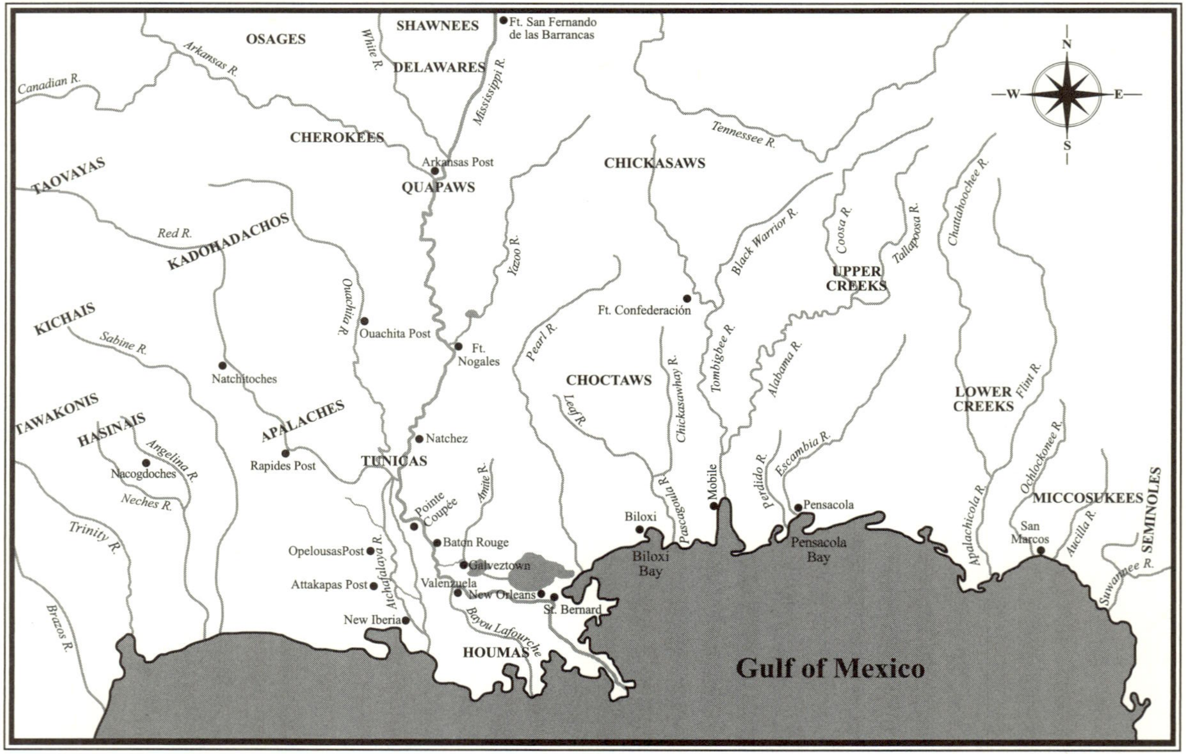

MAP 6. THE GULF SOUTH, 1763–1798

man Executive Council that governed the colony for two years. Granting land to prospective colonists was the Council's most important duty. In contrast to the Spaniards, the British had great plans to develop West Florida economically and therefore offered bounteous land grants in hopes of encouraging large-scale immigration to the colony. Family heads willing to immigrate received one hundred acres of land, with an additional fifty acres accorded to each family member or slave. If the governor approved, an applicant could supplement this free "family right" land by buying up to one thousand acres at very cheap prices. In addition to drawing people to the countryside, the Council also encouraged settlement in the towns of Pensacola and Mobile. Elias Durnford, provincial surveyor, drew a plan for the city of Pensacola, laying out a large grid that paralleled the bay shore. Fort George lay at the heart of Pensacola, surrounded by twenty-eight street blocks containing residential lots. Soon thereafter Mobile was laid out in a similar fashion, with a grid of streets established around Fort Charlotte. During the next few years a number of Anglo settlers from Great Britain (as well as from the American colonies) immigrated to the region, stretching from the east side of Pensacola Bay to the western shore of Mobile Bay. By 1766 nearly two thousand Euroamericans resided in the area, two-thirds of them living around Pensacola Bay. About one thousand slaves lived in the region; half were creole bondspeople of the French settlers in Mobile, while the other half had been recently shipped to West Florida from British Jamaica and the mainland colonies.

In view of the rapid rise of West Florida's population, in August 1766 Governor Johnstone issued a proclamation calling for the establishment of an assembly in the province, in accordance with the other British colonies in North America. Over the course of the following two months the male heads of the colony's households chose fourteen assemblymen for a lower house—eight from Pensacola Bay, six from Mobile Bay—and on November 3 the first representative body in the Gulf South held its primary meeting in Pensacola. The Executive Council served as the upper house. During the next half decade the West Florida Assembly passed a series of ordinances, such as the bonding of vessels, the licensing of the retail liquor trade, and the adjustment of wharf rates. The Assembly also enacted a harsh slave code, similar to those of Georgia and South Carolina, that defined slaves as property who were relegated to a restricted and subordinate place in society. Punishments for slaves were severe, including death for a series of grave offenses and dismemberment and whipping for lesser crimes, including running away. The code also made manumission an expensive endeavor by charging the emancipator a large sum to ensure that the freed slave would never become a burden on the colony.

Whereas Governor Johnstone worked harmoniously with the West Florida Assembly, he ran afoul of the military establishment that was so important to the fledgling frontier colony and was dismissed in January 1767. Confusion and uncertainty characterized the three-and-a-half-year period following the departure of the first civil governor. For two years after Johnstone's dismissal, Lieutenant Governor Montfort Browne served as interim governor amid charges of financial irregularities. Although John Eliot was appointed governor in early 1767, he did not arrive in West Florida until 1769, whereupon he hanged himself after only one month on the job. Elias Durnford then served as a caretaker governor, despite Browne's attempts to reclaim the position. Tensions between the two men escalated to the point that Browne killed one of Durnford's supporters in a duel and fled to England. Finally, in August 1770, Peter Chester, a professional soldier and administrator, arrived in Pensacola and took over as the governor, a position he held throughout the remainder of the colony's existence.

During West Florida's first half decade almost all the Anglo immigrants settled along the Gulf Coast between Pensacola and Mobile. The region's thin, sandy soil, however, was unsuitable to cash crops such as tobacco and indigo, and most of the settlers turned to raising food or livestock—principally cattle and hogs—on their land grants. A few planters with access to slaves established lumber mills, as the area's forest abounded in long-leaf yellow pine suitable for housing and for tar and pitch used in ships. In the meantime, as the poverty of the soil on the Gulf Coast became known throughout the British world, reports concerning the superiority of the land along the Mississippi from Manchac to Natchez began to be publicized. As a result, in 1768—despite the British evacuation of Forts Bute, York, and Panmure (as well as San Marcos de Apalache, which was technically in East Florida) for economic reasons the same year—immigration to West Florida shifted from Pensacola and Mobile to the province's western region. The rush of settlers included large numbers who arrived from the Atlantic seaboard colonies via the Ohio and Mississippi Rivers, while others traveled from Great Britain and the West Indies by sea. By 1774 the region had eclipsed the Gulf Coast in population, as about twenty-five hundred Anglos and six hundred slaves lived in the area. Settlement was concentrated at Bayou Manchac and the Amite River, northward along the east bank of the Mississippi past Baton Rouge, to Thompson's Creek opposite Pointe Coupée, and at Natchez. A few settlers established homesteads upstream from Natchez along the Walnut Hills region, stretching from Bayou Pierre to the mouth of the Yazoo River.

A few men in particular stand out among the many Britons who migrated to the Mississippi River section of West Florida during the period. Two immigrants made their marks as merchants and planters. Oliver Pollock was a Scots-Irish merchant who migrated from Ulster to Philadelphia in 1760. After spending some time in Cuba, where he converted to Catholicism, Pollock moved to Spanish New Orleans in 1769 and established a merchant house, making a fortune by importing dry goods from Great Britain and flour from Philadelphia, and by becoming a major slave trader. As a British citizen, Pollock also obtained a dozen tracts of land in West Florida, the most important being the Tunica Bend plantation across the Mississippi from Pointe Coupée. Following the Declaration of Independence, Pollock took up the Americans' cause and became the unofficial U.S. agent in New Orleans. John Fitzpatrick, an Irish Catholic, fought with the British in North America during the Seven Years' War before establishing a store and plantation at the confluence of Bayou Manchac and the Mississippi River in 1769. During the following two decades Fitzpatrick's store became a center of the region's activities, descriptions of which he recorded in his voluminous correspondences with customers, suppliers, and government officials.

Three other men traveled to West Florida as amateur scientists and provided important observations of the province's natural delights. Bernard Romans was a British civil engineer who spent a decade as the Georgia deputy surveyor before being sent to Pensacola in 1771 as the king's cartographer and botanist. After traveling extensively through West Florida he produced a fine map of the colony, and in 1775 published *A Concise History of East and West Florida,* containing his descriptions of the flora and fauna, as well as careful portrayals of the region's Indians and Anglo settlers. Two years after Romans arrived in Florida, William Bartram—the son of a wealthy Philadelphian—traveled to the South and began a four-year tour of the region, during which time he ventured to the British settlements at Pensacola, Mobile, and Manchac, as well as taking a trip to the Upper and Lower Creek villages. In 1791 Bartram published *Travels Through North & South Carolina, Georgia, East & West Florida,* a classic work of natural history containing observations of the province's geology, botany, zoology, anthropology, and geography. William Dunbar, a Scotsman residing in Philadelphia, moved to West Florida in 1773 and established a plantation a few miles north of Bayou Manchac near the fledgling community of Baton Rouge. Over the course of the next decade Dunbar acquired over thirty slaves and employed them in the successful cultivation of indigo and tobacco, as well as sawing wood for lumber products, such as barrel staves. Well educated, Dunbar kept an informative diary of the day-to-day operation of his plantation before moving to Natchez in 1784, after which he provided the United States with valuable information concerning the young republic's newly acquired territories in the region. Dunbar was also a scientist in the tradition of Benjamin Franklin, spending much of his life making astronomical observations and conducting experiments. He corresponded with Thomas Jefferson, who was instrumental in Dunbar's ultimately being accepted as a member of the American Philosophical Society.

British-Indian Relations

Through a series of conferences the British also moved quickly in regard to the Indians who now solely came under their purview after the French and Spanish withdrawal from the region east of the Mississippi River. In early 1763 Georgia governor James Wright invited Upper and Lower Creek leaders to Savannah and informed the startled headmen of the new diplomatic situation. In November, Creek, Choctaw, and Chickasaw representatives traveled to Augusta to hear John Stuart, Atkin's successor as Superintendent of Indian Affairs for the Southern district, discuss the establishment of formal relations and trade. Three months later Choctaw headmen descended on Mobile to meet Major Farmar, who promised that the British would provide them with the same trade and friendship as their former French allies. Chickasaw and Choctaw leaders met once more with Major Farmar at Mobile in June 1764.

Soon after these informal meetings the Indians learned the dire consequences of no longer being able to work the intercolonial rivalry in their favor. Almost immediately a new generation of British traders—freed from the fear of the French and from colonial trade restrictions—traveled to the Creek, Choctaw, and Chickasaw villages to ply their wares and make a quick profit. Veteran trader James Adair stated that most of the men who entered the business after 1763 were "the dregs and off-scourings of our colonies." Romans dismissed them as "monsters in human form, the very scum and out cast of the earth." The greedy traders brought chaos to the region, as they used any means to obtain deerskins from the various tribesmen. Not only did the traders employ false weights and measures to cheat the Indians, they also brought immense quantities of liquor to the villages, insulted and beat native men, and sexually abused the women. The rum trade in particular elicited complaints from Indian headmen. One Choctaw leader regretted that when the bells of the traders' packhorses were heard in the distance, "our Town is immediately deserted. Young & old Run out to meet them Joyfully buying Rum! Rum; they get Drunk . . . Confusion and Disorder are Consequences and this the Ruin of our Nation." The Indians responded by robbing the traders of their goods, assaulting them, and stealing or killing their horses and livestock.

Fearful that the dangerous situation might explode into outright warfare, Superintendent Stuart held another round of conferences with the tribes in 1765. Choctaw and Chickasaw leaders met with Stuart at Mobile in April and concluded a treaty in which the tribes pledged peace with the British and with one another. The agreement between the Choctaws and Chickasaws proved lasting, as members of the two nations began to intermarry and share hunting grounds soon thereafter. The treaty also called for greater trade regulations, including the establishment of fixed rates of exchange for goods, the licensing of traders, the stationing of official commissaries at principal Indian villages, and the prohibition of alcohol sales. In return for the distribution of a large amount of presents and the eradication of past debts, the Choctaws ceded land located along the Gulf Coast from Mobile to the Mississippi River to the British. Upper and Lower Creek leaders—including some Seminoles—met with Stuart the following month at Pensacola and entered into a similar agreement in which the Indians granted territory surrounding the West Florida capital to the British. Despite Stuart's efforts to regulate the trade and maintain the peace, the prohibitions proved impossible to enforce and, as a result, were scrapped by officials in Great Britain in March 1768. Disreputable traders, along with their pack trains loaded with rum, continued to enter the Indian villages unabated.

The unregulated trade, combined with the British refusal to distribute annual presents to Indian leaders as the French had done, threatened the authority of the chiefs by eradicating their role as the redistributors of gifts, thus rendering them politically weakened. Tribal leaders protested that their young men were uncontrollable without presents, but cost-cutting British officials disregarded their pleas. As a result of the lack of gifts, large numbers of Creek, Choctaw, and Chickasaw hunters entered the woods and began to seriously deplete the white-tailed deer population in their attempt to obtain trade goods, especially alcohol. Violence between the Creeks and the allied Choctaws and Chickasaws soon erupted over disputed hunting grounds. Colonists from Georgia, whose numbers had grown from eighty-five hundred people in 1761 to thirty-three thousand in 1773, also began to encroach upon Creek territory, hunting deer and allowing cattle to roam, leading to heightened tensions with the British.

Realizing that violence against their British suppliers promised disaster, in the spring of 1766 Creek and Choctaw headmen chose to go to war against one another in an effort to reestablish a degree of authority over the young men who would necessarily be forced to follow them in battle. Understanding that intertribal war took the pressure off settlements in West Florida and Georgia, British officials eagerly supplied both the Creeks and the Choctaws with weapons and other materials for a decade. In fact, in the winter of 1771–1772 the British held a conference in Mobile for the Choctaws and Chickasaws in which they distributed presents to various headmen—thus reinforcing chiefly power—for the first time since 1765. At this meeting a new generation of leaders emerged between the two tribes, namely Paya Mattaha of the Chickasaws and Franchimastabé and Taboca from the Western district of the Choctaws. The Creek-Choctaw war dragged on until 1776, when the Chickasaws finally intermediated between the two exhausted tribes. In October Choctaw and Creek peace delegations met in Pensacola and performed an elaborate ritual, overseen by Superintendent Stuart, to signify the end of the fighting. Stuart distributed a large number of gifts at the conference, thus helping ensure a degree of Indian loyalty to the British as the War for American Independence began, in addition to bolstering the position of native leaders within the Choctaw, Creek, and Chickasaw tribes. Throughout the rest of the period the British made sure to hold annual conferences in order to distribute presents to the Indian headmen. Despite the warfare and the disruption caused by the unregulated trade, the population of the tribes stabilized during the period, as the Creeks and Choctaws maintained about fourteen thousand people in each tribe, while the Chickasaw numbers stood at twenty-three hundred. The number of Seminoles residing in British Florida grew to fifteen hundred by the mid-1770s. The Seminoles lived in nine towns, located in the old Spanish provinces of Apalache and Timucua, where the women raised copious amounts of vegetables while the men hunted deer in the forests throughout the peninsula in addition to raising cattle and horses. The Miccosukee branch of the Seminoles residing in Apalache were now led by

Secoffee's successor, a mico named Kinache, while Cowkeeper continued to direct the Alachua Seminoles in Timucua from his town of Cuscowilla.

Other changes that took place during the era of British dominion of the region had long-lasting consequences for all three interior tribes. The stationing of British—often Scottish—commissaries among the groups led to intermarriage with native women and the emergence of a generation of educated, property-owning mixed-bloods. Whereas French and British traders had fathered mixed-blood children among the Choctaws, Chickasaws, and Creeks prior to 1763, maternal relatives had raised most of the offspring in a traditional native manner. The new generation of traders, however, tended to claim their children in accordance with European paternalistic traditions, often sending the boys to schools along the Atlantic Coast or in Britain. These mixed-bloods began to mature during the period of the American Revolution and would play a large part in the leadership of the tribes following the conclusion of the war. John McIntosh, John McGillivray, and James Colbert fathered children with Chickasaw women during the period, while John Pitchlynn, Nathaniel Folsom, Turner Brashears, and Louis and Michael LeFlore married Choctaw brides. Lachlan McGillivray, a Scottish trader among the Creeks, fathered a mixed-blood son named Alexander who was educated in Charleston before establishing a residence at Little Tallasee among the Upper Creeks. Lachlan McGillivray's nephew, William McIntosh, also had a son with the same name by a prominent Lower Creek woman. The British traders and commissaries who established settlements among the tribes and intermarried with their women also introduced animal husbandry and African slavery to the Indians. By the 1780s these men and their mixed-blood children, along with a few leading native chiefs, had established ranches manned by black bondspeople within the Creek, Choctaw, and Chickasaw territories.

Spanish Intransigence and the Rebellion of 1768

In contrast to the British in Florida, the Spaniards moved slowly and unsteadily to take possession of Louisiana, leaving management of the colony in a confused state for half a decade. Despite agreeing to accept Louisiana from France in the secret Treaty of Fontainebleau in November 1762, Spanish officials hesitated before taking control of the province, as they were in the midst of reorganizing their empire. As a result, France was forced to retain possession of the colony west of the Mississippi until the Spaniards arrived to take charge. In February 1763, in order to oversee the transfer of the trans-Appalachian territory to the British as called for in the Treaty of Paris, the French Minister of the Marine, the Duc de Choiseul, invested a naval officer, Jean-Jacques-Blaise d'Abbadie, with the powers and authority of the offices of both governor and finance officer, consolidated in the new position of director general. Choiseul also appointed Charles-Philippe Aubry, an officer stationed in Illinois, as commander of the colony's French troops. A Canadian bureaucrat, Denis-Nicolas Foucault, was named as financial comptroller of Louisiana. Despite these appointments, clearly established executive control of Louisiana remained fleeting. Soon after D'Abbadie arrived in New Orleans in June 1763, the director general relieved Governor Kerlérec of his duties and traveled to Mobile to facilitate the British occupation. In the meantime Foucault attempted to fill the power vacuum left by D'Abbadie's absence by serving on the Superior Council and by assisting the newly appointed attorney general, Chapitoulas planter Nicolas Chauvin de Lafrénière, in his successful effort to expel the Jesuits—who French officials considered to be too independent—from Louisiana, as called for by a directive from Choiseul.

Louisiana's transfer to Spain remained a secret until September 1764, when D'Abbadie, following his return to New Orleans, announced the terms of the Treaty of Fontainebleau to the colony's astonished French creole inhabitants. Expecting the prompt arrival of the Spaniards, the director general quickly implemented his orders for the colony's conveyance to Spanish dominion by transporting all but three hundred or so French soldiers to Saint-Domingue. In January 1765 merchants and planters in New Orleans, fearful that the Spaniards would enforce mercantile practices that might inhibit their accustomed trade with the French West Indies, held a meeting to protest the change of authority. In desperation, the group—led by Attorney General Lafrénière—sent Jean Milhet, a wealthy New Orleans merchant, to France on a fruitless mission to persuade Louis XV to maintain possession of Louisiana. The following month D'Abbadie suddenly fell ill and died, leaving the colony in the unsteady hands of Aubry and Foucault, who assumed control of the colony's military and administrative branches. In addition to reestablishing the traditional bipolar form of Louisiana's government, the appointments of Aubry as governor and Foucault as finance officer only reinforced the sense of confusion as to who was actually in charge of the colony in lieu of the Spanish arrival.

The appearance of Louisiana's first Spanish governor, Antonio de Ulloa, in New Orleans in March 1766 did little to alleviate the bewildering situation. Ulloa, a Spanish scientist who had previously been unsuccessful as governor of the Peruvian province of Huancavelica, arrived with only ninety Spanish troops and chose to postpone indefinitely the transfer of the colony from France to Spain. Instead, Ulloa left Louisiana in the hands of the French caretaker government while he made a tour of the colony's military posts before establishing himself in September 1766 at Balize, the small French outpost that guarded the mouth of the Mississippi, where he remained for nine months. Meanwhile it became necessary to institute formalities that would signify the extension of Spanish sovereignty over Louisiana. Therefore, in January 1767 Ulloa met with Aubry at Balize and conducted a muddled act of transfer in which Spain formally took possession of the colony, with the understanding that French troops would maintain order until the arrival of sufficient Spanish forces.

In the meantime, with Ulloa at Balize, and neither Aubry nor Foucault eager to assume control, Attorney General Lafrénière filled the void and employed the Superior Council to provide Louisiana with leadership. The use of the Superior Council, however, ran counter to Governor Ulloa's efforts, following his return to New Orleans in June 1767, to bring the colony firmly under Spanish authority. Ulloa began enforcing Spanish mercantile law by impounding a merchant vessel on a charge of smuggling, only to have the Superior Council overturn his decision and allow the ship's captain to unload his cargo. This incident, combined with other insubordinate actions taken by the Superior Council under Lafrénière's guidance, caused the Spanish governor to try and neutralize the body by asserting his own judicial authority. Ulloa also requested royal permission to replace the uncooperative French court with a *cabildo,* a Spanish local governmental entity that shared many of the Superior Council's administrative duties. Spurred by Attorney General Lafrénière, opposition to the Spanish governor grew until reaching a head in October 1768, when Ulloa issued a decree calling for the implementation of even tighter restrictions on Louisiana's trade. Lafrénière responded by calling a meeting of the Superior Council in which the body insisted that Ulloa submit to its demand for the restoration of free trade. When the Spanish governor refused to recognize the Superior Council's prerogative, the attorney general's wealthy and powerful kinsmen led armed bands of colonists, including a large number of Germans from Des Allemands, to New Orleans to expel Ulloa from Louisiana. Sensing a precarious situation, the beleaguered

Spanish governor boarded a French merchant ship on November 1 and sailed for Havana.

In the aftermath of the rebellion Louisiana's creoles renewed their effort to convince Louis XV to assert his sovereignty over the colony. Although Choiseul was sympathetic to the colonists' cause, on learning of his Spanish ally's decision in March 1769 to reclaim Louisiana, the French Minister of Marine declined the proposal. Nonetheless, the French creoles in Louisiana were surprised by the arrival in August 1769 of a new Spanish governor, Alejandro O'Reilly, along with an armada of twenty-one ships and over two thousand troops. O'Reilly, an Irish soldier of fortune who had fought brilliantly in Spain's previous two wars, swiftly and decisively established firm Spanish control of Louisiana. Taking clear possession of the colony from Aubry on August 18, O'Reilly quickly arrested and tried a dozen leaders of the rebellion, resulting in the execution by firing squad of five of them, including Lafrénière, Milhet, and Superior Council member Jean Baptiste Noyan, Bienville's nephew as well as the attorney general's son-in-law. Joseph Villeré, husband of German Coast commandant D'Arensbourg's granddaughter, was also sentenced to death for inciting the Des Allemands rebels, but had already died while resisting arrest. Although O'Reilly sent the other six men to be imprisoned in Havana, they were released soon thereafter.

O'Reilly only remained in Louisiana for eight months, during which time he fully implemented the new Spanish order. He dismantled the French administrative structure and placed the colony under the jurisdiction of the captaincy-general of Havana. The Irishman also nullified French laws and replaced them with a Spanish legal code, known as the "Code O'Reilly," as well as insisted that Spanish would replace French as the colony's legal language. The code acknowledged the extinction of the French Superior Council and the creation of the New Orleans Cabildo, a venerable Spanish institution that provided municipal government. O'Reilly chose six councilors to serve on the Cabildo, five of them from among the planters who had sided with Spain in the 1768 rebellion. He also implemented Spanish mercantile law by prohibiting trade with foreigners and foreign ports while expelling a number of British traders from New Orleans. In an effort to normalize commerce with other Spanish ports, he encouraged Cuban merchants to engage in trade with New Orleans, reducing many of the taxes for those who would reorient their trade with Louisiana. O'Reilly reformed the colony's military structure by reorganizing the Louisiana militia, forming twelve companies consisting of nearly one thousand men. The Irishman also transferred responsibility for Louisiana Catholics from Quebec to the Archdiocese of Santiago, Cuba. In March 1770, with the colony firmly under Spanish control, O'Reilly formally relinquished control to Luis de Unzaga y Amezaga and returned to Havana.

Spanish Louisiana and the Influx of Newcomers

Unzaga, an army officer from Málaga who had been stationed in Cuba, served as governor of Louisiana until January 1777, during which time he successfully reconciled the French creoles to Spanish control. While Unzaga's marriage to the daughter of New Orleans planter Gilbert Antoine de St. Maxent assisted him in this effort, Spanish policies that promoted Louisiana's economic well-being ultimately convinced the colony's French elites to accept Spain's control. Spain's accession of Louisiana coincided with the reign of Carlos III, the reform-minded Bourbon ruler who desired to implement Enlightenment methods of government in order to transform Spanish holdings into efficiently governed and economically productive territories. The king's so-called Bourbon Reforms strongly affected Spanish Louisiana because the colony was administered through the captaincy-general of Havana, the crucible in which many of the changes put forth by Carlos III were tested. Minister of the Indies José de Gálvez, the man the king chose to implement the Bourbon Reforms in America, was the uncle of Bernardo de Gálvez, Unzaga's gubernatorial successor and brother-in-law by his marriage to a St. Maxent daughter. As a result of the Spanish policy initiatives put forth under Unzaga and Gálvez, Louisiana's exports increased dramatically during the period, the population grew, and the colony enjoyed more economic prosperity and stability than had ever occurred under the French dominion.

After establishing firm control over Louisiana in 1769, Spanish officials sought to develop the export economy through various means. Although O'Reilly had forced Louisiana merchants to trade exclusively within the Spanish empire, most particularly with Cuba, Governor Unzaga recognized the necessity of illicit commerce with the British and thus permitted the renewal of the clandestine trade, while making a few symbolic seizures of English ships. With the outbreak of the American Revolution in 1775, however, the Spaniards took steps to weaken the British economic position prior to Spain's 1779 entrance in the war. Spanish officials decreed the opening of trade between Louisiana and France and the French West Indies in 1776, thus restoring the commercial channels that had developed during the first two-thirds of the eighteenth century. Gálvez, upon becoming governor in early 1777, enhanced the diversion of the colony's trade from Great Britain to France by confiscating a number of British vessels and ordering their departure from Louisiana. In addition to increasing the number of ports colonial merchants could deal with, Spanish officials also took steps to promote the expansion of Louisiana exports. Tobacco production, which had languished during the French period, took off after the Spanish Crown made Louisiana the sole supplier for Mexico in 1776. At the same time the colony was given a monopoly on the production of the wooden boxes in which sugar was exported throughout the Spanish empire, resulting in the development of the colony's cypress industry. As a result of these initiatives, by the 1780s Louisiana was annually exporting an average of 1 million livres' worth of tobacco, twice the amount produced during the French era, and another 1 million livres' worth of timber products, a five-fold increase. Although the Spanish Crown did not subsidize indigo production during the period, Louisiana planters more than doubled the amount exported, reaching 3 million livres' worth by the 1780s.

The renewed importation of African slaves to Louisiana during the Spanish regime enhanced the increase in indigo output, as well as that of tobacco and timber products. Realizing that the colony's export economy depended on unfree labor, Spanish officials gradually removed all barriers to slave imports, and large numbers of Africans began to arrive in Louisiana for the first time since 1731. As early as 1772 Governor Unzaga allowed British ships from Jamaica to land African slaves at New Orleans. As a result of the 1776 decree authorizing trade with France and its Caribbean islands, many ships loaded with African slaves arrived in New Orleans during the next two years. However, Spain's declaration of war against Great Britain in 1779 resulted in drastic trade reductions. As the fighting wound down in 1782 the Spanish Crown lifted the import duty on slave cargoes coming from neutral or friendly ports, and larger shipments of slaves began to arrive in Louisiana soon thereafter. Between 1772 and 1783, at least sixty ships—most from Jamaica, with a few from the French West Indies and British North America—brought three thousand or so African slaves to New Orleans. The imported newcomers, coupled with a rise in the rate of natural increase among the creole bondspeople, caused the slave population in Spanish Louisiana to triple during the period, reaching fifteen thousand people by 1785.

In addition to reopening the African slave trade, Spanish officials in Louisiana also attempted to more tightly regulate slave behavior, while at the same time providing a law code that granted more rights to the bondspeople than the previous French system. O'Reilly replaced the French Code Noir with Spanish laws concerning slavery, which could be traced back over one thousand years. Spanish legal tradition held that slaves were human beings who possessed rights as well as obligations and that they were entitled to personal security and property. If they were Christians, slaves gained additional rights through marriage, parenthood, and fraternization. The laws also made it easier for slaves to gain their freedom. Not only could a master free a slave without official permission, but bondspeople themselves could also initiate manumission proceedings on their own behalf. As a result of the new regime's laws, the number of *libres,* or free people of color, in Louisiana increased eleven-fold to just over one thousand people during the first decade and a half of Spanish rule. More than half of the libres resided in New Orleans, and most of them were the mistresses and offspring of French merchants and planters. In this initial phase of the libre community's development in New Orleans, free women of color tended to make a living as seamstresses or shopkeepers, while men worked as artisans or laborers. As with free men of color in other Spanish American colonial cities, New Orleans libre men were also mustered into their own free militia of color, an institution that would help promote group cohesiveness and stability, especially during the twenty years of Spanish rule following the end of the War for American Independence.

For a variety of reasons, numerous groups of free people also migrated to relatively uninhabited regions of Spanish Louisiana during the period. French-allied Indians residing east of the Mississippi River were the first people to move to the colony, mainly because they did not wish to submit to the authority of their erstwhile British enemies. In September 1763, soon after the arrival of British troops in Pensacola, the Catholic Apalaches living near Mobile requested permission from the French authorities to migrate westward. Director General D'Abbadie responded favorably and allowed the Apalaches to settle on the Red River near the newly established Rapides Post, located midway between Natchitoches and the Mississippi River. D'Abbadie welcomed the Apalaches to the area in early 1764, noting that they could give assistance to the boats heading upriver to Natchitoches as well as provide foodstuffs for New Orleans. During the following decade the few remaining French-allied Indians living along the Gulf Coast—now coalesced into the Pascagoula, Biloxi, and Taensa tribes—joined the Apalaches and settled on the Red River, as well as on nearby streams flowing south directly to the sea. By 1773 about one hundred Indians had established farms in the area and had successfully begun to raise livestock. The tribes once again maintained close ties with the local Euroamericans; the Apalaches even used the Catholic priest at Natchitoches to baptize their children, whose godparents were often leading citizens of the town.

Creek and Choctaw refugees from British West Florida also relocated to Louisiana following the Seven Years' War. In April 1764 a group of Alabama emigrants abandoned their Coosa River town and established a temporary village on the east bank of the Mississippi near Bayou Manchac. In the next few years this band, along with newly arriving Alabama groups, moved farther west to join the Indians residing near Rapides. The Yowanis, a Choctaw tribe from the Sixtowns district, also migrated to Rapides during the period. As with the emigrants from the Gulf Coast, the Alabamas and the Yowanis planted crops, raised livestock, and exchanged pelts for manufactured goods with the local French traders. By 1783 about three hundred emigrant Indians had taken refuge from the British by settling near Rapides. About 150 Tunicas crossed the Mississippi and moved to the lower reaches of the Red River during the period, while two hundred or so Houmas and Chitimachas migrated from the Mississippi westward to Bayous Plaquemine and Lafourche at around the same time.

The other immigrants to Spanish Louisiana were people of European descent, and the white population of the colony nearly tripled during the era, reaching about eleven thousand inhabitants by the 1780s. French Canadian exiles from British Nova Scotia began to arrive in Louisiana soon after the Spanish accession. They were the descendants of the initial three hundred colonists who had settled in the French province of Acadia, on the south shore of the Bay of Fundy, in 1632. French neglect of the colony throughout the seventeenth century had forced the Acadian pioneers to utilize their skills as backwoodsmen to support themselves. The Acadian families drained marshland in order to raise cereal crops and create grazing lands for livestock, and they supplemented their diet with small-scale fishing and hunting. The households were largely self-sufficient, as Acadian women produced woolen and linen clothing while the men made wooden furniture and agricultural tools and implements. By the mid-eighteenth century the fiercely independent Acadians had increased their population to nearly twenty thousand individuals. Unfortunately for the

Acadians, however, the British—who had assumed control of the region in 1713—did not trust the French Catholics and expelled them from their homes during the Seven Years' War. Most of the exiled Acadians initially took refuge either in France or in the British Atlantic colonies of Maryland and Pennsylvania. Although both colonies were known for their religious tolerance, the refugee Acadians were ostracized socially and denied access to the marketplace in each province, causing the exiles to respond favorably to the French caretaker government's suggestion that they reunite in Spanish Louisiana.

The first two hundred Acadians, led by Joseph Broussard *dit* Beausoleil, arrived in New Orleans in February 1765. Over the course of the next five years another eight hundred exiles migrated to Louisiana, mainly in family groups. Most of these Cajuns, as the Acadians came to be known, settled in two relatively uninhabited regions. Hoping to defend Louisiana from the British in West Florida, French and Spanish officials ordered one group of Acadians to settle on both banks of the Mississippi River downstream from Bayou Manchac. The Acadians, like other French residents on the Mississippi, were granted parcels of land in longlots with four to six arpents of river frontage. Lacking slaves at first, the Acadians raised vegetables, along with a small number of livestock, rather than engage in the cash crops of indigo and tobacco like the longer-established inhabitants on the river. Whereas nearly five hundred Acadians resided in this region by 1771, the settlers owned less than fifty bondspeople. The Mississippi River Acadians proliferated in their new homes, and their population nearly doubled to just over nine hundred residents within a decade and a half. The slave numbers increased as well; just over four hundred bondspeople lived in the sector by the 1780s, and four in ten Acadian households owned laborers. Nonetheless, most of the Acadian slaveholders living on the Mississippi owned fewer than five blacks, and therefore continued to raise foodstuffs instead of export crops.

The other Acadian group, led by Broussard and Louis Andry, a veteran military engineer, settled near the recently founded Attakapas Post in southwestern Louisiana in the spring of 1765. During the next few years other Acadians followed these pioneers to the region and, employing their backwoods skills, established subsistence farms and cattle ranches on the prairies between Bayou Teche and the Vermilion River, as far north as Opelousas Post. The Acadians also made their own clothes by learning to substitute cotton, which became an important crop soon after their arrival, for the wool they had been accustomed to in Canada. By 1771 nearly 450

Acadians had settled near the Attakapas and Opelousas Posts. Successful in their new homes, the Acadian population grew to about 750 people in 1777. A few Cajuns obtained slaves soon after establishing themselves on the prairies, and within a decade just over three hundred bondspeople toiled in the region. At this point, however, only one in ten Acadian families owned slaves. By the 1780s, with the increased importation of Africans to Louisiana, twice as many Cajuns held bondspeople, and the number of slaves increased fourfold to just under twelve hundred.

Due to an attempt by Bourbon officials to Hispanicize the French-dominated colony of Louisiana, Spaniards from Málaga soon joined the Acadians near Attakapas. They were led by Lieutenant Governor Francisco Bouligny, a native of Alicante who had arrived in the colony along with General O'Reilly and had subsequently presented a lengthy statement about Louisiana's economic and military conditions to José de Gálvez. In 1779 seventy Malagueños established the community of New Iberia on Bayou Teche. As with the Acadians who lived nearby, the Malagueños raised livestock on the vast prairies that surrounded their settlement. The Málaga immigrants eventually intermarried with their Acadian Catholic neighbors, and the white population of the region rose to just over twelve hundred people by the mid-1780s.

Spanish-speaking farming and fishing families from the Canary Islands migrated to Louisiana at the same time as the Malagueños, but did not fare as well as their fellow Spaniards or the Acadians in their new homes. In 1778, in order to increase the number of troops in the colony as tensions increased with Great Britain, Spanish officials authorized the recruitment of soldiers and their families to be transported to Louisiana from the Canary Islands for permanent settlement at royal expense. As a result, about sixteen hundred Isleños reached New Orleans between November 1778 and July 1779, with another three hundred or so coming in 1783. Dismayed by the large number of married military men with children who arrived at the capital, Governor Gálvez decided to employ the Canary Islanders as settlers rather than soldiers and placed them at three strategic sites where they could act as sentinels to help safeguard Spanish lands from the British in West Florida. In the spring of 1779 three Canarian communities were established almost simultaneously. About four hundred Isleños were sent to the south bank of the Amite River, near its junction with Bayou Manchac, where they founded the settlement of Galveztown. The low-lying area was subject to annual flooding, making it hard for the settlers to raise sufficient crops to feed themselves.

Hurricanes and disease also threatened the community, and by 1785 less than 250 Isleños remained at Galveztown. Another two hundred Canary Islanders established the community of Valenzuela on Bayou Lafourche, just downstream from its junction with the Mississippi River. Like their compatriots at Galveztown, the Valenzuela Canary Islanders suffered from epidemics and storms, but were able to set up small farms on which they raised pigs and chickens. By the mid-1780s just over three hundred Isleños resided at Valenzuela along with about fifty slaves. A third group of 150 Canary Islanders established the most successful of the three communities just east of New Orleans at St. Bernard, along the ridges of Bayou Terre-aux-Boeufs in 1779. Another three hundred Isleños joined them four years later. The St. Bernard Canary Islanders established farms along the bayou on which they produced vegetables for their own consumption and for sale in the capital, in addition to fishing in the nearby swamps that teemed with fish, shrimp, crabs, and oysters. As a result of their efforts, the St. Bernard population increased to around six hundred inhabitants by 1785.

The Lower Mississippi Valley

Despite the Acadian and Spanish immigration to Louisiana during the period, French creoles maintained their numerical majority and economic superiority within the colony. Most of the people and most of the wealth continued to be concentrated in New Orleans and the nearby plantation district, as the region's population grew from sixty-three hundred to fifteen thousand during the two decades following the Seven Years' War. The capital's population doubled, reaching five thousand inhabitants by 1785, with the free people—a mixed group of French creoles, Spaniards, libres, and a few Anglos—making up more than two-thirds of the town's residents. This heterogeneous group, which was also divided by class, increasingly expected the city to supply services that would improve the quality of life and protect their property. Whereas the French Superior Council had not been particularly successful in providing the capital with responsible municipal government, the newly established Spanish Cabildo took on such problems as floods, crime, health, fire hazards, sanitation, streets, and drainage, in addition to struggling with the consequences of damaging hurricanes that struck the city in successive Augusts in 1779 and 1780. Due to its impressive performance, the Cabildo reached its apogee of

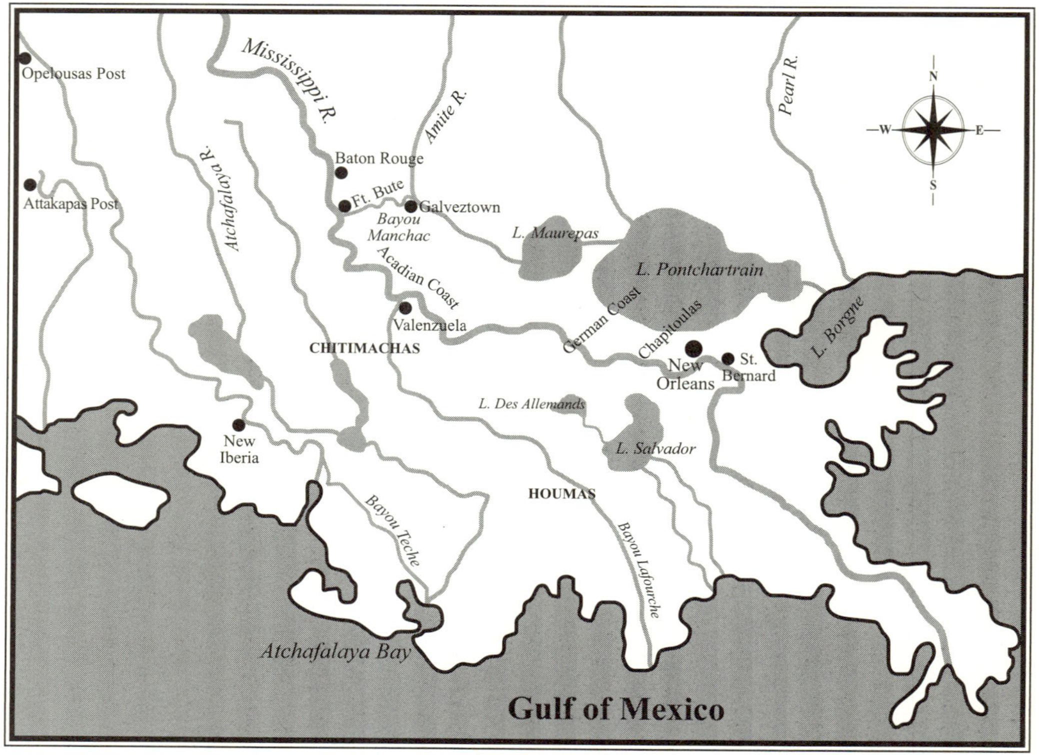

MAP 7. THE LOWER MISSISSIPPI, CA. 1780

power and prestige in the early 1780s, particularly under the leadership of Esteban Rodríguez Miró, a Catalonian soldier who was appointed acting governor of Louisiana in March 1782.

The plantation district that surrounded New Orleans upstream and downriver from Cannes Brulées to English Turn continued to be the colony's center of wealth and power. The region's population nearly tripled during the period, reaching ten thousand in 1785. Eight in ten of the area's inhabitants were enslaved laborers toiling on Louisiana's largest plantations, where they mainly concentrated on indigo production in the fields along the river, in addition to obtaining timber from the cypress swamps behind the settlements. Although a majority of the nearly eight thousand slaves were creoles, most of the three thousand Africans who arrived in the colony between 1772 and 1783 ended up on the farms just outside New Orleans. Whereas three-fourths of the plantation district's population, and many of the largest planters, continued to reside upstream at Chapitoulas, the rebellious actions of Lafrénière and his cronies caused O'Reilly to appoint downriver planters Francisco María de Reggio and Antonio Bienvenu to positions on the New Orleans Cabildo.

During the two decades following the transfer of Louisiana to Spain, the German Coast took on the characteristics of the plantation district farther downstream. French creoles became a majority of the district's white population, slaves emerged as a majority of the entire population, and, as a result, export crops provided the area with most of its wealth. The region experienced a huge population growth during the period, rising almost five times to reach thirty-two hundred people in 1785. The free population increased three times to just over thirteen hundred people. Meanwhile, because of intermarriage and new settlements, German households constituted only one-fourth of the area's farms and plantations. The slave numbers among the Germans rose most dramatically, however, increasing from two hundred in 1763 to eighteen hundred by the end of the era. Whereas two-thirds of the German Coast households contained no slaves in 1763, just under half owned bondspeople by the 1780s, with one in seven farms holding more than eight unfree laborers. As a result of the increase in slave labor, indigo became the region's foremost commercial product, along with tobacco, cotton, and timber products. Most Des Allemands planters, as well as farmers without slaves, also raised rice, corn, and beans, in addition to maintaining livestock.

French creoles, along with the above-mentioned Acadian and Canary Island immigrants, established farms along the Mississippi in the region between the German Coast and Pointe Coupée that had been occupied by the dwindling Indian groups during the French era. By 1785 almost three thousand people resided in the area, which consisted of the Spanish districts of Cabannocé, La Fourche des Chetimachas, Valenzuela des Chetimachas, Iberville, and Baton Rouge. In contrast to the rest of the Mississippi River settlements, less than one-third of the region's inhabitants were slaves, and thus most of the settlers raised foodstuffs and livestock during this period. Pointe Coupée planters, on the other hand, expanded their production of tobacco in response to the Bourbon policies that promoted the export of Louisiana's crop. Slave numbers nearly doubled during the period, reaching just over one thousand people by 1785, and unfree laborers made up over two-thirds of Pointe Coupée's fifteen hundred inhabitants.

Arkansas

Arkansas Post continued to stand in direct contrast to most of the rest of Louisiana during the Spanish period, as official efforts to develop export staples failed there. As during the French era, most of the 150 or so creole settlers who resided around the post at various times of the year continued to hunt deer and bear from camps they established along the upper reaches of the Arkansas, White, St. Francis, and Ouachita Rivers. The military fort, which had been moved downstream from the high ground near Écores Rouges in 1756, flooded so frequently that Commandant Balthazar de Villiers returned it to the bluffs upstream in 1779 and renamed it Fort Carlos III. Although the Quapaws at the Kappa, Osotouy, and Tourima villages formally transferred their allegiances from France to Spain following the latter's accession of Louisiana, the tribesmen quickly became displeased with their new allies, as the Spaniards provided little in the way of presents and trade. As a result, the Quapaws eagerly turned to British traders who established themselves on the east bank of the Mississippi opposite the mouth of the Arkansas. In fact, Angaska, the Tourima chief who became the spokesman for all the Quapaws during the 1770s, made a secret alliance with the British traders and accepted a medal and a flag from them. Through their friendship with the British, the Quapaws also made peace with their erstwhile Chickasaw enemies. In the late 1770s Chief Angaska craftily used his ties with the British and the Chickasaws to force the Spanish commandants—most of whom were actually French creoles—at the Arkansas Post to provide his people with more gifts than they had previously been receiving. The Spaniards also established two new posts, Avoyelles and Rapides, on the lower reaches of the Red River soon after the transfer of Louisiana, both of which had more in common with Arkansas Post than with the rest of the colony. By the 1780s about two hundred French creoles and a few Spaniards and Anglos resided near the posts, along with about 150 slaves. Most of the residents hunted along the Lower Ouachita, Tensas, and Little Rivers—Catahoula country—in addition to trading with the Indian groups who migrated to the area from British West Florida following the Treaty of Paris.

The Louisiana-Texas Frontier

Farther up the Red River at Natchitoches, the slave-owning residents of the community responded to the Spanish economic policies by fully turning to tobacco production in the late 1770s. Several French creoles purchased land along the river from the Natchitoches Indians in order to establish plantations, and by the end of the War for American Independence the community was well prepared to reap the benefits of Spain's promotion of tobacco cultivation in Louisiana. By the 1780s the town's slave population had nearly doubled to reach just over five hundred bondspeople, almost two-thirds of whom resided on plantations containing more than ten unfree laborers. Whereas a majority of the six hundred French creoles—double the number since the beginning of the Spanish regime—living in Natchitoches resided on plantations that raised tobacco, many of the nonslaveholding inhabitants turned to ranching, especially after 1779, when Spain opened up the livestock trade between Texas and Louisiana. Ranches were established throughout the area, most importantly at Campti and Bayou Pierre, north and west of town at sites that had formerly been occupied by Indians. In fact, the decline of the Indian population in the immediate area—only 150 Natchitoches, Yatasi, and Adaes Indians remained within fifty miles of the town—and in Texas reinforced the decision of the community's wealthier residents to abandon the formerly profitable Indian trade. By the 1780s only the poorest and least well-connected inhabitants of Natchitoches were involved in the rapidly declining Indian commerce.

Although Texas did not change hands like Louisiana and Florida following the Seven Years' War, the Spanish colony did experience great changes over the following two decades. As part of Carlos III's reordering of the

Spanish empire, in 1765 Spanish officials in Mexico City ordered the marqués de Rubí, a field marshal in the royal army, to inspect all presidios on the northern frontier of New Spain in order to determine whether the military outposts adequately defended the realm against Indians and foreign encroachments. The following year Rubí and his party, which included military engineer Nicolás de Lafora, began their tour in New Mexico, moved to Sonora, and then returned to Coahuila before entering Texas in the summer of 1767. After visiting the presidio and missions on the San Saba River, Rubí traveled to San Antonio and then on to East Texas. The party arrived at the three Franciscan missions among the Hasinais in September and discovered that there was not "one Indian to whom [the priests] could minister, nor had there been one during the more than forty years of [the missions'] existence." One priest was forced to admit that "there is no hope, not even a remote one" of converting any of the Hasinais to Christianity. Continuing on to Los Adaes, the marqués found it to be as worthless as the nearby missions. The garrison contained sixty-one men, but there were just twenty-five horses fit for service and only two functional muskets. The soldiers were dressed in rags, many without hats, shirts, or shoes. One of the men confessed to Rubí that his "company lacked arms, horses, coats, and in a word everything necessary to carry out its obligations." Convinced that the Spanish effort in East Texas was useless—especially now that Spain also controlled Louisiana—Rubí and his group returned to Mexico City, arriving at the capital in February 1768. In all, Rubí's inspection tour occupied him for twenty-three months, during which he traveled an estimated seventy-six hundred miles.

In the capital Rubí quickly put forth a report to the king based on his observations. The marqués called for the closure of the empty Franciscan missions in Texas and the establishment of a frontier, stretching from the Gulf of California to the Gulf of Mexico, that would be defended by a series of presidios spaced about one hundred miles apart. The new arrangement of forts included only two within the confines of Texas, one at San Antonio and the other at La Bahía, on the coast. Rubí recommended the total abandonment of East Texas and the removal of its citizens to Béxar, which was to become the new capital of the province. Having paid particularly close attention to the realities of Indian affairs during his tour of Texas, Rubí insisted that the Spaniards ally themselves with the Norteños—Comanches, Wichitas, and Caddos—and abandon all attempts at cooperation with the deceitful Lipan Apaches. Although the marqués sent his report to Spain in May 1768, it was not until September 1772 that Carlos III issued the New Regulations for Presidios, calling for the implementation of all of Rubí's proposals. At the same time the former governor of Texas, Hugo Oconor—an Irish Catholic serving in the Spanish army like his cousin, Alejandro O'Reilly—was appointed commandant inspector in charge of putting the new regulations into effect.

In early 1773 Viceroy Antonio María de Bucareli y Ursúa and Lieutenant Colonel Oconor ordered the present governor of Texas, Juan María Vicencio, Barón de Ripperdá, to bring about the immediate closure of the presidio and missions in East Texas and the prompt removal of the five hundred or so settlers who resided between Los Adaes and the Franciscan establishment at Nacogdoches. Whereas the isolated priests left the three missions without complaint, the settlers protested the forced evacuation of their homes and the abandonment of their crops and livestock, which they were not given enough time to round up before their exit. Nonetheless, most of them followed the lead of Antonio Gil Ibarvo, the owner of the El Lobanillo ranch, and accompanied the Spanish soldiers back to San Antonio in the summer of 1773. Immediately upon his arrival in Béxar, however, Gil Ibarvo traveled to Mexico City, where he convinced Viceroy Bucareli to permit the settlers to return to East Texas—but only as far as the Trinity River—in order to maintain friendly relations with the Hasinais and to make sure that Anglos from east of the Mississippi did not occupy the area. As a result, later that year Gil Ibarvo and a few of his compatriots founded the town of Nuestra Señora del Pilar de Bucareli where the royal road from San Antonio to Los Adaes crossed the Trinity River.

The frontier outpost of Bucareli prospered for the first four years of its existence, as about fifty families established residences there. Comanche raids and flooding, however, forced the settlers to abandon Bucareli in early 1779 and move east to the site of the abandoned mission at Nacogdoches. Following lengthy discussions, Spanish officials gave the relocation their approval in October 1779 and named Gil Ibarvo the captain of the militia and lieutenant governor of the civil post of Nacogdoches. Soon thereafter he began construction of a large house—now referred to as the Old Stone Fort—which served as a commissary, a trading post, and his own personal home. Gil Ibarvo also established an informal system of granting land verbally, and by the early 1780s about four hundred people lived in and around Nacogdoches, where they raised cattle and foodstuffs for their own consumption.

Whereas Rubí's recommendation that the Spaniards completely abandon East Texas was partially carried out in the 1770s, his proposal to form an alliance with the Norteños against the Lipan Apaches did not yield results for nearly two decades, mainly because of bureaucratic intransigence. The fact that Spain administered Louisiana and Texas separately caused many of the problems. Prior to his appointment as commandant inspector, Oconor had been the provisional governor of Texas between 1767 and 1770, charged with eradicating the smuggling between Natchitoches and Texas allowed by Spanish governors in the past. During his investigation Oconor became certain that French weapons from Louisiana had allowed the Norteños to destroy the mission on the San Saba River in 1758, as well as to successfully defend themselves against Ortiz Parrilla at the Taovaya village the following year. Despite the New Regulations for Presidios of 1772, Oconor continued to insist that the Wichitas and the Comanches, in particular, were enemies of Texas and that they should not be supplied with weapons and manufactured goods.

On the other hand, when Alejandro O'Reilly assumed control of Louisiana in 1769, he implemented a policy that allowed the Norteños to carry out their exchanges with traders from Natchitoches. O'Reilly understood that the eradication of this commerce would only drive the tribes into the hands of aggressive British traders, now poised on the east bank of the Mississippi River. O'Reilly insisted, however, that the Indians who had been French allies would now have to pledge an oath of fidelity to Spain. In return, the Spanish government would provide the tribes with annual presents and would designate distinguished leaders as chiefs, dignified by decoration with great and small medals. Although O'Reilly utilized French trading policies, he made significant modifications. Instead of being free to trade any items to any French trader who arrived at their villages, under the new policy the Indians could deal only with licensed traders, who were closely supervised by the government. The natives were also forbidden to deal in slaves and livestock, since Indian slavery was illegal in the Spanish empire and trading horses and cattle promoted theft from fellow Spaniards in Texas. To put such a policy into effect and establish an alliance with the Norteños, O'Reilly called upon the man who was said to have a knowledge of Texas and Louisiana and their native inhabitants "such as no one else possesses," Athanase de Mézières, son-in-law of St. Denis, the founder of Natchitoches. In late 1769 the Irishman named the Frenchman—both now in the employ of Spain—lieutenant governor of the all-important Natchitoches district.

De Mézières, who had resided in Natchitoches for more than twenty-five years, considered the allegiance of the Caddos—particularly the Kadohadachos who lived at the bend of the Red River—to be of the utmost importance to any peace plan, since the tribe occupied "the master-key of New Spain." Not only could the Caddos serve as a buffer against British incursions on the northeastern flank of Texas, but their influence with the Wichitas and Comanches might help bring about peace with those tribes as well. Therefore, in April 1770 de Mézières gathered the chiefs of the four Caddo tribes residing on the Red River at Natchitoches, where they officially transferred their allegiance from France to Spain. In return, the lieutenant governor designated the Kadohadacho and Yatasi leaders as medal chiefs, and the four tribes were granted an annual present and the right to have licensed traders from Natchitoches visit their villages. The following year de Mézières convinced the leaders of the four remaining Hasinai groups in East Texas to travel to San Antonio in order to reestablish their ties with the governor of Texas, the Baron de Ripperdá, since they were under his jurisdiction.

Although de Mézières had formed an alliance with the Caddos, Oconor, backed by Viceroy Bucareli and the Franciscan priests (who could not forget their martyred brothers at San Saba), blocked all of his efforts to establish peace with the other Norteños. Guided by Oconor, the viceroy barred communication between Governor Ripperdá and de Mézières and ordered Natchitoches traders to stop traveling to the Taovaya village to exchange goods with the Wichitas and the Comanches. Deprived of obtaining weapons from Louisiana, the Wichitas found themselves besieged by the rampaging Osages. Although the Osages were subject to the same official Spanish restrictions on trade issued from Louisiana, they had greater access to illegal trade and weapons since they lived between the Wichitas and the British. Well-armed with British guns and ammunition, increasing numbers of Osages moved into the Arkansas Valley, where the Spaniards were weakest, and stepped up their attacks on their traditional Wichita and Caddo enemies in an attempt to extend their territory southward and westward. According to de Mézières, the Osages had turned the region into a "pitiful theatre of outrageous robberies and bloody encounters." As a result of Osage pressure, the Tawakonis retreated southward to the Brazos River, where they established villages at the site of present Waco, while the Kichais moved from the Sabine River to the Trinity. Desperate for weapons, the Wichitas gained access to British goods through their fellow Caddoan speakers, the Skidi Pawnees, who lived on the Missouri River. The Skidis established commercial ties with British traders from Illinois, who supplied the Pawnees with arms and ammunition in return for horses. The Wichitas eagerly entered into this trade, using the Skidis as middlemen, and began raiding the horse herds at San Antonio and La Bahía, which only reinforced Oconor's contention that the Norteños were the Spaniards' enemies.

In 1777 Spanish officials finally allowed de Mézières to resume his attempts to establish peace with the Wichitas and Comanches. The previous year Spain created the Comandancia General of the Internal Provinces, a new administrative unit consisting of all the northern provinces of New Spain (including Texas, but not Louisiana) that was detached from the jurisdiction of the viceroy and brought under the control of a commandant general, who reported directly to the king. In effect, the Internal Provinces wrested control of Texas Indian affairs from Viceroy Bucareli and Commandant Inspector Oconor and placed them into the able hands of the first commandant general, Teodoro de Croix. Free to deal with the Indians as he pleased, in 1778 the commandant general authorized de Mézières to establish peace and trade with the Norteños in order to launch a campaign, in conjunction with Spanish troops, against the Lipan Apaches and the Osages. Before the plan could be put into effect, however, a smallpox epidemic swept through the region, reducing the Caddo and Wichita populations by one-third. By the time the sickness ran its course, only about three thousand Caddos and four thousand Wichitas remained in their villages located between the Red and the Brazos. The following year de Mézières died and Carlos III cancelled the joint Spanish-Norteño campaign due to Spain's entry into the struggle against Great Britain that had risen out of the War for American Independence. It would not be until after the Revolutionary War ended in September 1783 that the Norteños and the Spaniards would resume their peacemaking efforts.

The War for American Independence

Although the war between Great Britain and its rebellious colonists had begun in April 1775 along the eastern seaboard of North America, the conflict came to include France, which became an ally of the United States in February 1778, and Spain, which entered the war against the British in June 1779 as a partner of the French rather than of the thirteen states. While Spanish officials feared that the Americans' success might establish a dangerous precedent for their own colonies, their desire to drive the British out of the Lower Mississippi Valley and regain Florida led to the decision to join the fight against England. In contrast to the previous struggle between Great Britain, France, and Spain, large-scale hostilities actually took place within the Gulf South during the Revolutionary War, as American rebels and British and Spanish forces were active in the region. The outcome was also dramatically different; in this war the Spanish forces demonstrated the Bourbon Reforms' positive effects by aggressively carrying out well-organized campaigns that humiliated British troops throughout the Western Hemisphere, capped by a glorious victory in 1781 at Pensacola led by Louisiana governor Bernardo de Gálvez.

Spain, however, initially remained neutral when the war broke out between the colonists and Great Britain and maintained the impartial stance after the United States declared independence in July 1776. At this time most of the British subjects residing in West Florida were either neutral or pro-American in sentiment. Within a couple of years, however, a series of events caused the region to become a loyalist stronghold. In November 1775 British officials had ordered West Florida governor Peter Chester to issue a proclamation declaring his colony a haven for loyalists fleeing the colonies in rebellion and promising land grants for the newcomers. Although the refugees were slow in arriving at first, by April 1776 the loyalists were moving to West Florida in large numbers, nearly doubling the population by the end of the war. An American invasion of the colony during 1778 served to reinforce the growing loyalist sentiment in West Florida. Acting under a commission from the Commerce Committee of the Continental Congress, Captain James Willing—a former resident of Natchez—left Fort Pitt on the Ohio River in January 1778 with a force of about thirty volunteers, intending to capture British possessions on the east bank of the Mississippi. Moving swiftly down the swollen rivers, Willing's force grew to over one hundred men by the time it surprised the British residents of Natchez, who surrendered to the invaders in mid-February. Although Willing and his men did little damage to the Natchez settlers' property, as the force moved downstream it became a "body of banditti," plundering the sparsely settled region and instigating a wave of anti-American feelings throughout West Florida. After receiving supplies from Oliver Pollock, the American agent in New Orleans, Willing headed back to Fort Pitt, thus ending rebel activities in West Florida for the remainder of the war.

In addition to ensuring the loyalist attitude of a majority of the West Florida settlers, Willing's invasion impressed upon British officials the weak and defenseless state of the colony, which contained only about five hundred regular troops at the beginning of hostilities. In order to buttress the colony's defenses, in October 1778 nearly twelve hundred soldiers—including a contingent of German mercenaries and loyalists from Maryland and Pennsylvania—sailed from New York for Pensacola under the command of Brigadier General John Campbell. Upon their arrival in West Florida in January 1779, Campbell sent three hundred soldiers to the Mississippi River to reestablish Fort Bute at Manchac, in addition to shoring up Colonel Alexander Dickson's command of east bank British possessions upstream to Natchez. The rest of the troops set about repairing Fort Charlotte at Mobile and Fort George at Pensacola in preparation for another American invasion or war with Spain, which was expected following the establishment of the Franco-American alliance in early 1778.

In the meantime the talented Governor Gálvez also began to prepare for war with Great Britain. He hastened to set up a system of information gathering, receiving a copious amount of intelligence on the British situation in West Florida through various Spanish observers, as well as from Oliver Pollock. By the time Spain declared war on Great Britain in early summer 1779, Gálvez had already intercepted messages that the British planned to invade the colony from Canada and Pensacola. Rather than wait, Gálvez chose to immediately take the offensive, planning a campaign that would rapidly sweep upriver to surprise and defeat the British forts along the Lower Mississippi. Diego Joseph Navarro y Valladares, governor and captain general of Havana, supported Gálvez's plan and transferred over six hundred troops to New Orleans in late July. Gathering reports that the British were inadequately prepared to resist an attack, Gálvez mustered a force of five hundred regular army soldiers, along with sixty French creoles and eighty libres, and set out for Fort Bute at Manchac on August 27. Colonel Dickson, learning of the approaching force but unaware that a state of war officially existed between Spain and Great Britain, decided to transfer most of his troops from Fort Bute to a hastily constructed earthen redoubt at Baton Rouge in order to avoid a major confrontation. As a result, Gálvez easily overran the post in a dawn attack on September 7, taking twenty British soldiers prisoner. Exactly two weeks later the Spanish force surrounded the British troops at Baton Rouge and began an artillery barrage that forced Dickson to surrender after three hours. Gálvez captured nearly four hundred prisoners and took possession of eight transport ships sent from Pensacola. Dickson also agreed to Gálvez's stipulation that the British hand over Fort Panmure at Natchez to the Spaniards. Captain Jean de la Villebeuvre took possession of the fort on October 5. Gálvez spent the next few weeks defeating small enemy pockets around Lake Pontchartrain before returning to New Orleans in late October, having accomplished all his campaign's goals.

Flush with victory, Gálvez immediately turned his attention to the British forces along the Gulf Coast and requested more troops from Cuba. Although Navarro agreed to send reinforcements to Gálvez, his fear of leaving Havana defenseless caused him to approve fewer men than the Louisiana governor had requested for an assault on Pensacola. Therefore, Gálvez chose instead to attack the more lightly defended Fort Charlotte at Mobile. With a force of twelve hundred men, including regulars, militia, and a troop of libres, Gálvez left New Orleans in January 1780 in an armada of fourteen ships. Just as the force appeared at the mouth of Mobile Bay, a violent storm struck, sinking five ships and killing four hundred soldiers. Rather than retreat, the Louisiana governor pressed on and set up a base on the Dog River, just nine miles below Mobile. As the Spaniards prepared to attack Fort Charlotte, which was defended by only three hundred or so British troops, five ships carrying over fourteen hundred men, equipment, and supplies arrived from Havana. Learning that General Campbell had launched a relief expedition from Pensacola, Gálvez hurriedly attacked Fort Charlotte on March 12. After a daylong exchange of fire, the British force ran out of ammunition and surrendered. They turned the post over to Gálvez two days later. Pleased with the victory at Mobile, Carlos III promoted Gálvez to field marshal and put him in charge of all Spanish military operations on the North American continent. Gálvez headed to Havana soon thereafter to plan the upcoming campaign against Pensacola, leaving Mobile in the hands of Colonel José de Ezpeleta y Galdeano.

By October 1780 Gálvez had gathered a force of thirty-eight hundred men that left Havana in fifty transports accompanied by twelve warships. Two days after leaving port, however, a hurricane scattered the armada, sinking a few ships and forcing the survivors to return to Havana. The storm provided General Campbell a bit more time to gather his forces, which by early 1781 numbered approximately twenty-five hundred men, including one thousand or so Choctaw, Chickasaw, and Creek allies and a few hundred black slaves. Eager to attack Pensacola as soon as possible, Gálvez departed Havana on February 28, 1781, with just over thirteen hundred troops. Cuban officials, however, had sent fifteen hundred soldiers to New Orleans and Mobile the previous December and promised Gálvez that reinforcements would soon be following him to Pensacola. On March 19, with Gálvez himself leading the way, the Spanish force ran past the British battery that guarded the entrance to Pensacola Bay and anchored on the inside of Santa Rosa Island. A few days later twenty-three hundred men from Mobile and New Orleans arrived, allowing Gálvez to aggressively establish a base within cannon shot of Fort George. On April 19, as the Spaniards began to besiege the British force, a joint Spanish-French fleet carrying twenty-four hundred soldiers entered Pensacola Bay, increasing Gálvez's troop strength to more than seven thousand men. The Spanish artillery, commanded by Colonel Ezpeleta, now began to wear down the outmanned and outgunned British forces. Finally, on May 7, a Spanish shot scored a direct hit on the British powder magazine, killing more than one hundred soldiers and creating a major breach in the walls of Fort George. Spanish troops eagerly moved in. Following a bit of skirmishing, General Campbell surrendered, turning the fort and the town over to Gálvez on May 10. The British troops, along with Governor Chester, were allowed to leave Pensacola a few weeks later. On June 4 Gálvez headed to Havana to assume command of the Spanish war effort in the Gulf of Mexico, leaving Pensacola under the command of Colonel Arturo O'Neill, another Irishman in the service of Spain. Ultimately, the Spanish Crown rewarded Gálvez's efforts by promoting him to governor and captain general of Cuba in 1784, and to viceroy of New Spain the following year.

Although the Franco-American victory over Lord Cornwallis at Yorktown in September 1781 ended the fighting in North America, hostilities between Great Britain and the French and Spanish allies continued until the signing of an armistice in Paris between all parties in January 1783. Nine months later, on September 20, 1783, Great Britain recognized the independence of the United States and the extension of its western boundary all the way to the Mississippi River. In a separate accord signed the same day, the British officially recognized West Florida as a Spanish possession and surrendered East Florida to Spain, even though St. Augustine remained in British hands at the end of the war. For the first time since the establishment of colonies along the northern reaches of the Gulf of Mexico in the late seventeenth century, Texas, Louisiana, and Florida would now be administered by the same European power, Spain.

6

The Anglo Protestant Influx and the Consequences of the French Revolution 1783–1803

Although Spain administered Texas, Louisiana, and Florida following the signing of the Treaty of Paris, the diplomacy of the Gulf South proved to be very complicated over the course of the next two decades, due to the establishment of the expansionist United States and the consequences of the wars of the French Revolution. Spanish Texas remained fairly well isolated from the burgeoning power of the United States, and it would not be affected by the world political situation until the middle of the first decade of the nineteenth century. Spanish Louisiana and Florida, on the other hand, bordered the young republic, and both colonies were immediately pressured by Anglo Protestant immigration into the lands west of the Appalachian Mountains and south of the Ohio River after 1783. Already overwhelmed by the American incursions, Spain was further weakened by its involvement in the wars caused by the French Revolution, forcing the Spaniards to submit to humiliating treaties with France and the United States that left the Americans in possession of Louisiana and various powerful Indian groups dominant in East Texas and West Florida by December 1803. Throughout all of this, despite the diplomatic uncertainty in the region, Louisiana's economy continued to grow at a fantastic pace. Thousands of African slaves were sent to the Mississippi Valley to work on plantations that were converted to cotton and sugar production in the final decade of the eighteenth century. Finally, the United States initiated an Indian policy in the Gulf South designed to "civilize" the region's Native Americans, resulting in the exacerbation of tensions between indigenous full-bloods and the burgeoning class of market-oriented mixed-bloods that ultimately would lead to civil war among the Creeks early in the nineteenth century.

Spanish-United States Diplomacy

Although Spain had triumphed over Great Britain during the War for American Independence, the Spanish Gulf South was immediately threatened by the astonishing number of Anglo Protestants who moved across the Appalachian Mountains from the United States in the aftermath of the Revolution. Whereas a few colonists had settled in the region prior to the end of the war, following the signing of the 1783 Treaty of Paris their numbers grew rapidly, reaching seventy-five thousand people in Kentucky and thirty-five thousand in Tennessee by 1790. The two states' population tripled during the following decade, reaching over 300,000 (one-fifth of them slaves) in 1800, seven times as many inhabitants as in Spanish Louisiana and Florida. Another 160,000 people—one-third of whom were enslaved—resided in Georgia, on Spanish Florida's northeastern flank, by the turn of the century. While the Georgians mainly pressured the Creeks for land, many of the Kentuckians and Tennesseans—an unruly set of English and Scots-Irish Protestants with no powerful government or religious institutions to reign in their avaricious desires for land and wealth—raised foodstuffs that they floated downriver to sell in the markets of Spanish New Orleans. Other Anglo Americans, attracted by land and marketing opportunities in Louisiana, filtered across the international border to establish farms and businesses in Spanish territory.

Spanish officials had mixed feelings concerning Anglo American commerce and immigration, and the situation was complicated further by a dispute between Spain and the United States concerning the northern border of Florida. Like the British following the Seven Years' War, Spain quickly established control of Florida after the War for American Independence and governed the colony as two distinct political units. Although Spanish officials never drew a clear line to separate the two provinces, West Florida extended from the Mississippi River eastward to include San Marcos de Apalache, which was shifted from the jurisdiction of St. Augustine to more accessible Pensacola. The northern boundary of West Florida, however, remained undetermined, as the 1783 treaty had failed to specify a clear border. American officials insisted that the 31st Parallel was the demarcation line, while Spain placed the border over one hundred miles north of there, at 32 degrees, 28 minutes, the British boundary of West Florida since 1764. Spain also claimed the east side of the Mississippi up to the Ohio and Tennessee Rivers. Pensacola remained the capital of West Florida, but the province's officials came under the de facto supervision of the governor at New Orleans, as the colony was essentially administered as an extension of Spanish Louisiana. Because the important West Florida district of Natchez was located within the area contested by Spain and the United States, the governor of Louisiana maintained direct responsibility for this disputed region. Spain also introduced the position of intendant, who mainly functioned as a finance officer, to Louisiana during this period. Louisiana and Florida both fell under the jurisdiction of the captaincy-general of Havana, while Texas continued to be administered by the viceroyalty of New Spain.

For the first decade following the Treaty of Paris, Spanish officials in Louisiana tried to protect the region from being overwhelmed by Anglo Americans through the implementation of policies designed to regulate commerce, control immigration, and create a barrier of pro-Spanish Indians. Ministers in Spain initially tried to stop the flow of Americans into the Mississippi Valley by blocking their access to the marketplace in New Orleans. In 1784 they closed the Lower Mississippi River to all but Spanish shipping while at the same time allowing their citizens in New Orleans to trade with certain French ports in order to obtain much-needed foodstuffs, particularly flour, for the colony's inhabitants. Louisiana's Governor Miró quickly ascertained the unfeasibility of this plan and defied his superiors by opening up the Mississippi to American shipping. As a result, flatboats laden with flour, bacon, and bulky produce descended the river from Kentucky and Tennessee at the same time ships from the Atlantic Coast, mainly from Philadelphia, also arrived in New Orleans to ply their wares.

James Wilkinson, a retired brigadier general in the U.S. Army who had relocated from Philadelphia to Kentucky in 1783, was one of the many Anglo Americans who journeyed downriver to New Orleans during this period. Arriving at the provincial capital in the summer of 1787, Wilkinson met with Miró and warned him that disgruntled trans-Appalachian American settlers might attack Louisiana if the Spanish Crown overturned the governor's liberal trade policy. Wilkinson, presently a colonel in the Kentucky militia, also raised the prospect of Spain forming a political association with the territory, which he stated was on the verge of seceding from the United States. Hoping to establish himself as the foremost intermediary between the trans-Appalachian Anglos and Spain, in addition to seeking profit from the expansion of trade between Kentucky and Louisiana, Wilkinson pledged a secret loyalty oath to the Spanish Crown during his meeting with Governor Miró. Following Wilkinson's visit, the Louisiana governor forwarded the Kentuckian's warnings to Madrid, leading Spanish officials to formalize Miró's trade policy by allowing Americans to ship their produce to New Orleans, subject to a 15 percent import duty. The pace of trade increased greatly with this stimulus; for example, between February and July 1790 forty-one flatboats arrived in New Orleans from upstream carrying nearly five thousand barrels of flour and thirty-four thousand pounds of meat, in addition to numerous other items, including large amounts of whiskey. Although Wilkinson saw little monetary profit from the expansion of trade, the ever-ready opportunist used his position and military experience to obtain reappointment as a brigadier general in the American army in 1792. Despite being in the service of the United States, Wilkinson maintained his influence in New Orleans by passing along information concerning the western Americans to Spanish officials in return for an annual pension. For the next two decades Wilkinson would play a leading role—generally self-serving—in the international diplomacy of Louisiana and the Gulf South frontier.

At the same time as Spanish officials opened the Mississippi River to American shipping, they also established a policy designed to control, rather than prohibit, American immigration to Louisiana and Florida. Whereas Spain had eagerly allowed French Acadians and Spanish Canary Islanders to migrate to Louisiana prior to 1783, few other Catholic immigrants were willing to settle in the region following the War for American Independence. On the other hand, Anglo American Protestants flocked to the wealthy Natchez district, which by 1785 contained about eleven hundred free non-Catholics, along with nine hundred or so slaves. Fearful that the residents of this disputed region might tip the balance in favor of the United States if they were not granted Spanish citizenship, Governor Miró devised a plan, which he submitted to the Crown, by which the illegal Protestants might be converted and assimilated through the use of English-speaking Irish priests. In August 1787 officials in Spain not only approved Miró's scheme, but expanded on it by granting Anglo Americans in general the right to settle in Louisiana and to continue to practice their religion as long as they obeyed Spanish laws and swore an oath of allegiance. As a result of the edict, a few thousand Anglo Protestants migrated to Louisiana and Florida over the course of the next fifteen years, settling in various districts throughout both colonies. Americans were particularly drawn to Natchez, where they developed tobacco and indigo plantations. By 1792 nearly twenty-five hundred free people and nineteen hundred slaves resided in the Natchez district. The Spanish Crown responded to the Anglo influx by appointing Manuel Gayoso de Lemos, an English-speaking Spanish naval officer, to the position of governor of the Natchez district in 1789.

Whereas the commercial and immigration policies failed to stem the tide of American encroachment, the Spaniards met with greater success by establishing alliances with the Creeks, Choctaws, and Chickasaws. Spanish interests in this domain coincided with that of many tribal leaders, who regarded the burgeoning Anglo population as a threat to their lands. For the first half-decade or so after the Treaty of Paris, as long as the United States was governed by the weak Articles of Confederation, the Spanish-Indian alliance thwarted American expansion into the disputed territory. Although the Articles provided that Congress had sole authority to manage Indian affairs, the state of Georgia laid claim to portions of the territory north of the 31st Parallel extending all the way to the Mississippi River. In November 1783 Georgia officials dictated a treaty—unchallenged by the unsteady federal government—to a small group of Creek chiefs who surrendered eight hundred square miles of land in return for trade rights. Many Creeks refused to recognize the land cession, most particularly Alexander McGillivray, the mixed-blood Creek entrepreneur who had established a plantation just above Mobile. McGillivray also had a second residence at Little Tallassee on the Coosa River among the Upper Creeks, and taking advantage of an Upper Creek power vacuum, the literate and well-read McGillivray became the group's leading spokesman, advocating the development of an alliance with the Spaniards in West Florida in order to counteract the aggressive Georgians.

In January 1784 McGillivray wrote to Florida governor Arturo O'Neill offering his services to the Spaniards, stating that the king would "Gain & Secure a powerful barrier in these parts against the ambitious and encroaching Americans." Six months later McGillivray traveled to Pensacola and met with Miró and O'Neill to negotiate a treaty that officially established relations between the Creeks and Spain. Mindful of the extreme importance of keeping McGillivray attached to the Spanish interest, Miró appointed him as Spain's salaried agent to the Creeks, giving the mixed-blood the power to distribute gifts and to regulate trade. Claiming that the Indians "will attach themselves to and serve them best [those] who supply their necessities," McGillivray also arranged that Spain grant Panton, Leslie, and Company—a firm owned by a group of Scottish traders who had previously dealt with the Creeks and Seminoles through St. Augustine—a monopoly on the Indian trade, as the Spaniards were ill-equipped to fulfill that part of the agreement. As a result, Panton, Leslie, and Company employed McGillivray as a silent partner and established trading posts at San Marcos de Apalache, Pensacola, and Mobile soon thereafter. In July 1784 Choctaw representatives from all three divisions, along with Chickasaw headmen, met with Governor Miró in Mobile and signed a similar treaty of mutual friendship and support. Although another British firm, Mather and Strother, was initially granted the rights to the Choctaw and Chickasaw trade, within a few years the successful Panton, Leslie, and Company obtained these two tribes' commerce as well.

In late 1785 U.S. officials attempted to counteract the Spanish-Indian alliances by inviting the Choctaws, Chickasaws, and Creeks to a conference at Hopewell, on the Keowee River in South Carolina. Although there was a faction of Creeks who opposed McGillivray's centralization of power and his pro-Spanish stance, the mixed-blood leader successfully used his position to force his tribe to boycott the meeting with the Americans. On the other hand, the Choctaws and Chickasaws, feeling less threatened by Anglo encroachment than the Georgia-bordering Creeks, sent representatives to Hopewell in order to establish a counterweight against the Spaniards. In January 1786 both tribes agreed to terms with the United States, establishing peace with the young republic in return for promises of trade. Although neither tribe ceded land to the Americans, officials inserted articles in the treaties granting the United States the right to establish trading posts at Muscle Shoals in Chickasaw territory and at three unnamed locations among the Choctaws. Although commerce with the unorganized and undersupplied Americans generally failed to materialize following the signing of the Treaty of Hopewell, Chickasaw and Choctaw leaders—particularly Franchimastabé of the Western district—used the American alliance to gain further trade benefits from the Spaniards, such as limiting the rum trade and lowering prices for European-manufactured merchandise.

In the meantime the McGillivray-led Creeks used the weapons provided by Panton, Leslie, and Company to attack American settlers on the Georgia frontier. In addition to killing the Georgians, the Creek warriors also burned their homes and absconded with black slaves, cattle, and horses. Creeks also joined forces with a group of Cherokees to terrorize American frontiersmen in Tennessee. Whereas the state of Georgia and the Articles of Confederation government proved helpless to thwart the Creek aggression, the strong federal government established by the Constitution of 1787 took firm steps to establish peace with the Indians. In the summer of 1790 President George Washington and Secretary of War Henry Knox (the War Department had been assigned responsibility for Indian affairs) invited McGillivray and other Creek leaders to the temporary capital at New York. Serving as the Creek spokesman, McGillivray softened his pro-Spanish stance—in part, because the United States granted him the title and salary of brigadier general—and settled the disputed Georgia-Creek boundary by acknowledging the loss of territory in return for a perpetual annuity for the tribe and an allotment of trade goods. The treaty also transferred the remaining Creek territory claimed by Georgia from state to federal jurisdiction, and the United States pledged to prevent Americans from crossing onto Indian lands. For the next three years, until his death due to illness at Panton's store in Pensacola in February 1793, McGillivray used his ties with the Spaniards and the Americans to enrich himself and to maintain the peace along the Georgia-Creek frontier.

The Spaniards responded to the stronger, more centralized power of the United States by asking the Indians for permission to establish forts in their territory. Fearing that the Americans planned on occupying the Walnut Hills at the junction of the Yazoo and Mississippi Rivers, in May 1792 Governor Gayoso held a conference at Natchez in which the Chickasaws and the Western Division of the Choctaws agreed to allow Spain to establish Fort Nogales at the site, near present-day Vicksburg. William Blount, who President Washington had appointed governor of the American territory south of the Ohio River, answered the following month by holding a conference in Nashville with all three Choctaw divisions and the Chickasaws. Governor Blount reaffirmed the pledges made in the 1786 Treaty of Hopewell with both tribes and named James Robertson as the new federal Indian agent for the Choctaws and Chickasaws. Following the Nashville conference Eastern Choctaws and Chickasaws began to trade regularly with the Americans in Tennessee.

François-Louis Hector, barón de Carondelet, the energetic but impulsive career officer who succeeded Miró as governor of Louisiana in late 1791, responded forcefully to the increased American activity in the region. In early 1793, fearing that the United States might take advantage of the outbreak of war between revolutionary France and Spain and its ally, Great Britain—as well as a host of other countries—and seize the Mississippi

River, Carondelet ordered construction of a fleet of armed galleys to meet any waterborne invaders. The governor supplemented this move by attempting to combine the Creeks, Choctaws, and Chickasaws into a military alliance that would aggressively block American expansion. In October 1793 Governor Carondelet arranged a meeting at Fort Nogales, officiated by Gayoso, in which all three tribes agreed to the plan on paper, with the Choctaws also allowing the Spaniards to establish a new fort, named Confederación in honor of the occasion, on the Tombigbee River near the site where the French had erected a post in 1736. Two summers later in June 1795 Carondelet obtained permission from the Chickasaws to establish another fort, called San Fernando de las Barrancas, at the Chickasaw Bluffs on the Mississippi River, the site of present-day Memphis. Despite agreeing to the Treaty of Nogales, the Creeks, Choctaws, and Chickasaws never joined forces to fight the Americans, who, in any case, chose to win the boundary dispute through diplomacy rather than military invasion.

Deteriorating fortunes in Europe, rather than in North America, ultimately forced Spain to sign a treaty with the United States in 1795 that yielded to all of the American demands. The first sign of Spanish decline came in 1787 with the death of José de Gálvez, the man who, along with King Carlos III (who died the very next year), had been most responsible for the implementation of the Bourbon Reforms, the policies that had reinvigorated Spain's situation in the Western Hemisphere. The new monarch, Carlos IV, shared little of his father's energy or ability, and found himself immediately overwhelmed by the overthrow and execution of his Bourbon cousin, King Louis XVI of France, during the early stages of the French Revolution. In November 1792 the Spanish king irresponsibly appointed his wife's young lover, Manuel Godoy, to the position of prime minister. Three months later the inexperienced Godoy foolishly joined Great Britain in its war against the French Republic, whose troops swept across the Pyrenees the following year, forcing Spain to sue for peace in July 1795. Now threatened by war with the British, Godoy decided to settle with the United States and humbly began talks with Thomas Pinckney, the American envoy President Washington had sent to Madrid in November 1794 to negotiate a treaty with Spain. In the resulting October 1795 Treaty of San Lorenzo de El Escorial (better known as Pinckney's Treaty in America), Spain accepted the 31st Parallel as the northern border of West Florida, granted Americans free navigation of the Mississippi River without paying duties, and gave U.S. merchants the right to deposit their goods at New Orleans for reshipment on oceangoing vessels.

Although the treaty was formally ratified by both nations in April 1796, two years lapsed before the United States actually took possession of the region. Believing rumors that Great Britain and the United States planned to join forces and invade Louisiana, in October 1796 Minister Godoy decided to delay the execution of the treaty. Governor Carondelet, however, did not obtain Godoy's instructions until Spanish troops had already evacuated Forts Confederación and San Fernando de las Barrancas. American forces took possession of the posts soon thereafter, renaming them Forts St. Stephens and Pickering, respectively. Following the reception of Godoy's orders in New Orleans, Carondelet insisted on maintaining possession of Natchez and Fort Nogales, despite the arrival of Andrew Ellicott and Thomas Freeman, President Washington's appointees to survey the international boundary, at Natchez in February 1797. The situation remained unresolved in August, when Carondelet resigned his position and left New Orleans to become the president of the Royal Audiencia of Quito. Fearing that the United States might go to war over the impasse, Spanish officials once again reversed course the following month and ordered Gayoso, the new governor of Louisiana, to evacuate the remaining Spanish possessions. Finally, in March 1798, U.S. troops took possession of Natchez and Nogales, with the Spanish soldiers retreating to Baton Rouge. The Spanish consul, José Vidal, crossed the Mississippi River and established Concordia Post on the east bank opposite Natchez in order to block American entry. In May the American boundary commissioners met with their Spanish counterparts, Stephen Minor—Gayoso's replacement as Natchez district governor—and the planter-scientist William Dunbar, to begin surveying the northern boundary of Florida. Their task was completed two years later.

Mississippi Territory

The federal government of the United States officially took control of the region in April 1798 when Congress created the Mississippi Territory, ultimately consisting of all the area between the Chattahoochee and Mississippi Rivers north of the 31st Parallel and south of Tennessee. Applying the same principles to this territory that its predecessor had to the Northwest Territory in 1787, Congress centralized power in the hands of five officials—a governor, a secretary, and three judges—all appointed by the president. Accordingly, John Adams named a fellow New Englander and Harvard graduate, Winthrop Sargent, as first governor of the Mississippi Territory. Sargent arrived in Natchez in August 1798 and quickly organized militia units, enacted a legal code, and divided the territory into six counties. Approving of Sargent's progress, in 1800 Congress passed a bill granting Mississippians the second grade of territorial government, allowing for an elected house of representatives. General Wilkinson, who had recently been assigned command of all American forces west of the Appalachians, arrived in the territory soon after Sargent and immediately began the construction of Fort Adams on Loftus Heights, a bluff overlooking the Mississippi River just north of the 31st Parallel. The following year American troops established Fort Stoddert on the Tensaw River just above the boundary line near Mobile Bay.

Despite Sargent's work, the Yankee never won the favor of the Natchez frontiersmen, who characterized him as a "haughty, over-bearing man," with a "phlegmatic and austere disposition." As a result, few Mississippi residents were unhappy when the newly elected president, Thomas Jefferson, named his Virginia compatriot William Charles Cole Claiborne as Mississippi territorial governor in May 1801. Conflicting land claims posed the most important challenge facing Governor Claiborne. Three European governments had at one time or another controlled portions of the territory, and all had granted lands to both actual and potential settlers, leaving land titles in a chaotic state. Adding further confusion was Georgia's decision in 1795 to grant the same lands to several prominent speculators, known as the Yazoo claimants, who in turn quickly disposed of their claims to a second set of fortune seekers. In 1802, after years of negotiations, Georgia ceded its western lands to the federal government in exchange for partial guarantees to the Yazoo claimants. Secretary of State James Madison ordered Claiborne to investigate the situation, and the governor submitted a report that Congress incorporated into a comprehensive land act passed in March 1803. It confirmed the claims of residents holding a British or Spanish patent before 1795 and empowered the president to appoint commissioners to resolve land claims. Despite a few complaints, the new system served its purpose in settling the confusing situation of land titles. As a result of the establishment of federal power in the Mississippi Territory, Americans rushed to the region, and by 1800 the population in the Natchez district had climbed to forty-five hundred free people and three thousand slaves, with another fifteen hundred people—most of them Anglo Americans without slaves—residing along the Tombigbee and Tensaw Rivers in Washington County, the area lying east of the Pearl River.

U.S. Indian Policy

American control of the Mississippi Territory allowed the federal government to proceed with the implementation of a new and different Indian policy than the European powers had employed with the Creeks, Choctaws, and Chickasaws, one that would have dramatic consequences for the three tribes. Convinced that the eastern Indians were doomed to extinction if they did not adopt the superior Anglo culture, President Washington and Secretary of War Knox, in accordance with theories posited by Secretary of State Thomas Jefferson, devised a highly optimistic "civilization" policy designed to achieve the complete transformation of the tribes' way of life. Believing that the natives were by nature equal to Euroamericans but that their culture was inferior, these three architects of U.S. Indian policy focused on agriculture, education, and Christianity as the means of convincing the tribes to accept the white man's civilization. Transforming the native men from hunters to commercial farmers, who held their own private property, lay at the heart of the federal program, thus the government was committed to providing the tribes with livestock, agricultural implements, and instruction on their use. This fit well with the program's second purpose, which was to peacefully obtain tribal lands for American citizens. Theoretically, as the Indians settled down to become productive farmers and livestock raisers, they would need less land and, as a result, would happily sell their excess territory to the United States in exchange for trade goods and other annuities. The federal government fully accepted the country's Protestant churches as allies in its civilizing endeavor and promoted the establishment of missions among the tribes that would impart Christianity, as well as traditional learning and industrious work habits, to the native children. Congress outlined the workings of the federal Indian policy in a series of Trade and Intercourse Acts that were passed during the 1790s, with a final one being enacted in 1802. They authorized the president to appoint agents to the various Indian tribes. Their duties were to win the natives' allegiance through the supervision of the civilization program and to keep unauthorized whites out of Indian territory. The 1796 law called for the establishment of a system of government trading posts, called factories, to be located throughout Indian country in an attempt to regulate trade by setting fair prices, and by banishing alcohol as a means of exchange.

In 1796 President Washington appointed Benjamin Hawkins, a former North Carolina senator and negotiator of various treaties, as Indian agent for the southern Indians. He was charged with the responsibility of implementing the federal government's civilization program among the Creeks, Choctaws, and Chickasaws. Hawkins initially settled among the Lower Creeks at Coweta and quickly won the tribe's confidence by using federal troops to remove unlawful Anglo intruders from their lands and by establishing a government trading factory for the Creeks at Fort Wilkinson, on the Oconee River. In 1803 the Creek factory was moved westward to Fort Hawkins on the Ocmulgee River at present Macon, Georgia. The Creeks rewarded Hawkins by giving him the high-ranking title of "beloved man," denoting wisdom, accomplishment, and trust. Although Hawkins initially was responsible for the Choctaws and Chickasaws as well as the Creeks, Samuel Mitchell became his assistant with jurisdiction over the two western tribes in 1798. The following year that position was split, and John Mckee was named Choctaw agent, establishing the new agency headquarters near present-day Jackson, Mississippi. Mitchell maintained responsibility for the Chickasaws and built their agency at Pontotoc, in present Chickasaw County, Mississippi. Following President Jefferson's inauguration Hawkins became solely responsible for the Creeks and in 1803 moved their headquarters westward to the Flint River. As with the Creeks, the United States established official trading factories for each tribe in 1802: the Choctaw post was located at Fort St. Stephens along the Lower Tombigbee River, while the Chickasaw factory was housed near Fort Pickering on the Mississippi River.

Soon after his appointment as agent to the southern tribes in 1796, Hawkins and his associates began to apply the federal government's civilization policy. The agents encouraged several revolutionary changes among the tribes: the transformation of Indian men from hunters to farmers, moving Indian women from agriculture to being producers of household manufactures, and the abandonment of communal fields for private farmsteads. Although most of the Indian men refused to farm, the great decline in the white-tailed deer population forced many Creek, Choctaw, and Chickasaw males to accept stock raising as a gender-acceptable alternative to hunting. Cattle, horses, and hogs took the place of deer, as tribal men allowed their stock to range freely in the spring and summer before rounding up the animals in the fall and driving them to market or butchering them for home consumption. As an increased number of tribesmen turned to livestock, there was a dispersal away from the major towns and river valleys so that the livestock could have access to undisturbed grazing lands. Many Creek families moved to nearby narrow floodplains of secondary streams, while some Choctaws migrated to prairie lands to the northeast and west of their traditional homeland. Chickasaws dispersed westward as well in order to allow their stock to find pastureland. Despite these migrations, which the agents optimistically mistook for the development of private farms, most of the native women continued to use traditional techniques to raise corn, beans, and squash in communal fields. A few women, however, did add cotton to their gardens for use in weaving clothes and blankets. As a result, the agents provided the tribes with cotton gins and taught the women how to use spinning wheels and looms. For the most part, however, the American agents' initial attempts to reverse gender roles and radically transform the tribes' traditional culture met with only very limited success by the beginning of the nineteenth century.

The civilization program exacerbated the gulf between mixed-blood tribal members and the traditionalists, as it was mainly only the descendants of Euroamerican traders and their native wives—in addition to many recently arrived Anglos who married Indian women—who adopted the new way of life. These bicultural men grew up accustomed to both their mother's traditional native culture and their father's concern for profit. As a result, they used their positions to obtain land through their matrilineal line in order to develop private farms and ranches, often using black slave laborers to fence their fields, on which the bondspeople raised commercial crops such as cotton and wheat, in addition to acting as herdsmen for their owners' livestock. Others employed their slaves to build and operate ferries, inns, and taverns—or "stands," as they were often called—to service Anglo travelers. By the turn of the century many of these mixed-bloods—such as the Chickasaw Colberts, the Choctaw LeFlores, and the Creek McIntoshes—also had assumed important positions within the tribal political hierarchies, in addition to becoming the leading spokesmen for their tribes in dealings with U.S. officials. Among the Creeks, for instance, wealthy, market-oriented mixed-bloods were able to take control of the National Council, a newly created body that attempted to unify the traditional separate town polities in order to better organize tribal policies. As a means of protecting their own property and to stop young Creek men from raiding the ever increasing number of nearby Anglo homesteads, the National Council passed decrees revoking the right of blood revenge, instituting punishments for horse thieves and murderers, and appointing a body of warrior police to enforce the laws. Although these edicts were rarely actually put into effect, they exemplified the growing distance and increased tensions between tribal "progressives" and "traditionalists" that would erupt in violence and civil war in the second decade of the nineteenth century.

Despite the adoption of commercial farming and stock raising among some tribal members, the Creeks, Choctaws, and Chickasaws continued to be indebted to various trading firms, such as Panton, Leslie, and Company, as well as to the government factories. The United States eagerly used this debt as a means to obtain access to tribal lands. In the 1796 Treaty of Colerain, the Creeks ceded lands between the Ogeechee and Oconee Rivers to Georgia in return for $6,000 worth of goods. By 1802 the Creeks had run up a $10,000 debt to the Fort Wilkinson trading factory and could not afford to purchase needed goods. As a result, American officials forced the Creeks to cede a portion of land between the Oconee and the Ocmulgee Rivers in return for $25,000, three-fifths of which went to retiring the tribal debt and paying damages claimed by Georgia citizens. Realizing the need for dependable communication between Natchez and Nashville, in the fall of 1801 General Wilkinson and Agent Hawkins negotiated separate treaties with the Chickasaws and Choctaws in which the tribes assented to the widening of the extant Indian trail, called the Natchez Trace, through their territory. In the Treaty of Chickasaw Bluffs, the Chickasaws received about $700 worth of trade goods and a guarantee that only tribal members would be allowed to operate taverns and ferries, the latter clause designed to protect the lucrative ferry of George Colbert, the mixed-blood son of an Indian trader, on the Tennessee River. In the Treaty of Fort Adams, the Choctaws obtained $2,000 worth of goods for their consent to the construction of a road from Natchez to the Tombigbee River. In subsequent treaties during the next two years—the 1802 Treaty of Fort Confederation and the 1803 Treaty of Fort St. Stephens—the indebted Choctaws agreed to the establishment of a formal southern boundary between the Chickasawhay and Tombigbee Rivers and the cession of eight hundred thousand acres north of Mobile, the first actual diminution of the tribal domain at the hands of the Americans. Tribal land cessions would only increase during the first two decades of the nineteenth century as the acre replaced the deerskin as a unit of trade.

Spanish, French, and American Diplomacy, 1795–1803

In the meantime, Spain continued its retreat in North America, ultimately resulting in the ambitious United States' gaining possession of Louisiana. In December 1795, at the same time that Minister Godoy was hesitating to hand over Natchez to the United States, he began to consider returning Louisiana to France in order to let Spain's new ally shoulder the burden of defending the costly buffer zone along the Mississippi. France initially declined Godoy's offer, but the loss of the incredibly wealthy sugar island of Saint-Domingue to slave rebels led by Toussaint L'Ouverture and the rise to power of Napoleon Bonaparte had changed the minds of French diplomats by the turn of the century. In 1800 Bonaparte and his foreign minister, Charles Maurice de Talleyrand, conceived of a plan to send troops to the West Indies to reclaim Saint-Domingue in order to restore slavery and sugar production on the island. To supply the colony with food, Bonaparte desired possession of Louisiana, which would also help realign the balance of power in North America to the detriment of his British enemy as well as please Spain by serving as a brake on American ambitions. As a result, France and Spain negotiated the Second Treaty of San Ildefonso in October 1800 by which Carlos IV secretly ceded Louisiana to Napoleon. Spain, however, did not officially turn Louisiana over to France until October 1802, after Bonaparte promised not to relinquish the colony to a third party. Six months later the French leader broke that promise by selling the entire colony of Louisiana to James Monroe and Robert Livingston, the American envoys that President Thomas Jefferson had sent to France to purchase New Orleans after learning of the Spanish retrocession, and after Napoleon had received news that French troops had failed to retake Saint-Domingue. In October 1803 the U.S. Senate ratified the Louisiana Purchase, and American officials took possession of the territory in New Orleans on December 20.

The diplomatic situation concerning the transfer of Louisiana from Spain to France, and then to the United States, was complicated by the province's overall inefficiency in governmental administration during its final years as a colony. Whereas Miró and Carondelet had ably directed Louisiana between 1781 and 1797, from the death of Governor General Gayoso during a yellow fever outbreak in July 1799 to December 1803, when the American authorities took charge of the territory, four men served as governor of the province. Francisco Bouligny, commandant of the Spanish military in Louisiana, became acting military governor upon Gayoso's demise, but only held the position for two months, until the Marqués de Casa-Calvo took charge as interim governor in September 1799. Casa-Calvo, who had accompanied O'Reilly's expedition to Louisiana in 1769 and had fought with Gálvez at Mobile and Pensacola, kept the affairs of the colony running fairly smoothly until Manuel Juan de Salcedo arrived in New Orleans as official governor in July 1801. Unlike Casa-Calvo, Salcedo quarreled with the Cabildo by boycotting its meetings and humiliating its members. Salcedo also sought to profit from his post, abused his authority, and was ultimately charged with corruption. When France regained Louisiana in 1802, Pierre Clément, Baron de Laussat, was appointed as prefect, the highest civilian post in the new French colonial government. Laussat did not arrive in New Orleans until March 1803, only a month before Napoleon sold the colony to the United States. As a result, Laussat became the commissioner charged with receiving Louisiana from Spain and delivering it to the Americans. Because Spanish officials did not believe that Governor Salcedo was fit to surrender the colony to the French, Casa-Calvo was sent back to Louisiana to handle the transfer. Ultimately, Laussat did not take official possession of the colony until November 30, 1803, whereupon he turned Louisiana over to U.S. officials only twenty days later.

Introduction of Cotton and Sugar

The confusion caused by the international diplomatic situation and the final years of Spanish governance did nothing to hinder the fantastic growth of Louisiana's economy during the period. In fact, the trade with the Anglo Americans in foodstuffs allowed the colony's planters to concentrate even further during the 1780s on the cash crops of indigo and tobacco. When the profitability of these crops declined in the mid-1790s, the planters used their growing numbers of slaves to quickly adapt to the cultivation of sugar and cotton, the two staples that would dominate the region's economy during the nineteenth century. During the first decade following the Treaty of Paris indigo continued to be the colony's most valuable staple crop, and plantations raising the item lined both sides of the Mississippi from below New Orleans north to Baton Rouge. Prices and production remained high throughout the decade, as Louisiana planters harvested between four hundred thousand and six hundred thousand pounds per year at prices that varied from 5 to 7 livres per pound. In the

1790s, however, the crop suffered a series of setbacks from which the industry did not recover. Crop failures caused by adverse weather occurred from 1791 to 1793, and a worm ferociously attacked the indigo the following year, destroying the roots and leaving only naked stems standing in the fields. Most planters, discouraged by successive crop failures, declined to replant the crop, and by 1801 only eighty thousand pounds of indigo was raised in the colony.

Tobacco production in Louisiana suffered a similar fate. In the 1770s Spanish officials had decreed that the colony would be the sole supplier of tobacco manufactured for consumption in Mexico. Spain's declaration of war against Great Britain, however, postponed the tobacco boom until the mid-1780s, when Louisiana planters—mainly in Natchez and Natchitoches—raised more than 2 million pounds annually through the end of the decade. In 1790 the colony produced just under 3 million pounds of tobacco (263 planters in Natchez raised over half of the total, eighty-three Natchitoches households raised one-fourth, and Pointe Coupée, Attakapas, and Opelousas provided the rest). Unfortunately for Louisiana's tobacco planters, by the fall of 1789 Mexican storehouses were overloaded with the leaf, causing the viceroy of New Spain to suspend all further imports in October. Although tobacco shipments to Spain temporarily compensated for the decline in demand from Mexico, in late 1790 Spanish officials decided to accept only forty thousand pounds from the following year's crop. Over the next couple of years Natchitoches residents only raised about twenty thousand pounds per annum, while planters elsewhere in Louisiana abandoned the crop altogether. In 1795, when Spanish officials increased the colony's tobacco quota to 200,000 pounds, Natchitoches producers, who raised just under 150,000 pounds, were the only Louisiana planters to respond.

Luckily for the colony's planters, just as the indigo and tobacco crops became unfeasible to grow, technological advances in cotton and sugar cultivation made the large-scale commercial production of these staples available as replacements. Cotton had been raised in Louisiana since the 1730s, but the great labor entailed in separating the fiber from the seed retarded further development of the crop. In the 1770s Acadian and German residents raised a small amount of cotton, as did the Anglo settlers around Natchez. But it was only in the mid-1790s, with the spread of efficient ginning techniques, that Louisiana planters along the Mississippi River upstream from Baton Rouge, as well as property owners along the Red River all the way to Natchitoches, fully turned to cotton production.

In 1796, one year after Daniel Clark—who had emigrated the previous decade from Ireland to New Orleans, where he formed an alliance with Philadelphia merchants—introduced the first cotton gin to the region after reading a report of Eli Whitney's design, Natchez planters produced 750,000 pounds for export. Within a few years cotton cultivation in Louisiana and the Mississippi Territory had increased to the point that New Orleans received over 5 million pounds of the crop in the six months between October 1801 and May 1802. On the eve of the acquisition of Louisiana by the United States, most of the region's tobacco planters had made the transition to cotton, a profitable move that allowed them to recover financially from the Spanish decision to stop promoting the leaf.

The demise of Louisiana's indigo crop, coupled with the disruption of sugar production in the West Indies by war and revolution, provided the impetus for Étienne de Boré to begin experimenting with cane on his plantation upstream from New Orleans, at present Audubon Park. Previous attempts to raise sugar in Louisiana had failed when frost killed the cane in the ground. De Boré, however, with the aid of a few Frenchmen who had escaped from the slave rebellion on Saint-Domingue, successfully produced a crop of sugar for export in 1795. Within a year sugar cane cultivation had replaced indigo as the great staple crop along the Lower Mississippi River. Over the next half decade de Boré, along with his brother-in-law, Jean Noel Destréhan, continued to test new varieties of cane and methods of distillation. As a result, by 1803 there were seventy-five sugar plantations located between Baton Rouge and English Turn, yielding over 5 million pounds of sugar per year.

Slaves and Libres

The expansion of Louisiana agriculture was necessarily coupled with an increase in the importation of slaves from Africa. Whereas about three thousand slaves had been sent to Louisiana in the 1770s, following the end of the war even larger shipments of bondspeople, nearly all from Africa, began to arrive in New Orleans. From 1784 through 1792 over one hundred ships—most of which had picked up their cargoes in the British free ports of Kingston, Jamaica, and Roseau, Dominica—brought over seven thousand slaves to Louisiana. The overall trade to New Orleans underwent a sharp decrease in 1793 due to the outbreak of war, and because Spanish officials banned all imports from the French West Indies out of fears caused by the August 1791 slave uprising in Saint-Domingue. Continued qualms concerning rebellions directed by newly arrived African males caused Governor Carondelet to ban all further slave shipments to Louisiana in early 1796. As a result of the restrictions, only eleven ships arrived in New Orleans between 1793 and 1796, carrying just over two hundred African slaves. Following the development of cotton and the labor-intensive crop of sugar during the mid-1790s, however, Louisiana planters convinced Spanish authorities to reopen the slave trade from Africa in November 1800. During the course of the final three years of Spanish Louisiana, eighty-five ships, mainly from Havana, brought another one thousand slaves to the colony. Whereas most of the slaves sent to Louisiana from Africa during the French period had come from the Senegambia region, during the Spanish era they came in relatively equal numbers from the Bight of Benin, the Bight of Biafra, Central Africa, and Senegambia. On the eve of the Louisiana Purchase nearly twenty-five thousand slaves toiled in the colony, more than half being recently imported Africans.

Whereas most of the new arrivals were ultimately forced to submit to the overwhelmingly dominant power of the planters and the Spanish government, there were a few incidents of slave independence that slightly challenged the Euroamericans' hegemonic authority. During the war with Great Britain a number of slaves ran away from their plantations and established a maroon camp, led by a man called San Malo, downstream from New Orleans in the marshy region near Lake Borgne. The runaways stole food from plantations and killed some livestock, but only after they murdered a couple of Anglos did the Spanish authorities take action. In June 1784 Lieutenant Colonel Bouligny, acting under orders from Governor Miró, organized a force that destroyed the maroon outpost and captured sixty runaway slaves, including San Malo. Soon thereafter the leader, along with three other cimarrones, were executed in the Plaza de Armas, and most of the others received up to three hundred lashes as punishment. In the aftermath of the San Malo affair Governor Miró, with the support of the planter-dominated New Orleans Cabildo, imposed a tax on all of the colony's slave owners in order to establish a fugitive slave fund that would reimburse masters for runaways killed as they were recaptured. Despite the large African influx into the colony, and the reluctance of slaveholders in the interior region to pay the tax they felt would only benefit the large plantation owners near New Orleans, *grand marronage* was brought under control and independent maroon communities never were able to form again in Louisiana.

The outbreak of the French Revolution and the slave uprising in Saint-Domingue, however, heightened the fears of the colony's planters in the 1790s. In July 1791 an uprising at heavily Africanized Pointe Coupée—where Bight of Benin slaves conspired to overthrow their masters, and killed a French planter before the plot was uncovered and suppressed—increased the plantation owners' anxieties. Whereas the planters called for stricter measures to help them control their bondspeople, in July 1792 Governor Carondelet issued a decree designed to ameliorate the slaves' situation in order to prevent revolts. The order called for owners to provide their slaves with adequate food and clothing, regulated work hours (including Sundays completely free), and limited punishment to thirty consecutive lashes. Masters who abused their slaves would be fined, while overseers could be imprisoned. Slaveowners, already unhappy with Carondelet's lenient regulations, were outraged when yet another slave conspiracy was discovered at Pointe Coupée in the spring of 1795. The panicky governor, fearing an uprising similar to Saint-Domingue, brutally reacted to the planned revolt and ordered the execution of fifteen slaves—including eight who were hung at separate locations on the levee upstream from New Orleans as examples of the punishment exacted on conspirators—and imprisoned and flogged another thirty or so. Despite his violent response, in June 1795 Carondelet also issued a new set of lenient regulations designed to keep the slaves in a state of contentment and subordination so that they would "banish from their minds the notion of acquiring liberty." Although the decree called for the greater policing of the slaves' mobility, once again it reiterated and specified the benign treatment owners had to provide their laborers, including advising masters to assign garden plots for their bondspeople to cultivate. Although planters tried and failed to secure harsher laws against the slaves during the final years of Spanish Louisiana, Carondelet's amelioration policy proved effective, as no major uprisings occurred during the remainder of the colonial period.

Carondelet's 1795 decree also took note of the incredible rise in the number of free people of color during the prior decade, and reiterated that Louisiana libres enjoyed the same privileges as other free persons, while forbidding anyone from injuring them or taking their possessions. Most of the libres continued to reside in New Orleans, where the number of manumissions per year increased from just over forty in the 1770s to slightly more than sixty in the final quarter-century of Spanish rule. The libre population gave birth to free children and thereby also augmented its numbers through natural growth. By the first decade of the nineteenth century over fifteen hundred free people of color lived in New Orleans, making up one-fifth of the city's total population and one-third of the free total. Like libres in other urban areas throughout the Western Hemisphere, those in New Orleans labored at middle and lower sector tasks, competing with poor whites and slaves but offering little threat to the middle and upper classes. Policy and practice excluded them from the professions, clergy, and government positions, and relegated most of them to manual or skilled labor. Although increasingly creating a separate identity from whites and slaves at the end of the Spanish period, libres still did not constitute a uniform group whose interests and character were one. Persistent dependency and downward mobility plagued newly freed blacks, while libres manumitted long ago or born free, by contrast, frequently attained economic independence as smallholding farmers, slave owners, traders, and business people.

Despite the barriers to the development of a group cohesiveness and identity among libres in colonial New Orleans, service in the militia provided the city's free people of color their best opportunity to promote a sense of corporate identity. Spanish governors called upon the libre militia to provide defense for Louisiana especially during the tumultuous 1790s, in addition to relying on it to police runaway slaves, repair levee breaks, fight fires, and patrol city streets at night. While the free black militia existed in New Orleans during the 1780s, it did not meet very regularly or in an organized form. However, fearing the consequences of the French Revolution, in July 1791 Governor Carondelet reorganized and expanded the militias, creating two companies of free *pardos* (light-skinned blacks) and one company of free *morenos* (dark-skinned blacks). During the 1790s promotions occurred rapidly, enhancing the loyalty of free black militiamen to the Spanish government. By 1801 over 450 libres served in the three free black companies. In addition to its defensive role, by the turn of the century the free black militia in New Orleans began to function as a corporate group in society, wielding its strength on behalf of all libres. Individual members, especially officers, used their position to attain increased material and social influence. Free blacks actively participated in the activities of the Catholic Church, and libres increasingly chose people from their own class—particularly members of the militia—to be the godparents of their children during the final years of Spanish Louisiana.

Whereas a majority of the free people of color in New Orleans were able to form families and households independent of whites, outside the city most of the one thousand or so libres in Louisiana resided in mixed-race households dominated by Euroamerican males. One exception to this rule occurred in Natchitoches, where Pierre Metoyer freed Marie Thérèse *dit* Coincoin, his morena slave and the mother of ten of his children, in 1778. Eight years later Metoyer granted her a tract of land fronting both sides of the Red River, upon which she began to raise tobacco and livestock. With her modest economic success, Coincoin purchased and freed a number of enslaved relatives whom Metoyer had failed to emancipate, including some of her children and her sister. Upon Metoyer's death, she and her children inherited other tracts of land at Isle Brevelle, located along nearby Cane River, and they increased their holdings in the area during the 1790s through purchase or by petitioning the Spanish government. Coincoin's eldest son by Metoyer, Nicolas Augustin, was the first Isle Brevelle libre to acquire slaves, and eventually most Metoyers *de couleur* also came to own and employ enslaved laborers. By the early nineteenth century, the Metoyers had established flourishing plantations at Isle Brevelle that were comparable to the most productive French creole–owned farms in the Natchitoches area. Despite the Metoyers' success, most libres in Natchitoches—as with most free people of color outside of New Orleans—lived in households dominated by white males, like that of François Grappe, who resided on a plantation in nearby Campti that consisted of his numerous morena concubines and pardo children.

Acadia and the Lower Mississippi Valley

Louisiana's white population increased as well during the period, but at a slower rate than that of the slaves or the libres. By 1803 about seventeen thousand whites resided in the colony, a gain of nearly six thousand inhabitants over the course of two decades. In addition to the few thousand Anglos who immigrated to Louisiana during the era, in 1785 another sixteen hundred Acadians exiled in France moved to the colony to join their fellow refugees who had begun to arrive in the 1760s. Whereas a few of the second wave Acadians settled with their brethren in Attakapas and Opelousas, nearly one-third of the arrivals chose to establish small farms on vacant lands located along the Mississippi between Manchac and Baton Rouge. Most of the newcomers, however, settled along Bayou Lafourche, downstream from the Canary Islanders who had established Valenzuela in the late 1770s. During the next two decades other Acadians, mainly from the Mississippi River, joined their fellows on Bayou Lafourche and established narrow, contiguous farms—usually six by forty arpents—on the natural levee. By 1803 nearly twenty-five hundred Acadians and Isleños resided on Bayou Lafourche, along with seven hundred or so slaves. Most of the residents raised livestock and foodstuffs on their farms, as less than one in ten households in the region contained bondspeople. The Acadian occupation of Bayou Lafourche caused the few hundred remaining Houma Indians to move even farther downstream and into the nearby swamps. In the Opelousas and Attakapas districts about thirty-five hundred whites—mainly Acadians interspersed with Anglo immigrants—resided alongside three thousand or so slaves. Although most of the region's inhabitants also were involved in animal husbandry, many planters made the transformation from tobacco to cotton, as more than one-third of the households owned slaves.

As with the previous eras, most of Louisiana's forty-five thousand inhabitants—up from twenty-seven thousand in the 1780s—continued to dwell along the Lower Mississippi River between English Turn and Pointe Coupee. Outside the confines of New Orleans, plantations filled up the banks on both sides of the river. The ten thousand slaves who toiled in the area—many being newly arrived Africans—easily outnumbered the six thousand or so whites and five hundred libres. Whereas French creoles continued to dominate the wealthy Chapitoulas district just above New Orleans, Acadians, Germans, French creoles, and Anglos lived interspersed among the various districts farther upstream. Using the huge profits obtained from their sugar and indigo plantations, many planters in the region constructed great dwellings during this period, such as the Caribbean-influenced house built for Jean-Baptiste Destréhan in 1787 that still stands in present St. Charles Parish, by a libre carpenter named Charles.

New Orleans certainly had the colony's most heterogeneous population by the end of the Spanish era, as about thirty-five hundred whites, fifteen hundred free blacks, and three thousand slaves resided within the city's confines at the turn of the century. The slave population consisted of both Africans and creoles, while French creoles made up half of the city's white population, Spaniards about a quarter, and the rest being newly arrived Anglos, refugees from Saint-Domingue, Germans, and others. Reflecting the city's diversity, the Ursuline Sisters opened their convent to Spanish creole nuns and accepted the introduction of the daughters of Spanish officials and Anglo American merchants, as well as free girls of color, into

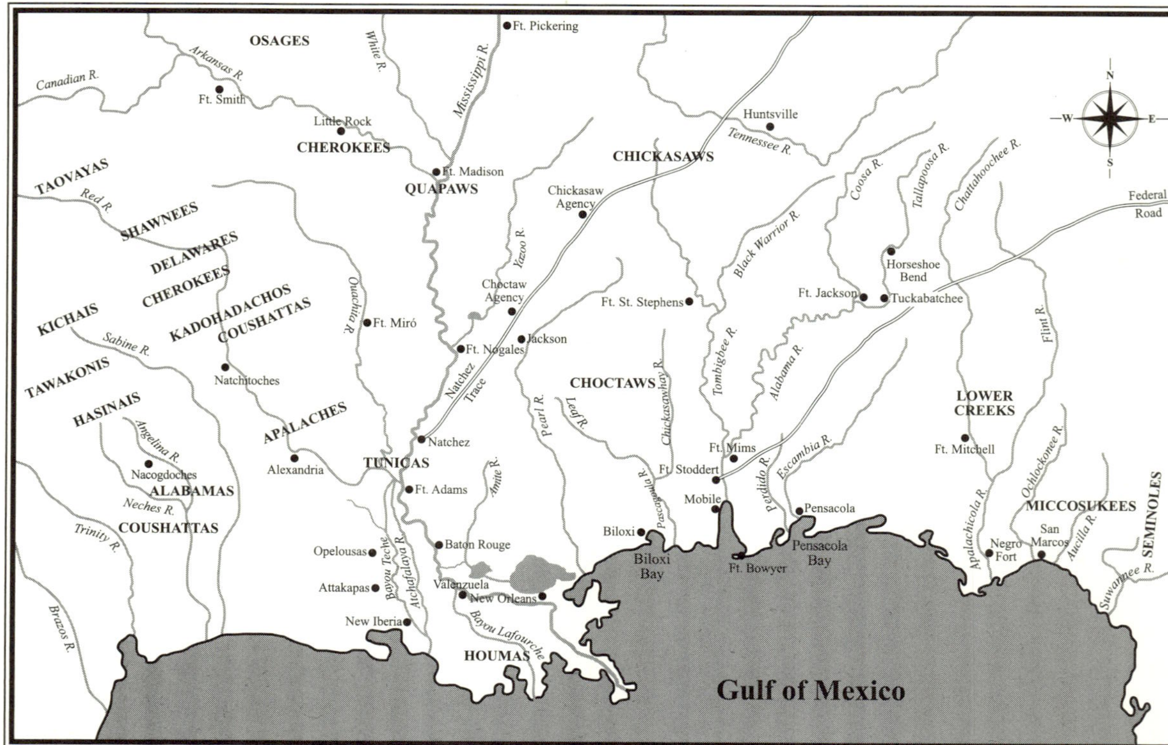

MAP 8. THE GULF SOUTH, 1798–1821

their classrooms. If not for a series of disasters that occurred during the period, the city's population might have been much larger. A smallpox epidemic broke out in 1787 and attacked the townspeople periodically until it was brought under control in 1803, hurricanes struck during successive Augusts in 1793 and 1794, and yellow fever claimed hundreds of lives during an outbreak in 1796.

Fires in the city, however, provided the most devastation. In March 1788 a fire broke out that burned nearly 80 percent of the buildings in New Orleans. Many homeless people left the city, moving into the countryside temporarily or permanently. Much of the town had been rebuilt by December 1794 when a second fire occurred, destroying nearly one-third of the city. The new town that rose out of the ashes formed the basis of today's French Quarter, with masonry and stucco replacing wood as the main components of the buildings, which now adjoined each other in order to accommodate the city's growing population. St. Louis church—which became a cathedral in 1793 with the creation of the Diocese of Louisiana and Florida—and its surrounding buildings on the Plaza de Armas, the Cabildo and the Presbytere, were also rebuilt in the aftermath of the fires, with the financial assistance of New Orleans's first great philanthropist, Andrés Almonaster y Roxas, a royal notary who had arrived in the colony with O'Reilly. Despite the city's reputation for disorderliness and chaos—one visitor complained that "the city abounds with tippling houses . . . places of riot and intoxication" that were crowded day and night—Governors Miró and Carondelet, along with the members of the Cabildo, continued to provide New Orleans with effective municipal government and services throughout the turbulent period.

Although Anglos were probably the most numerous people to relocate to New Orleans during the last years of Spanish Louisiana, Francophones escaping from the 1791 slave uprising in Saint-Domingue countered the influence of the English-speaking, Protestant arrivals. The first refugees from the wealthy French colony arrived in 1792, followed by another one thousand or so over the following decade. Most came as families directly from Saint-Domingue, while others arrived via Jamaica or various American Atlantic ports, where they had first gained safety. Although the arrivals from Saint-Domingue had various backgrounds, many were well-educated men who made a lasting impact on their new city. In summer 1793 Louis Duclos, a printer and engraver, fled from Cap-Français directly to New Orleans, where he began publishing *Le Moniteur de la Louisiane,* the colony's first newspaper, the following spring. In 1797 Duclos's associate in Saint-Domingue, Jean-Baptiste Le Sueur Fontaine, became the journal's editor following his arrival from New York the previous year. Jean-François Pitot also landed in New Orleans, in 1796, after first taking refuge in Philadelphia. In addition to writing a book based on his observations of the region, Pitot established a residence on Bayou St. John and became the mayor of New Orleans in May 1804. Three other arrivals from Saint-Domingue, planters Pierre Berquin-Duvallon and François Perrin du Lac and physician Paul Alliot also penned memoirs concerning their experiences in Louisiana.

Outlying Louisiana Settlements

Many of the areas outside the Lower Mississippi also experienced population growth and economic prosperity during the last years of Spanish Louisiana. During the decade following the end of the War for American Independence, Natchitoches planters took full advantage of the Spanish efforts to promote tobacco cultivation, and by 1790 nearly two-thirds of the district's households raised the leaf. Accordingly, the slave population in Natchitoches nearly doubled during the final two decades of Spanish rule, reaching 950 people by 1803, a slight majority over the 900 or so free residents of the town. Although African imports augmented the slave numbers, the incredible fecundity of the district's creole slave women accounted for most of the increase in the number of bondspeople. Those residents who did not concentrate on tobacco production raised livestock instead, generally in the regions outside of town, such as Bayou Pierre, Campti, and Lac Noir, located on upstream tributaries of the Red River, in addition to establishing new ranches during the late 1790s in the swampy scrublands downstream from Natchitoches. Due to the profitability of plantation agriculture and ranching, few Natchitoches inhabitants bothered to remain involved in the Indian trade, as the nearby natives continued to be decimated by disease, and the Spaniards in Texas were granted responsibility for the commerce of that province's indigenous inhabitants.

The official Spanish decision to suspend tobacco shipments from Louisiana obviously had disastrous results for most Natchitoches planters, causing Commandant Louis de Blanc to report that they "are very much in debt and almost on the point of financial ruin." A few disgruntled planters complained that "the government bought [tobacco] from them under contract . . . [and that] suddenly discontinuing taking any at all . . .

[has] brought them to the threshold of poverty." Within a few years the economic situation among the planters had become so dire that there was an outbreak of violence at the post in the summer of 1795. Spurred by the arrival and support of a controversial priest named Jean Delvaux, about twenty young Natchitoches creole planters formed a group they christened *Les Revenants,* or "the ghosts." The drunken Revenants terrorized the community by riding around on horseback, firing pistols in the air, and denouncing various Spanish officials, including Commandant de Blanc. When de Blanc sought to remove Delvaux from his position as priest, the Revenants protested and signed a petition asking Carondelet to allow the clergyman to remain in Natchitoches. In August, upon learning that the governor had rejected their plea, the Revenants unleashed a new wave of unruly behavior and threatened anyone who opposed them.

An alarmed Carondelet consequently sent Antonio Argote and fifteen soldiers to Natchitoches with instructions to put down the rebellion, investigate the matter, and identify and arrest the instigators. By the time Argote arrived at the post in January 1796, Father Delvaux had already surrendered to Spanish authorities and had been sent to Cuba for confinement in a monastery. The troublemakers apparently lost their momentum without the priest's leadership, and Argote found Natchitoches to be calm and orderly. Ultimately, Carondelet temporarily expelled three Revenants from Louisiana and relieved de Blanc as commandant, transferring the grandson of the founder of Natchitoches to Attakapas. Soon thereafter cotton took the place of tobacco as the district's primary cash crop, and by 1802 the placated inhabitants of Natchitoches had built twenty-five gins along the Red River and had shipped nine hundred thousand pounds of the fiber to New Orleans. Downstream from Natchitoches, the nine hundred or so free residents of the Rapides and Avoyelles districts also began to raise cotton, but their efforts were hampered by their lack of slaves, who numbered only about 250 by the end of the era.

Arkansas Post continued to be immune to plantation agriculture during the final years of Spanish Louisiana. Nonetheless, the district's population nearly doubled during the period, reaching four hundred or so residents by 1803, including fifty slaves. The Spanish fort, built on Écores Rouges in 1779, fell into the river in 1788 and was replaced by an amateurish effort described as "two ill-constructed huts . . . surrounded with great palisades, without ditch or parapet." Between 1796 and 1803, however, the residents built a new fort consisting of a stockade containing four buildings. A small village emerged just upriver from the fort consisting of about thirty houses laid out on two streets. Although most of the Arkansas Post residents continued to hunt game as their main source of income, about a dozen families established wheat farms on lands just downstream from the fort. While the Euroamerican population grew during the final two decades of Spanish control, the Quapaw numbers declined to less than eight hundred people, and the Indians still resided in three separate villages on the south bank of the Arkansas near the Spanish fort.

Whereas the French creoles and the Quapaws continued to maintain their domiciles near the mouth of the Arkansas River during the final years of the eighteenth century, other Indian groups crossed the Mississippi in the 1790s to hunt farther upstream. Following the American Revolution, various Algonquian-speaking tribes located north of the Ohio River clashed with colonists crossing the Appalachians before finally succumbing to the U.S. Army at the Battle of Fallen Timbers in 1794. In the Treaty of Greenville the following year the nations of the Ohio Valley made peace by ceding vast amounts of land in the Northwest Territory. The traumas of war and the aftermath of land cessions drove many Shawnees, Delawares, Miamis, Abenakis, and Illinois to seek refuge in Spanish territory, where they settled along the White and St. Francis Rivers. At the same time, Iroquoian Cherokees from Georgia and Tennessee also fled the Americans and moved west of the Mississippi, where they established homes south of the Arkansas River at the invitation of the Quapaws.

Soon after their arrival the newcomers clashed with the Osages, who considered the central Arkansas Valley to be their own private hunting grounds, as they had already gone to war with the Caddos and Wichitas to secure the area. In fact, by the mid-1780s some Osage hunting bands, led by young men who desired opportunities for hunting, trading, and raiding so as to increase their prestige within the nation, had begun living on the Arkansas most of the year in order to protect the region from rivals. Led by a man named Cashesegra, the independent Arkansas band of Osages continued to make raids on the Caddos and Wichitas to the southwest, in addition to stepping up attacks on the newly arrived tribes on their eastern flank. Young warriors also occasionally robbed and killed French hunters along the Red, Ouachita, and Arkansas Rivers, despite attempts by Great Osage leaders to rein them in. In 1792 Governor Carondelet responded to the Arkansas band's rampage by ordering St. Louis officials to suspend trade with all of the Osages and by attempting to organize an Indian coalition against them. The campaign against the Osages proved to be an utter failure, as the tribe continued to receive weapons from independent traders and the Indians that had been urged to attack them either refused or only skirmished with small raiding parties. Finally, in 1795 the governor allowed two St. Louis traders, Auguste and Pierre Chouteau, to establish Fort Carondelet on the Upper Osage River and granted them a monopoly on the Osage commerce. Over the next few years the Chouteaus used their influence and power to form an alliance with a Great Osage chief named Pawhuska, who was able to convince the Arkansas band of Osages to at least raid less frequently than they had in the past.

In order to prevent Anglo Americans from crossing the Mississippi and settling in the sparsely inhabited Ouachita Valley, in February 1783 Governor Miró ordered Jean Baptiste Filhiol, a French native residing at Opelousas, to establish a post as far up the river as possible and concentrate the scattered inhabitants at the settlement. Filhiol located his first post at Écore a Fabri, a longtime gathering spot for the French creole hunters of the region, but found it too isolated and moved downstream to Prairie des Canots, site of present-day Monroe, Louisiana, in 1785. Although he tried to convince the two hundred or so residents of the Ouachita Valley to follow him downriver and abandon hunting in favor of tobacco planting, few chose to give up their independent lifestyle. Over the next few years, however, about twenty-five families from Pointe Coupée and Natchitoches moved to the Ouachita Post and established small farms and ranches on the left-bank prairies. Following the construction of Fort Miró in 1791, Filhiol decided to allow a few Americans from Natchez to establish homesteads near the post, as he could not persuade any other residents of Spanish Louisiana to relocate to the area. Hoping to prevent further American immigration, in March 1795 Governor Carondelet signed a contract with the Marquis de Maison Rouge, a French nobleman who had fled the Revolution to settle in Baltimore with other refugees, granting him a huge tract of land downstream from the Ouachita Post, on which he was to settle European families. The following year Carondelet made a similar agreement with a Dutchman of noble pretensions, the baron de Bastrop, and allocated him an even larger parcel of land upstream from Fort Miró. Neither man came close to fulfilling his obligations, as Maison Rouge died in 1799 and Bastrop fled to Texas soon after the Louisiana Purchase. Disposal of their land grants were tied up in litigation for years, however, thus hindering settlement in the Ouachita Valley well into the following century. By the turn of the century less than three hundred free people—mainly French creoles along with a few Americans and thirty libres—and seventy-five slaves resided near the Ouachita Post, raising foodstuffs and a bit of cotton on their small homesteads. In the early 1790s a few hundred Choctaws also established settlements near Fort Miró at the invitation of Spanish officials, who hoped they might provide a barrier to Anglo encroachment and be a counterweight to the Osage threat. The Spaniards soon regretted summoning the Choctaws, as the newcomers instead began to attack the Indians near Rapides, as well as the Caddos upstream from Natchitoches.

West Florida

West Florida, despite being isolated from the dynamic Mississippi Valley, also experienced a bit of growth during the final years of the eighteenth century. Since the governor of Louisiana maintained control over the disputed Natchez district for most of the period, Arturo O'Neill, who ably held the position of West Florida governor between 1781 and 1794, was only responsible for the region located between Mobile Bay and Apalache Bay. Upon taking control of the province, O'Neill immediately set about repairing the damages suffered by the British fortifications during the previous war. Whereas the British had concentrated their troops at Fort George in the center of Pensacola, the Spaniards' top military priority was the strengthening of the fortifications at the entrance of the bay. Accordingly, Spanish engineers established Fort San Carlos de Barrancas on the bluffs overlooking the mouth of Pensacola Bay, and most of the five hundred or so soldiers stationed in West Florida were located there. A few other Spanish troops manned the forts at Mobile and San Marcos de Apalache, the latter of which was rebuilt in 1787. Following O'Neill's reassignment, Colonel Vicente Folch y Juan, a native of Catalán, was appointed governor in 1796 and served in Pensacola until 1811.

Unlike the British, Spanish officials made little effort to economically develop West Florida, and the colony's productive capabilities languished for the remainder of the eighteenth century. Although many of the thirteen hundred British settlers around Pensacola abandoned the area immediately following the Spanish occupation, the population rebounded to nearly three hundred free residents—a mixed group of Anglos, French creoles, and Spanish Canary Islanders—and three hundred slaves by the mid-1780s. Despite being an economic backwater that mainly depended on the Indian trade and raising foodstuffs for the military garrison, by 1803 Pensacola's population had grown to about one thousand people, nearly half being unfree laborers. In contrast to the Anglos in Pensacola, the French creole inhabitants of Mobile welcomed the Catholic Spaniards to West Florida and remained in their homes after the occupation. As result, Mobile's population rose from over seven hundred residents in 1781 to more than fifteen hundred people two decades later. Slaves made up one-fifth of Mobile's inhabitants, while libres accounted for about one-third of the district's free people. Only a few planters in Mobile raised tobacco for export, most being content to tend to livestock and grow corn for local consumption.

Beyond the strongholds of Mobile and Pensacola, however, Spanish control over West Florida was extremely limited, as the two thousand or so Seminoles exerted their strength in the hinterlands. Whereas Payne, Cowkeeper's successor as leader of the Alachua Seminoles, strove to maintain the peace and keep commercial ties open with the Spaniards at the East Florida capital of St. Augustine, Kinache and the Miccosukees in the former Apalache province frequently raided Spanish settlements and were disinclined to trade through the Panton, Leslie, and Company stores at San Marcos and Pensacola. The situation became more complicated in 1791 when the Spanish Crown rescinded its policy of providing sanctuary for slaves who had escaped from their masters in South Carolina and Georgia in order to protect the growing plantation economy in East Florida and to appease the United States. As a result, fugitive slaves began to seek their freedom among both groups of Seminoles in Florida, alarming Spaniards and Americans alike. Although a few Seminole leaders obtained black slaves for their own private use, most of the escapees were allowed to establish semiautonomous villages near the Seminole towns, where they paid tribute in the form of agricultural produce to the local mico and acted as military allies in a subordinate position to the Indians. Throughout the 1790s Spanish officials were helpless to stop the runaway slaves from joining the Seminoles, despite the protests of the Americans and the occasional assistance of Creek mixed-bloods.

William Augustus Bowles, a Maryland native who had fought with the Redcoats as a Loyalist in the Revolutionary War, attempted to exploit the Spanish weakness and the Seminoles' independence, in addition to Lower Creek discontent with the United States, in order to take control of the region's Indian trade and to reassert British power in West Florida. While stationed at Pensacola during the war, Bowles had deserted from the British forces to marry the daughter of William Perryman, a mixed-blood Lower Creek chief whose village was situated on the Lower Chattahoochee River. Following the Spanish victory at Pensacola in 1781, Bowles traveled between the Bahamas and West Florida throughout the rest of the decade in a failed attempt to wrest control of the Creek trade from McGillivray and his partners at Panton, Leslie, and Company in favor of firms in Nassau and New Providence. Undaunted, Bowles—now clad in buckskins, beads, and feathers—returned to West Florida in the summer of 1791 and claimed the title of director general of the independent state of Muskogee, gaining support from its purported Seminole and Lower Creek citizens by distributing presents to various tribal leaders. Denounced by McGillivray and given the cold shoulder by Spanish officials, Bowles and a thousand Creek and Seminole allies responded by seizing the Panton, Leslie, and Company store at San Marcos in January 1792. Realizing their forces were hopelessly outnumbered, Spanish officers from the nearby presidio persuaded Bowles to travel with them to New Orleans by promising the adventurer an audience with Governor Carondelet in order to obtain official permission to trade. Instead, the Spaniards placed Bowles under arrest at the capital and sent him to a prison in the Philippines.

Incredibly, in 1798 Bowles escaped from Spanish authorities in Africa while being transported back to Spain. He first made his way to London, then headed to Jamaica and the Bahamas, where he rousted up associates and trade goods in yet another attempt to establish the independent state of Muskogee. Despite losing most of his supplies while grounding his ship at the entrance of the Apalachicola River, Bowles traveled to his father-in-law's village on the Chattahoochee in October 1799 and claimed formation of the Supreme Council of Muskogee, with himself holding the position of director general. Although the Spaniards in Louisiana and West Florida tried to capture the interloper, acute shortages in manpower, war materials, and funds seriously hampered their ability to meet Bowles's challenge, especially now that Spain was at war with Great Britain. Pledging the contents of the Panton, Leslie, and Company store at San Marcos to Indian allies, Bowles picked up the support of Kinache's Miccosukees, along with other Seminoles and Lower Creeks, and seized the property in early 1800. Bowles and his army then besieged the Spanish post of San Marcos de Apalache, forcing Captain Tomás Portell to surrender and evacuate his troops from the presidio in May 1800. Bowles's triumph was short-lived, however, as Spanish soldiers from Pensacola retook the post a few months later, and intensive patrolling prevented the at-large Bowles from receiving trade goods from his Bahamian associates, thus slowly but surely depriving him of his Indian allies' support. Finally, in

August 1802, Kinache succumbed to Upper Creek pressure and signed a treaty with the Spaniards at San Marcos de Apalache in which, in return for gifts and promises of debt cancellation, the Miccosukee mico pledged to maintain the peace with Spain and assist in the capture of Bowles. As a result of the treaty, Creek leaders seized Bowles at the Hickory Ground conference on the Coosa River in May 1803 and turned him over to Spanish authorities in New Orleans. Bowles was then sent to Havana, where he died in prison in December 1805. Despite the agreement with the Seminoles, Spanish authority in West Florida remained weak throughout the following two decades, allowing the British to exploit Indian discontent in the area during the War of 1812 by following the example set by Bowles, their American sympathizer.

Louisiana Indians

In contrast with West Florida, the rise in Louisiana's Euroamerican population, combined with Spanish officials' inability to provide them with protection, forced many of the colony's declining Indian tribes to relocate their settlements during the period. The small Caddoan-speaking groups living near Natchitoches continued to lose people during the final years of the eighteenth century, and survived only by combining their forces with their linguistic kinsmen. Less than fifty Yatasis remained in their village on Bayou Pierre, and the few surviving Adaes joined them in the 1790s. The Natchitoches tribe, which Commandant de Blanc stated "is almost finished," sold their lands, located only about six miles above the French town, and moved about twenty miles farther up the Red River, where they established a village and planted crops. Due to the transformation of the Natchitoches economy from the Indian trade to plantation agriculture and ranching, the two Caddo tribes—the Kadohadachos and the Petit Caddos—who lived in separate villages near the Great Bend of the Red River, were constantly short of arms and ammunition during the final years of Spanish Louisiana, especially compared to their better-equipped enemies to the east. The main threat to peace continued to be the Osages, who not only had access to legally authorized Spanish traders but also received numerous supplies and weapons from American traders east of the Mississippi. Prodded by the Anglos and their desire for horses and furs, the Osages resumed their raids upon the Indians of Texas and Louisiana in the late 1780s. In 1790 the Kadohadachos gave in to Osage pressure and moved their village downstream to take refuge with the Petit Caddos. Direct Osage attacks upon the Kadohadachos declined following the unification with the Petit Caddos, yet they continued to assault Indian and French hunters above Natchitoches in the valleys of the Red and Ouachita Rivers. Commandant de Blanc complained that while an abundance of game existed between the Kadohadacho and Panis Pique villages, the post of Natchitoches was "deprived of these provisions by the treacherous Osages who constantly wage war upon us in the region as well as upon our Indian allies."

Osage hostilities dwindled over the next few years as internal dissension divided the tribe and St. Louis traders successfully applied economic pressure on them to maintain the peace. In the wake of the Osages, however, several Choctaw bands, who Spanish officials had encouraged to expand west of the Mississippi, invaded the region and began attacking Indian and Euroamerican settlements alike while trying to take control of the rich hunting grounds between Natchitoches and Nacogdoches. By 1792 de Blanc was complaining that the Choctaws "come in great numbers and cause me a great deal of trouble by their thefts of horses and cattle," which they then delivered to American traders. For the next decade or so, the Spaniards were unable to control the American-supplied Choctaws, who intensified their violent raids in the region as the eighteenth century came to a close. In October 1797 Spanish officials mediated a two-day conference between Kadohadacho and Choctaw leaders in which both groups agreed to peace. By the following summer, however, the Choctaws had resumed their hostilities, forcing the one thousand or so remaining Kadohadachos and Petit Caddos to take refuge on Caddo Lake, about thirty-five miles west of the main branch of the Red River. In 1801 the two tribes united under the leadership of a new caddí, Dehahuit, who was described by observers as being a "very fine looking man" and a remarkably "shrewd and sensible fellow." For the following three decades Dehahuit would provide the Indians on the Louisiana-Texas frontier with inspired leadership through extremely trying times.

Although the Euroamerican and slave populations at Rapides increased during the period, the Indian numbers also rose as tribesmen continued to cross the Mississippi River to settle with their kinsmen in Spanish Louisiana. By the mid-1790s about two hundred Apalaches, Taensas, and Alabamas lived in contiguous settlements on the Red River, about twenty miles above Rapides. All three tribes maintained a close relationship with the settlers of Natchitoches and Rapides, and were said to be "highly esteemed by the French inhabitants." The tribes impressed their neighbors by successfully raising crops, tending livestock, and adopting Euroamerican dress. In addition, many Taensas, living in close proximity to the Christian Apalaches since 1763, adopted Catholicism as well. Between 1792 and 1799 local priests baptized forty-five members of both tribes, with Natchitoches citizens often acting as godparents. Both Étienne, the Apalache chief, and Louis, the Taensa leader, claimed to be Catholics. In 1800 a small party of Coushattas, led by Soulier Rouge (Red Shoes), crossed the Mississippi River to join with their close Alabama associates at the Red River settlements.

The groups living near the French settlers above Rapides experienced few problems with the inhabitants, but by the 1790s the other tribes in the area began to feel the pressure from recent immigrants, many of them Americans from east of the Mississippi. These tribes included the five hundred or so Pascagoulas, Yowani Choctaws, and Biloxis that resided on Bayou Bouef. Although all three tribes engaged in agriculture and raised cattle and horses, American settlers illegally sold the Indians alcohol and allowed their livestock to destroy the natives' cornfields. A couple of traders, Alexander Fulton and William Miller, formed a firm whose actions were representative of the American shift of interests from engaging with the Indians as merchants to acquiring their land as speculators. In October 1800 Fulton and Miller obtained the exclusive rights to the Indian trade of the Rapides district. The traders allowed the Indians extensive lines of credit, and within a year or so all the tribes had run up huge debts. Fulton and Miller quickly realized that obtaining Indians' land in order to sell it to Anglo cotton planters would be greatly more profitable than continuing the undependable trade. Therefore, in May 1802 Fulton and Miller purchased over forty thousand acres from the three tribes in return for extinguishing their debts. Following the sale the Biloxis remained near Bayou Bouef on a small parcel granted to them by Fulton and Miller, while the Pascagoulas moved to the Red River and settled just above the Apalache village. The Yowani Choctaws, however, began a westward movement toward Texas that ultimately most of the Louisiana Indians would be forced to follow. The Yowanis moved to a prairie, located between the Red and the Sabine, about forty miles southwest of Natchitoches, where they established a village, planted fields, put up fences, and raised cattle. At about the same time Soulier Rouge led a party of Coushattas from the Red River to the east bank of the Sabine, about forty miles from the Yowanis. Another group of Coushattas, led by Pia Mingo, joined their kinsmen on the Sabine soon thereafter, bringing the total number of tribal members living in the village to about six hundred. By the end of 1803 the Coushattas, along with the Alabamas, Yowanis, and Biloxis, were crossing into Texas to hunt and obtain horses. It would not be long before many of these tribes actually settled in Texas. Other Rapides-area tribes moved farther downstream toward the river's mouth, where they took refuge with the one hundred or so remaining Tunicas.

Texas

The situation in Texas remained diametrically opposite that of Louisiana, as the twenty thousand or so Indians greatly outnumbered the three thousand Spanish settlers. Nonetheless, the Spaniards in Texas achieved a bit of stability from the establishment of peace with the two main Norteño tribes, the Comanches and the Wichitas. Negotiations between the Norteños and Texas officials began in 1784 when Governor Domingo Cabello sent Natchitoches trader Jean Baptiste Bousquet to the Taovaya village on the Red River in order to establish ties with the Wichitas and hopefully begin talks with the Kotsotekas, the eastern branch of the Comanches. Bousquet found one Spaniard and two Frenchmen, including blacksmith Pierre Vial, living in the village and convinced them to accompany him and the Taoavaya chief back to San Antonio, where the alliance between the Wichitas and Spain was confirmed. After pardoning Vial for the crime of living illegally among Indians, Governor Cabello ordered him to return to the Taovaya village to negotiate a treaty with the Comanches. Vial entered the Panis Pique town in August 1785 and met with twelve principal Kotsoteka chiefs a few weeks later. Following a round of negotiations, all the Comanche headmen agreed to peace. Three chiefs returned to San Antonio with Vial, and in October the Spaniards and Comanches finally reached the accord that both had been trying to achieve for a decade. Each party agreed to refrain from fighting the other, and the Spaniards promised to distribute annual gifts and send traders to the Comanche villages.

The Norteño-Spanish alliance initially proved to be a great success. Within a month of the establishment of peace a succession of Kotsoteka groups visited their new Spanish allies in San Antonio to celebrate the treaty. In addition to distributing gifts to the Comanches, Governor Cabello exhorted them, as well as visiting Wichita bands, to attack the Lipan Apaches. As a result, over the next few years Comanche and Wichita warriors continually raided Apache villages, culminating in the formation of a joint Spaniard-Norteño campaign in January 1790, when the allied force surprised a large Lipan encampment on Soledad Creek, a small tributary of the Medina River. About sixty Apaches died, and the Spaniards captured a large number of women and children, in addition to taking eight hundred horses from the Lipans. Continued Norteño pressure forced the Lipans to agree to a peace agreement with the Spaniards in April 1793 in which they agreed to stop stealing livestock in return for being granted the right to exchange buffalo skins for metal goods at various Spanish settlements. For the most part, the treaty would successfully maintain the peace between the Lipans and Spaniards for the rest of the eighteenth century.

The Norteño peace and the defeat of the Lipan Apaches allowed the Spanish settlers at Nacogdoches to expand their ranching operations throughout East Texas, and the district's population increased to about seven hundred people by the turn of the century. Although most of the settlers were Hispanic, about one hundred French residents from Louisiana also established ranches in the region, as did a few Anglos from east of the Mississippi. Most of the French creoles and Anglos settled, along with a few libres, in the region between the Sabine River and Attoyac Bayou, where they raised cattle and horses that were sold legally in Louisiana, and illegally to American residents in Natchez. Lieutenant Governor Gil Ibarvo was suspected of being involved in the smuggling, and in 1791 he was arrested and incarcerated in San Antonio. Although he was eventually cleared of all charges, Gil Ibarvo was banished from Nacogdoches, where his presence was deemed "contrary to the union and best harmony of its inhabitants." Texas officials found it hard to replace the founder of Nacogdoches, as no less than eighteen military commandants and interim commanders supervised the district between 1791 and 1812.

Throughout the era Nacogdoches remained the official Indian trading post for Texas, even though keeping the various tribes well supplied with goods proved to be a very difficult task for the Spaniards. Items still had to be transported from Europe to New Orleans, and then up the Red River to be deposited at Natchitoches. Goods for the Indians of Texas then had to be transported overland to the trading post at Nacogdoches, where Joseph María Armant, a French merchant from Natchitoches, had been granted a monopoly as the colony's official trader. All of the Texas Indians, except the Comanches, were expected to travel to Nacogdoches to receive their annual presents. Armant also sent traders, mostly Frenchmen from Louisiana, to the various Indian villages. Other goods and presents were sent to San Antonio for the governor to distribute as the annual gifts for the Comanches, in addition to providing Indian visitors with items each time they arrived. While this was the plan for dealing with the Indians of Texas, the Spaniards found it almost impossible to adequately supply their Indian allies, for the colony was located at the extremities of a global empire that Spain could barely maintain even during peacetime. Following the outbreak of the wars of the French Revolution in 1793, ties between Spain and its American colonies were almost completely severed. As a result, the legal flow of Indian trade items to the Louisiana-Texas frontier, light during the best of times, slowed to a trickle. An ample supply of illegal goods, however, existed among the Anglo American traders east of the Mississippi River, and the Indians of the region defied their Spanish allies by eagerly tapping into these sources. Since the Americans desired horses in addition to furs, the illicit trade caused the Indians to resume their raids on Tejano livestock in San Antonio and La Bahía.

Trade that the Spaniards maintained for the Comanches proved to be the most successful of any in Texas. Aware of its great importance, Spanish officials awarded the Comanche commerce the highest priority and strove to keep the tribe well supplied with goods and presents. To maintain the peace and the flow of trade goods, Kotsoteka chiefs tried to prevent their young men from raiding Tejano ranches in order to gain wealth and prestige. Although they were only partly successful, the Comanche leaders often paid restitution for their warriors' transgressions and, for the most part, the tribe maintained the all-important peace with the Spaniards of Texas for the better part of a decade. The Spaniards had a more difficult time providing the other Texas tribes with trade goods, and relations with the non-Comanche Norteños—the Wichitas and Hasinais—suffered as a result. Armant quickly fell into debt and was unable to acquire an ample supply of merchandise for the Indians. Texas governor Manuel Muñoz revoked Armant's trading monopoly in 1790 and granted permission for independent traders, mainly Spaniards, to visit the various Indian villages. The new system did not fare much better, and by 1794 Wichita and Hasinai leaders were forced to travel to Natchitoches to complain to Commandant de Blanc. They told the Frenchman that, although they had made peace with the Spaniards in Texas in order to receive traders in their villages, they had actually been deprived of goods "in such a way that currently they are in most major misery." They begged de Blanc to send them traders from Louisiana, but he refused since Texas was not in his jurisdiction.

To remedy the situation, Texas officials granted exclusive rights to the Indian trade to two Irishmen from Pennsylvania, William Barr and Samuel Davenport. In 1798 the two men, naturalized citizens of New Spain, set up shop in Nacogdoches and sent traders to the Hasinai, Tawakoni, and Kichai villages. While the tribes were pleased with the increase in trade goods that resulted from the Barr and Davenport monopoly, most of the tribes had already developed ties with illicit traders and continued to jealously guard these crucial sources of goods. The number of traders increased during the last years of the eighteenth century as Americans from east of the Mississippi River crossed the border into Spanish territory. As early as August 1786 illegal traders headed up the Red River to encourage the Taovayas to steal horses from San Antonio. Beginning in the 1790s Anglos from mount-poor Natchez traveled to the Texas plains to capture horses from among the huge wild herds that roamed near the Wichita villages. The first of these men to cross into Spanish lands, Philip Nolan of Belfast, legally entered Texas from Natchez in 1791 with a passport obtained from the Louisiana governor through the Irishman's business partner, James Wilkinson. Nolan established relations with the Wichitas and realized that, in addition to obtaining mustangs in Texas, he might supplement his income by providing the desperate tribes with trade goods. Nolan again received a passport to make legal trips to Texas in 1794 and 1797, and on both occasions he conducted illicit commerce with the Wichitas.

Trade with the Anglos led to strained relations between the Spaniards and the Wichitas, a dangerous situation that was exacerbated by a smallpox epidemic that swept through the area in the late 1790s and killed a "great number" of tribal members. As a result of the sickness, two aggressively anti-Spanish chiefs, Eriascoc and Awahakei, emerged as leaders of the Panis Piques. Both men considered the Spaniards to be undependable and untrustworthy and were disappointed in the alliance that netted them few trade effects and scant protection from enemies such as the Osages and the Choctaws. Therefore, following Eriascoc's accession as Taovaya medal chief in July 1799, Panis Pique warriors stood up to a troop of Spanish soldiers that tried to thwart the tribes' exchange of goods with a party of Chickasaws that had come to their village from east of the Mississippi. Spanish officials further angered the Wichitas with their efforts to stop the incursion of American traders into Texas. Nolan, whose activities over the past decade had raised the suspicions of the Spaniards, illegally entered Texas in October 1800 with thirty or so

Anglos. Nolan's well-armed force established a camp on a tributary of the Brazos River, upstream from the Tawakoni villages, where they erected a small fortification, including some corrals, and began rounding up wild horses. In March 1801 Spanish troops from Nacogdoches located the camp and attempted to arrest Nolan's party. When the Americans resisted, the Spaniards killed Nolan and captured most of his band of mustangers, who were later tried and imprisoned in Chihuahua. However, a few of Nolan's men escaped and returned to Mississippi, intent on returning to Texas to trade with the Wichitas and capture horses.

In early 1803 hostilities broke out between the Spaniards and Wichitas that threatened to spill over to the Comanches. In February Spanish troops killed nine Taovayas who had stolen horses from outside San Antonio. Enraged by what they considered an excessive use of force, the Panis Piques called on their fellow Wichitas, as well as their Comanche allies, to assist them in obtaining retribution. Although Kotsoteka leaders rejected the call to war and met with Governor Juan Bautista Elguézabal in San Antonio to reiterate their desire for peace, in August 1803 Spanish troops encountered a group of Comanches outside San Antonio and placed them under arrest for stealing horses and charged them with the murder of a citizen who had recently been killed by unidentified Indians. In October Kotsoteka chief Chihuahua negotiated a settlement with the Texas governor, who released all of the prisoners except two who admitted they had stolen the horses. Although war had been averted between the Comanches and the Spaniards, many Kotsoteka warriors sided with their Wichita allies and felt no great compunction to maintain the peace in Texas. On the eve of the American accession of Louisiana, relations between the Norteños and the Spaniards had reached their lowest point since peace had been achieved in 1785. As a result of the hostilities, the United States would be able to take advantage of the situation and convince most of the province's Indians to favor the Americans in a dispute concerning the Louisiana-Texas boundary following the Louisiana Purchase.

7

The Establishment of Anglo Protestant Hegemony, 1804–1821

During the two decades following the Louisiana Purchase, Anglo Protestants from the United States established firm control over the various groups who had competed for power on relatively equal terms for more than two centuries. During the first decade of the nineteenth century American officials, unlike the Spaniards four decades prior, set up administrative control over Louisiana—leading to statehood in 1812—without causing the French creoles to rebel. In the following decade the United States destroyed Creek and Seminole resistance and repelled a British invasion of Louisiana. In the wake of the military victories, Anglo Protestants and their slaves poured into the region, resulting in statehood for Mississippi and Alabama. American pressure, combined with problems emerging from renewed wars in Europe, then forced Spain to cede Florida in 1821, opening up the region even further to the Anglo Americans, who would maintain and extend their hegemony over the course of the following century and a half.

Claiborne and the Creoles

On December 20, 1803, newly appointed territorial governor William Claiborne, along with General Wilkinson and five hundred U.S. troops, took possession of Louisiana for the United States in a ceremony held in New Orleans. For the second time in forty years Louisiana had actually been transferred to another nation. And this one was much different from the monarchist, Catholic Spain that the French creoles had rebelled against soon after the Bourbon takeover. Unlike Spain, the United States was a predominantly Protestant nation that was dedicated to representative government. Governor Claiborne realized that in order to calm the fears of the conservative, Catholic French creole majority, he needed to move slowly in imposing the American system in Louisiana. Ultimately, Claiborne succeeded brilliantly. Like his Spanish predecessors, he married into a wealthy creole family soon after assuming the gubernatorial position, and with the assistance of a thriving plantation economy he had won the loyalty of the French creoles by the time a British army stood at New Orleans's gates in 1814.

Local creoles feared that the republican Americans would impose a legal system that was radically different than the previous royal structure, but U.S. officials initially provided the territory with a government that was relatively similar to the prior French and Spanish regimes. Congress, employing a plan authored by President Jefferson, passed an act in March 1804 creating the Territory of Orleans, consisting of the present boundaries of the state of Louisiana, except for the area between the Mississippi and the Pearl Rivers encompassed by Spanish West Florida. Executive power was vested in a governor who was commander in chief of the militia and who appointed all civil and military officers. The governor, whose authority resembled that of the French and Spanish colonial executives, worked with a territorial legislature called the Legislative Council, a body similar in nature to the Cabildo, for it was composed of thirteen individuals appointed by the president. Jefferson, however, signed blank appointments and allowed Governor Claiborne to fill in the names of his council, half of whom were wealthy French creoles. In April 1805 the Legislative Council divided the territory into twelve counties, based mainly on the Spanish administrative districts, each manned by a sheriff, judge, coroner, clerk, and treasurer appointed by the governor. This act provided for a local government that was similar to the Spanish system introduced by Carondelet in 1792, in which each district was provided with a syndic, or justice of the peace, to support the local commandant. As a result, the new American arrangement was very familiar to the Louisiana creoles.

In March 1805, however, Congress introduced a more democratic form of government to the Orleans Territory by passing an act calling for a popularly elected lower legislative house of twenty-five men and an upper body of five men appointed by the president. Only property owners of at least two hundred acres could vote for the lower house, a requirement reduced to fifty acres before the second election. The first territorial legislature, composed mostly of French creoles, was chosen in early 1806.

In May 1807 the legislature divided the territory into nineteen parishes, with a twentieth added the following year. Although the previously created counties remained as electoral units until 1845, all the other functions of the county were bestowed upon the parish judge. Over the next few years the legislature created what came to be known as the "police jury," a group of twelve citizens from each parish who met annually to oversee levees and roads and to police the district.

Whereas the executive and legislative systems put forth for the Orleans Territory were not that different from their French and Spanish predecessors, Anglo American common law clashed dramatically with the colonial system, which was based on civil law. The general jurisprudential theory of civil law is that the law is primarily based on doctrines set forth by legislation or decree, while the common law is derived from prior court decisions which themselves represent law. Although President Jefferson and Governor Claiborne fully intended to introduce the common law system into the Orleans Territory, they allowed the civil laws in force at the time of the Louisiana Purchase to remain in effect out of fear that the French creoles might resist the American occupation and rebel if they proceeded too swiftly. Aware of Claiborne's views, the predominantly creole territorial legislature passed an act in May 1806 that retained the Spanish system of civil law. Although Governor Claiborne promptly vetoed the act, he signed a measure a few weeks later assigning James Brown (a lawyer from Virginia) and Saint-Domingue jurist Louis Casimir Moreau-Lislet to the task of devising a civil code for the territory modeled on Spanish law and the French Napoleonic Code. The two men submitted a draft less than two years later, and in March 1808 the territorial legislature approved the new code, which provided law for the settlement of noncriminal cases until 1825. Claiborne, despite his initial opposition, signed the bill with the understanding that the civil law code was a political compromise that constituted the creole population's acceptance of permanent American rule. Essentially, Claiborne and Jefferson surrendered their desire for total Americanization in return for a faster and smoother absorption of the territory into the United States.

Governor Claiborne softened his position on the law code in favor of the French creoles in part due to the intrigue caused by Aaron Burr, former vice president of the United States, just as lawyers Brown and Moreau-Lislet began their task of writing a new civil code. In the spring of 1805, soon after leaving office in disgrace after killing Alexander Hamilton in a duel, Burr headed to the Mississippi Valley and met with General

Wilkinson (who was still in the pay of the Spanish Crown) and other Anglos, including Daniel Clark, Louisiana's territorial delegate to Congress and Claiborne's leading political enemy. By the summer of 1806 rumors abounded that Burr—who had meanwhile returned to the Atlantic Coast—and his associates planned to pry the area west of the Appalachians from the United States, or to invade Mexico and establish an independent state, or both. In fall 1806, as Burr and a small group of followers descended the Mississippi River toward New Orleans to carry out their undetermined plan, Wilkinson denounced his co-conspirator and conducted a bloodless "reign of terror" in New Orleans, climaxed by the arrests of Burr's local Anglo associates and the imposition of martial law. Realizing what was happening, Burr tried to avoid the authorities but was arrested for treason and transported for trial to Virginia, where he was ultimately acquitted by Chief Justice John Marshall. Although the threat caused by Burr had subsided in New Orleans by early 1807, the political life of the territory had been transformed. Whereas Claiborne had been suspicious of the local French creoles during his first few years as territorial governor, his greatest political clashes had actually been with Anglos, such as Clark and the lawyer Edward Livingston, both of whom were associated with Burr. On the other hand, the leading Francophone representatives in the territorial legislature, particularly Julien Poydras and Jean Baptiste Macarty, had stood by Governor Claiborne during the crisis and had demonstrated their loyalty to the United States. As a result of their actions, Claiborne and the creoles firmed up their alliance in the aftermath of the Burr Conspiracy, leading to Poydras—who was actually born in France and resided in Saint-Domingue before migrating to Louisiana in 1768—being named as territorial delegate to Congress in 1809 following Clark's resignation.

The issue of slavery and the slave trade also threatened to drive a wedge between the incoming Americans and the Louisiana French creoles, but ultimately wound up bringing the two groups even closer together. Whereas the creole planters who were profiting from the boom in sugar and cotton had convinced the Spanish authorities to reopen the slave trade from Africa in 1800, the 1804 act creating the Orleans Territory banned the importation of all foreign slaves. The U.S. Constitution also stated that the Atlantic slave trade would become illegal in 1808. Thus, it seemed that the Louisiana planters would be denied further slave imports just when they claimed they needed them the most. American officials, however, defused the creole planters' outrage in 1805 by ruling that slaves imported to the rest of the United States could legally be introduced into

Louisiana. As a result, a few thousand Africans—most of whom had landed in Charleston, South Carolina—were re-exported to New Orleans between 1805 and 1808. In addition, French privateers illegally brought countless other slaves to Louisiana even after the constitutional ban on importation. Brothers Jean and Pierre Lafitte, natives of France as well as refugees from Saint-Domingue, directed the smuggling from the base they established on Grand Terre, the barrier island at the mouth of Barataria Bay. In addition to African slaves, the Lafitte brothers also introduced all sorts of untaxed merchandise into New Orleans by using shallow draft pirogues to traverse the bayous and swamps between Barataria Bay and the Mississippi River. Although American officials and Governor Claiborne initially differed with the creole planters on the African trade, both groups agreed that the Spanish slave laws promulgated by Carondelet were far too liberal. As a result, in 1806 the planter-dominated territorial legislature, with Claiborne's full approval, enacted the most repressive slave code in Louisiana history, bringing it fully in line with the American South's draconian laws that defined the bondspeople first and foremost as property devoid of almost all rights. Ironically, American democracy actually allowed the planters, as property owners, to have more freedom to control their slaves than the absolutist monarchies of France and Spain.

Governor Claiborne furthermore won the French creoles' approval by supporting the emigration of Saint-Domingue refugees from Cuba in 1809. As a result of Napoleon's invasion of Spain the previous year, in March 1809 Cuban authorities decided to expel the French escapees from Saint-Domingue who had settled on the Spanish island following the 1791 slave rebellion. Understanding that a few Saint-Domingue refugees had already successfully established residences in Louisiana, the French in Cuba began boarding ships headed for the mouth of the Mississippi River, the first arriving in May 1809. By January 1810 at least 9,059 refugees—2,731 whites, 3,102 free people of color, and 3,226 slaves had reached Louisiana, almost all departing from Santiago in the southeastern part of the island. Most of the migrants settled in New Orleans, thus doubling the number of French-speakers in the city at a time when Anglos were threatening to become the majority. For the most part, the Saint-Domingue refugees from Cuba received a warm welcome from the citizens of Louisiana. Although Governor Claiborne reported that "many good Americans are dissatisfied with so great an influx of foreigners," no measures were adopted to block the settlement of the new arrivals. To the contrary, government officials and the French-speaking community of New Orleans actively took steps to ease the refugees' troubled situation. Mayor James Mather called for and received from the municipal council the adoption of measures designed to provide the arrivals with assistance, such as the securing of temporary accommodations, the collection of blankets, and the formation of a welfare committee to procure them with relief and work. In addition to the local government, the principal French-language newspapers served as conduits of aid to the refugees, allowing them to advertise their talents free of charge and announcing events organized on the arrivals' behalf. Whereas these initiatives were intended for white refugees, local free people of color collected money for a fund to assist poverty-stricken arrivals of their own caste. Finally, residents of New Orleans put pressure on Governor Claiborne to provide an exception to the 1808 federal law prohibiting the importation of foreign slaves in order to allow the bondspeople accompanying the refugees to disembark. Claiborne won the favor of the French community by forwarding their petitions to the federal government, resulting in Congress passing a law in June 1809 that remitted penalties concerning the slaves belonging to the refugees from Cuba.

Soon thereafter, Claiborne—despite his initial opposition—supported the French creoles' call for statehood, and in February 1811 Congress authorized a convention to draw up a constitution. Elections were held in September, with French speakers winning twenty-six of the forty-five seats. In November the constitutional convention met in New Orleans and chose Julien Poydras as its presiding officer. During the following two months the constituents drew up a fairly conservative document, based on the 1799 Kentucky constitution, that was scarcely distinguishable from those of the other states at the time. The legislature was bicameral, and only men of property could aspire to office, while only men who paid taxes could vote. In keeping with Louisiana's colonial tradition, however, the governor's powers were extensive in that he appointed all state officials, including judges, some with the approval of the legislature, some without. The governor was also to be selected indirectly; the voters would nominate candidates in a general election and the legislature would select the winner from the two who received the highest number of votes. In January 1812 the convention officially adopted the document and sent it to Congress, which approved the constitution soon thereafter, opening the way for Louisiana to enter the Union on April 30, 1812. Elections were held in late June, and the voters, who were predominantly French creole planters, rewarded Claiborne for his support by giving him more than twenty-seven hundred votes. Less than twelve hundred votes went to his creole planter rivals, Jacques Villeré and Jean Noel Destréhan. The French creole-dominated legislature chose to go along with the voters, and Claiborne was inaugurated as state governor on July 31. Following nine years of effort, Claiborne had successfully shepherded the authoritarian French Catholics of Louisiana into a union with the republican Anglo Protestants of the United States with as little conflict as possible.

The Lower Mississippi Valley and Acadia

Louisiana was eligible for statehood because the decennial census of 1810 showed that the population had increased from about forty-five thousand at the time of the purchase to over seventy-five thousand by the end of the decade. The white population doubled—due mainly to natural increase and Anglo migration—to thirty-four thousand people, while the number of free people of color more than tripled—aided primarily by the Saint-Domingue refugees—to reach seventy-five hundred residents. Despite the initial ban on the importation of Africans into the Orleans Territory, the slave population in the state rose from twenty-five thousand to thirty-four thousand. While Louisiana's two-thirds population growth during the decade was impressive, it still could not match the incredible numbers of people—mainly Anglo Protestants and their slaves—residing in Kentucky and Tennessee, as those states' populations had doubled to 665,000 in 1810. Georgia grew at a slightly lesser rate, climbing from 160,000 at the turn of the century to 250,000 a decade later. These three states would provide most of the people who would overwhelm the rest of the Gulf South in the upcoming decades.

Following the pattern set in the colonial era, more than two-thirds of the people in Louisiana resided along the Mississippi River downstream from Baton Rouge. About seventeen thousand whites—French creoles, Acadians, Spaniards, Germans, and Anglos—lived in the region, alongside nearly twenty-thousand creole and African slaves, as well as sixty-five hundred free people of color. More than half of these forty-three thousand people lived in New Orleans, where the population tripled to reach twenty-four thousand residents in 1810. Most of the city's growth was from immigration rather than natural increase, as yellow fever epidemics killed thousands in 1804, 1807, and 1808. Whereas many of the migrants to New Orleans were Anglos from the United States, most of the newcomers were the nine thousand French refugees—from all three castes—who arrived from Cuba in 1809. As a result, by 1810 the population of New Orleans consisted of eight thousand whites, fifty-seven hundred free people of color, and eleven thousand slaves. The city's huge population growth during the decade led, for the first time, to the development of residential districts located outside the grid of the French Quarter. In 1805 Bernard Marigny subdivided his plantation just downstream from the French Quarter, laying out streets and lots alongside a filled-in sawmill canal that he named Les Champs-Elysées, or Elysian Fields. Whereas most of the residents of Faubourg Marigny were French-speakers—many being refugees from Cuba, including a large concentration of free people of color—Anglos from the United States tended to settle in Faubourg St. Mary, located upstream from the French Quarter across the thoroughfare that would eventually be called Canal Street.

The presence of such a large proportion of free people of color—more than 40 percent of the city's free population—greatly troubled the incoming Americans, who had little familiarity with the French and Spanish legal recognition of a caste between free whites and black slaves. The presence of the libre militia particularly bothered Governor Claiborne and General Wilkinson, both of whom viewed the battalion as a threat, but hesitated to disband it out of fear of an uprising. Recognizing Claiborne's uncertainty, in January 1804 fifty-five members of the free colored militia addressed a memorial to the governor professing their sincere attachment to the United States, whose democratic and revolutionary principles they believed would forever assure them their "personal and political freedom." In June 1804 Claiborne responded through compromise, allowing the free colored militia to remain intact while replacing the libre officers with a French creole and an Anglo. Whereas the governor desired to bring the free colored militia under control through the implementation of white officers, in April 1805 the French creole-dominated Legislative Council disbanded it altogether by omitting any mention of the libre battalion in the territory's militia law. Although the libres protested, and Claiborne urged the Legislative Council to reconsider its decision, the governor refrained from vetoing the measure. In 1807, with Claiborne's approval, the French planters of the Territorial Legislature further attacked the liberal Spanish policies concerning the free people of color by eliminating the right of self-purchase altogether and prohibiting the in-migration of free blacks to Louisiana. As with the issue of slavery, Louisiana's French creoles were discovering that the democratic American federal system—along with Anglo anxiety toward libres—allowed them to curb the state's free people of color in a manner that had been forbidden during the French and Spanish regimes.

The creoles also found that the American system provided them with more control over the Catholic Church than they had previously experienced, resulting in the Schism of 1805. In 1801 the Diocese of Louisiana and Florida's first bishop, Luis Peñalver y Cárdenas, was transferred to Guatemala, and the Louisiana Purchase delayed the naming of his replacement. By 1804 Father Patrick Walsh, an Irishman who Peñalver had appointed vicar general, began to function as if he held the diocesan authority in New Orleans. The following year, when Walsh attempted to remove Padre Antonio de Sedella, known as "Père Antoine," from his position as the beloved pastor of Saint Louis Cathedral, the French creole laity rose up in a tumultuous meeting held in the cathedral and raucously proclaimed the Capuchin Spaniard as their spiritual leader. Walsh was forced to withdraw to the Ursuline nuns' chapel, which he proclaimed to be the legitimate parish church. He also announced that sacraments performed elsewhere would be null and void. The schism ended in 1806 when Walsh died and the entire Louisiana Purchase was put under the administration of Bishop John Carroll of Baltimore, the only American bishop at the time. While Sedella remained pastor of Saint Louis Cathedral until his death in 1829, Carroll acted as the apostolic administrator of the diocese until 1812, when he appointed Louis-Guillaume Dubourg, a refugee from Saint-Domingue, as his representative.

The continuing boom in sugar and cotton production was yet another reason the creole planters easily adapted to American rule. By 1810 the ninety-one sugar works located downstream from Baton Rouge produced almost 10 million pounds of sugar, twice the amount that had been raised in 1802. Accordingly, the sugar plantations contained a large number of slaves. The ninety-five hundred bondspeople outnumbered the eight thousand or so whites and free people of color. In contrast to the sugar-producing area along the Mississippi, St. Bernard's six hundred Canary Islanders continued to raise produce and poultry, alongside their four hundred slaves, for the New Orleans market. According to Governor Claiborne, they were a "useful portion of our society," as they were "industrious, honest, obedient to the laws, and content with their situation."

Upstream from Baton Rouge sugar gave way to cotton, and Louisiana planters and their slaves increased production from eighteen thousand to forty-two thousand bales during the first decade of the nineteenth century. The French creole planters of Pointe Coupée, along with newly arrived

Anglos in Concordia Parish, dominated Louisiana's cotton industry. In these two districts, the five thousand or so slaves outnumbered the free people by a ratio of two to one by 1810. The Red River communities of Natchitoches and Rapides—the latter of which grew dramatically due to Anglo migration—also raised cotton, but at a lower rate than those along the Mississippi, and the four thousand or so free people in these districts outnumbered the thirty-three hundred slaves. To the southwest, in Opelousas, Attakapas, and Lafourche, most of the residents—mainly Acadians with an intermixture of Anglos—continued to be small farmers, ranchers, fishermen, or trappers. As a result, the fifty-six hundred slaves of the region only made up one-third of the total population. A few Cajuns, located mainly along Bayou Teche, did establish cotton plantations during this period.

Louisiana Indians

The dramatic rise in Louisiana's free and slave populations put great pressure on the province's Indians, causing most of the Native Americans to relocate within half a decade of the American takeover. The groups living along the Red River near Rapides were the first to move, most of them heading to Spanish Texas. In January 1804 Taensa chief Louis, claiming to have the consent of the nearby Apalaches, set the emigration in motion by selling over eleven thousand arpents of land situated on both sides of the Red River to the Miller and Fulton firm for $5,200, half of which the Indians already owed the trading house. Chief Louis then traveled to Nacogdoches in March and obtained permission to settle in Texas from Spanish officials, who characterized the Apalaches and Taensas as being "industrious, civilized, and inclined toward the Catholic religion." Whereas only a few Apalaches and Taensas abandoned the Red River and moved westward at the time, the other Rapides tribes took advantage of the Spanish ruling and began crossing west of the Sabine River in the summer of 1804. One band of Alabamas settled on the Angelina River, just below the mouth of the Attoyac Bayou, while others, along with Coushatta and Yowani Choctaw tribesmen, established small villages between the Trinity and the Neches. Over the next couple of years headmen from these tribes, as well as Biloxi and Pascagoula leaders, often visited Nacogdoches to meet with Spanish officials. By 1806 the chiefs had persuaded Commandant General Nemesio Salcedo that they could be used as a reliable buffer against the encroaching Americans, and he granted them all permission to settle in Texas.

Many of the Indians, however, remained in their Louisiana villages, unwilling to abandon their homes, livestock, and fields. Continued Anglo immigration, which resulted in outbreaks of violence, soon convinced most of them to move to Texas. In January 1807 an Anglo settler murdered the brother of Coushatta headman Soulier Rouge near Natchitoches, causing a fellow tribesman to kill an American in revenge. U.S. troops were sent to the Coushatta village to apprehend the culprit, but most of the tribesmen had already moved to Texas to escape retribution. Most of the remaining Alabamas and Coushattas crossed west of the Sabine in the summer of 1808 following the execution by Louisiana territorial officials of two Alabama men who had been convicted of murdering an American in Opelousas. By the end of the year nearly six hundred Alabamas and Coushattas lived in two southeastern Texas villages: the Alabamas settled on the west bank of the Neches River, nearly twenty-five miles above its confluence with the Angelina; the Coushattas, under Soulier Rouge and Pia Mingo, moved about fifty miles west to the east bank of the Trinity River. The tensions in Louisiana encouraged members of the other tribes also to seek refuge in Texas, as Yowani Choctaws, Biloxis, and Pascagoulas, as well as Apalache and Taensas tribesmen, established villages near the Alabamas on the Neches River. By 1810 perhaps one thousand Indians had immigrated to the heavily forested region south of Nacogdoches—soon to be called the "Big Thicket"—between the Neches and the Trinity River.

Other Louisiana tribesmen moved up the Red River and settled on the unoccupied Kadohadacho lands above Natchitoches that were protected from Euroamerican settlement by the Great Raft, a huge logjam that had developed during the late eighteenth century. In 1804 Apalache headman Étienne secured permission from Chief Dehahuit to establish a town within Kadohadacho territory. As a result, about 350 Apalaches, Alabamas, and Coushattas built houses and planted corn on the east bank of the Red River, about twenty miles above the head of the huge obstacle. The Kadohadachos gladly accepted the settlement—which the confused Americans designated as being a Coushatta village—because they could be used as allies against the Osages and Choctaws. The success of the Coushatta settlement on the Red River encouraged further emigration, and the Indians moved upstream in 1809 to a site known today as Coushatta Bluffs, situated on the east bank of the river. Although most of the Indians that lived in Rapides Parish abandoned the area following the transfer of Louisiana, about two hundred Pascagoulas, Apalaches, and Taensas continued to live on the Red River in settlements located just above the newly christened town of Alexandria.

Following the sale of their lands to Miller and Fulton in 1804, the remaining Apalaches had protested to the U.S. Board of Land Commissioners, claiming that Taensa chief Louis did not represent them and, therefore, had no right to vend their territory. As a result, the land sale was held up until 1812, when the land commissioners voided the Apalache half of the sale and allowed the tribe to maintain title to nearly three thousand acres on the Red River. Despite the continued pressure of American settlers, the Apalaches, along with members of the other two tribes, lived on this tract for the next two decades. About one hundred or so Tunicas, along with a few Biloxis, continued to reside on the Red River about fifty miles downstream from the Apalaches. Another one hundred Houmas occupied the marshes between the Atchafalaya and Bayou Lafourche.

Arkansas

The Louisiana Purchase by the United States did little to change the pattern of settlement that had existed for nearly a century in the Arkansas Valley. In the March 1804 act that created the Orleans Territory, Congress also established the Louisiana District north of the 33rd Parallel, which was placed under the control of the territorial government of Indiana. The following year, when Congress created the Louisiana Territory, with its capital at St. Louis, Arkansas was placed in the New Madrid District, the southernmost jurisdiction of the province. Soon thereafter the U.S. Army stationed a captain and sixteen troops at Arkansas Post, rechristened Fort Madison. The region's isolation caused the territorial government to create a separate Arkansas District in 1806 and a local court began to operate at the post in 1808. Despite the uncertainty of the territory's status, a few Anglos crossed the Mississippi to settle along the lower reaches of the Arkansas River, and by 1810 the population doubled to about nine hundred whites, along with one hundred or so slaves. Most of the settlers continued to combine hunting and small-scale vegetable farming to make their livings. Nearly six hundred Quapaws maintained their three villages near Fort Madison and established friendly relations with the newcomers by selling them horses and corn. In 1805 the United States built a trading factory near the Quapaw towns and, after a delay of three years, Indian agent John Treat was authorized to distribute up to $1,000 worth of presents to the tribe annually.

The six thousand remaining Osages in the region quickly befriended the United States as well, for they hoped the young republic would replace the Spaniards as a source of goods and provide control over the eastern Indians that continued to cross the Mississippi River to encroach upon their territory. In the spring of 1804 Chief Pawhuska and eleven other Great and Little Osages eagerly accepted President Jefferson's invitation to become the first Indian delegation from the Louisiana Purchase to visit Washington. At the capital, Jefferson conformed to the Osage ideal of a good ally, giving them medals, showering them with gifts, promising them trade, and appointing their longtime trader, Pierre Chouteau, as their agent. Following the chiefs' return to their villages, in September 1805 U.S. officials stepped in to negotiate a treaty between the Osages and a host of Algonquian tribes from the Great Lakes region, in which the various tribes agreed to settle their disputes through mediation by the Americans rather than through violence. The following year Arkansas River Osages, now led by a rival of Pawhuska named Clermont II, began trading regularly with the Americans at the Arkansas Post factory. Due to continued immigration by Cherokee bands into the area between the White and the Arkansas Rivers, in September 1808 Chief Pawhuska signed a treaty ceding fifty thousand square miles of land on the tribe's eastern borders to the United States for the use of the newly arrived Indians. In return, the United States promised to build a fort in Osage territory to house a garrison for their protection, provide an increased number of goods for their benefit, and provide a blacksmith to mend their weapons and tools. Although the Arkansas Osages initially protested the treaty, Clermont II eventually agreed to the land cession after being promised more presents and diplomatic attention than the tribe had received in the past. In general, the Osages were content with their relationship with the United States, as the young republic seemed to be helping them protect their status as the leading tribe in the region.

The Louisiana-Texas Frontier

Whereas American officials had little difficulty in establishing their authority in the French creole provinces located just west of the Mississippi

River, the 1803 purchase created great tension between the United States and Spain on the Louisiana-Texas frontier, for France had sold the huge expanse of territory without ever defining its western borders. Thus, the boundary between Louisiana and Texas became subject to various interpretations, the most extreme being that of President Jefferson, who held that the border was the Rio Grande. Understandably, Spain scoffed at this claim, interpreting the line to be just a few miles west of the Red River, where it had been when France controlled Louisiana in the early eighteenth century. Since the situation was so tenuous, Spanish and American officials understood that the loyalty of the native tribes along the border would be crucial in any boundary determination. The Caddos, Wichitas, and Comanches were particularly central to this dispute because American officials held that the tribes formerly allied to France were now under their jurisdiction. In addition, both nations fully expected war with each other and realized that native allies might make the difference. Therefore, the Americans of Louisiana and the Spaniards of Texas both courted the Red River Caddoans and the Comanches, and representatives of both nations realized that trade was crucial to win the tribes' favor. Despite the Spaniards' comprehension of the situation, their lack of resources and general ineffectualness would prove no match for the wealthy and energetic Americans in winning the Indians' allegiances.

Kadohadacho leader Dehahuit understood the situation and adeptly used the boundary issue to his tribe's advantage. Officials of both the United States and Spain desired to win Dehahuit's favor because they realized that the Kadohadachos had clearly become the dominant Caddo tribe by the beginning of the nineteenth century. The Kadohadachos were by far the largest of the Caddo tribes, consisting of about one thousand people. Among the Indians influenced by the Kadohadachos were the one hundred or so remaining Natchitoches, Yatasi, and Adaes tribesmen, who lived upstream from Natchitoches on Bayou Pierre and the Red River. The Hasinais—with a population as large as the Kadohadachos—continued to live in their traditional villages on the Neches and Angelina Rivers "in great amity" with Dehahuit's tribe, that also was allied with the Wichitas and Comanches farther upstream. The Kadohadacho leader quickly made the Americans realize his tribe's influential position on the Louisiana-Texas frontier and forced the country's representatives to take measures to gain his favor. Dehahuit made a number of trips to Natchitoches to meet with John Sibley, the U.S. Indian agent for the region, who arranged a peace treaty between the Kadohadachos and the Choctaws in May 1804. Three months later Dehahuit visited Natchitoches and received gifts of powder, lead, and tobacco, as well as an American flag to fly over his village, for he explained that it was "customary to have the Flag of the Nation who claimed his Country in which they lived." In December 1804 Sibley sent traders up the Red River to distribute presents and American flags to the Taovayas, as well as sending invitations to the Hasinais and Comanches of Texas to visit him at Natchitoches in order to initiate trade. Upon the establishment of an official U.S. Indian trading factory at Natchitoches in early 1806, the American trade advantage over the Spaniards on the Louisiana-Texas frontier became complete.

In the meantime President Jefferson began to arrange an exploratory venture—similar to the concurrent Lewis and Clark expedition on the Missouri River—along the Arkansas and Red Rivers in order to more firmly establish the United States' claims along the border. In April 1804 the president chose William Dunbar, the Natchez scientist who had only recently helped set the southern boundary of the United States along the 31st Parallel, and George Hunter, a Philadelphia chemist born in Scotland, to lead the so-called Grand Expedition westward to the Rocky Mountains sources of both rivers. However, fears of Spanish resistance along the Red, and possibly hostile Osages on the Arkansas, caused Dunbar and Hunter to ask and receive permission to explore the Ouachita River instead. Obtaining a $3,000 appropriation from Congress, the expedition, consisting of nineteen men, including soldiers and a few slaves, departed from Natchez in a flatboat in October 1804. Two weeks later the party arrived at Fort Miró, obtained a less cumbersome vessel, and headed upstream with a French creole guide. In early December the Grand Expedition reached the hot springs near the Ouachita's source, where they spent a month investigating the flora and fauna of the region before returning to Natchez. Following their arrival in late January 1805, Hunter reported that the Ouachita Valley was "generally fertile and capable of the highest cultivation," claiming that the hot springs were "among the greatest natural curiosities in the country . . . [possessing] extraordinary medical virtues." The following year Dunbar and Hunter published their accounts of the Ouachita River expedition. Due, in part, to the two men's favorable views of the region, Anglos eagerly crossed the Mississippi to establish residences near Fort Miró, and by 1810 the Ouachita district's population had tripled to just over one thousand people, one-fourth of whom were slaves.

By early 1806, after receiving reports of the establishment of friendly relations with the Kadohadachos and their allies, President Jefferson decided the time was right to go forth with the previously planned Red River expedition. Jefferson chose Major Thomas Freeman, an Irish-born surveyor who had helped Ellicott and Dunbar run the northern boundary of Spanish Florida in 1798, and Peter Custis, a doctoral student in the medical and natural history program at the University of Pennsylvania, to ascend to the source of the Red River in an attempt to define the border between Louisiana and Texas. In addition, Freeman and Custis were instructed to "court an intercourse with the natives as intensively as you can" and to instruct the tribes that they were no longer subjects of Spain but "henceforth [the United States would] become their fathers and friends." The Freeman-Custis expedition—consisting of three boats, twenty-one soldiers, and a black servant—entered the Red River in April 1806, doubled their numbers upon reaching Natchitoches the following month, and headed upriver once more in early June. After two weeks of struggling with the Great Raft, the Americans reached the Coushatta village on June 24 and held a conference with the town's inhabitants, as well as with Dehahuit and a contingent of Kadohadachos, in which the Americans explained that the United States would "protect them and supply their wants" in the future. The Kadohadacho leader gladly accepted this pledge and ordered three tribesmen to guide the expedition on to the Taoavaya village.

Dehahuit also warned Freeman and Custis that he had heard rumors that Spanish troops were en route from Nacogdoches to intercept the Americans, and he promised to send messengers from his village with information concerning the enemy force. Dehahuit was correct about the Spanish disposition, as Lieutenant Colonel Simon Herrera had been ordered to take one thousand troops to the Red River to stop the expedition. On the way to the Red, the Spanish force passed through the Kadohadacho village on Caddo Lake, where Herrera brusquely tore down the American flag that was flying above it, informing Dehahuit that the town lay on Spanish soil. A couple of weeks later the overwhelming Spanish force met Freeman and Custis on the Red River, and the expedition was obliged to retreat. In late August the Americans reached Natchitoches and informed Governor Claiborne of their fate. The governor immediately sent a letter to Herrera protesting the Spanish troops' having stopped the expedition on U.S. soil and their having committed "another outrage" by chopping down the American flag in the Kadohadacho village. Lieutenant Colonel Herrera responded by dismissing Claiborne's claims, asserting that the Indian town was not on American soil "and on the Contrary the place which they inhabit is very far from it and belongs to Spain." Tensions between the two countries continued to mount, but war was averted in November 1806 when General Wilkinson and Herrera struck a deal, known as the Neutral Ground Agreement. The accord established a demilitarized zone between Louisiana and Texas that, though claimed by both countries, would remain ungoverned and unoccupied by Spain and the United States. This agreement remained in force until 1821, by which time the neutral zone had become a notorious home to fugitive slaves, outlaws, smugglers, and squatters from the United States, as well as a staging ground for filibustering expeditions into Texas.

The Freeman-Custis expedition and Spain's reaction served only to propel the Kadohadachos further toward the Americans. Two weeks after the expedition was repelled, Dehahuit and a delegation of fourteen warriors met with Claiborne in Natchitoches and accepted the governor's claim that the Kadohadachos were now subjects of the United States. Although the Spaniards had stopped Freeman and Custis before they could reach the Taovaya village, in the fall of 1806 Agent Sibley took advantage of the Neutral Ground Agreement and sent traders up the Red River, where they met and exchanged goods with Wichita and Comanche tribesmen. The Texas Indians and the United States drew even closer together the following year. In August 1807 Dehahuit enhanced his prestigious position on the Louisiana-Texas frontier by arranging a grand council at Natchitoches between Agent Sibley and the Caddos, Wichitas, and Comanches. Sibley addressed a gathering of the visiting headmen, inviting the Indians to deposit their goods at Natchitoches and to accept American traders in their villages regardless of which side of the undefined border they lived on. As a result of the grand council, the Taovayas welcomed Anthony Glass, a Natchez merchant familiar with the exploits of Philip Nolan and his cronies, into their village the following summer. Glass and his men spent the fall and winter on the Red River obtaining horses and exchanging goods with various Comanche and Wichita warriors. Although the Spaniards attempted to match the Americans' efforts, by 1808 it had become clear that ample trade goods and skilled diplomacy had won the Red River Caddoans, as well as many Comanches, over to the American side of the boundary dispute.

Consequences of Napoleon's Invasion of Spain

Although war had been avoided between Spain and the United States on the Louisiana-Texas frontier, a new round of fighting in Europe threw the Gulf South into even more turmoil by the end of the decade. Following a brief lull in the wars of the French Revolution, in 1803 France and Great Britain resumed their struggle, with Austria, Prussia, and Russia joining the anti-Napoleonic coalition a couple of years later. After defeating Austria and Prussia and signing an armistice with Russia, in February 1808 Napoleon invaded Spain, forced Carlos IV to abdicate, and captured his son and heir, Ferdinand VII, who was placed under house arrest in France. The French emperor then put his brother, Joseph Bonaparte, on the throne of Spain, resulting in a nationalist uprising by Spanish patriots in March. Opposition to Napoleon's pretensions in Spain came from guerrilla units, who were soon joined by British forces under the command of the duke of Wellington. News of these events reached the Americas in the summer of 1808, producing a flurry of events in the Gulf South region that, among other things, ultimately resulted in the United States obtaining Florida and the destruction and abandonment of East Texas, opening up the area for Anglo settlement after Mexico gained its independence from Spain.

The movement of Saint-Domingue refugees from Cuba to New Orleans in 1809 was the first outcome of Napoleon's invasion of Spain the prior year. The second consequence occurred in the summer of 1810 when the residents of the westernmost districts of West Florida rebelled against Spain, resulting in annexation by the United States. Whereas many Anglos had settled in the region during the era of British control, most had left Florida after its return to Spain in 1783. Following the 1787 edict allowing Anglo Protestants to settle on Spanish territory, a few thousand Americans moved to the area, for land was easily obtainable through Spanish land grants, and the Spanish government—led by Commandant Carlos de Grand Pré—provided the region with stability and order. Following the Louisiana Purchase, the eastern border with Florida, as with the western boundary with Texas, was disputed between Spain and the United States. President Jefferson insisted that the border between Louisiana and Florida lay not at Spain's claim of the Mississippi River, but at the Perdido River, the boundary between the French and Spanish colonies before 1763. At Jefferson's instigation, in February 1804 Congress passed the Mobile Act, claiming the territory between the Mississippi and the Perdido for the United States. Spanish protests resulted in American troops taking no direct action to seize the land, but in the summer of 1804 a group of Anglos, led by three Kemper brothers from Virginia, crossed the border from Mississippi and tried and failed to instigate a rebellion in Spanish West Florida. Nonetheless, the president remained optimistic; following Napoleon's 1808 invasion of Spain, Jefferson notified Secretary of State James Madison that soon "a moment may occur favorable" for the United States to obtain possession of the disputed land.

Ultimately, the Anglo settlers in the region took matters into their own hands to transfer the region from Spain to the United States. In the years since the Louisiana Purchase the Anglo residents had gradually become dissatisfied with the local Spanish government, as the liberal land granting policies were tightened and crime and general instability were on the rise. (The proximity of the unpoliced international boundary line allowed bandits, such as the Kemper gang, to easily cross at will.) Following the death of the well-liked Grand Pré in April 1809, and the arrival of his despised successor, Carlos Dehault De lassus, a group of Anglo landowners used the crisis in Spain as an excuse for holding a convention of fourteen delegates for the purpose of securing peace in the area. Although De lassus permitted the convention to meet in Baton Rouge in August 1810, during which time the delegates made no attempt to subvert the laws of Spain or overthrow the local administration, West Florida's Governor Folch suspected treason and decided to lead Spanish troops from Pensacola to quell the uprising.

Upon learning of Folch's decision, the convention issued a preliminary declaration of independence and organized a militia to attack the Spanish fort at Baton Rouge, which fell to the attackers within minutes on September 23. Three days later a newly reconvened convention formally declared independence, and in October a constitution modeled on that of the United States was adopted for the independent West Florida Republic. Immediately the new nation appealed to Jefferson's successor, President Madison, for annexation. Madison quickly responded by officially proclaiming that the Louisiana Purchase had included West Florida and by ordering Governor Claiborne to take possession of the area between the Mississippi and the Pearl River. On December 10, American troops entered Baton Rouge and replaced the flag of the West Florida Republic—a single white star in a blue field—with the Stars and Stripes. Although a few convention members raised a body of men, led by Reuben Kemper, to extend the territory all the way to the Perdido River, President Madison preferred not to stir up tensions with Spain any more than necessary and the plot fizzled in the face of opposing American troops.

Just as the events in West Florida began to unfold, a popular insurgency led by Father Miguel Hidalgo y Costilla broke out in Querétaro, about two hundred miles north of Mexico City, which would affect the entire Western Hemisphere. Hidalgo and his creole associates hoped to free Mexico from Spanish rule by advancing a radical agenda that called for social and economic justice, in addition to proclaiming the abolition of slavery and death to slaveowners who refused to free their chattel. The conspirators assembled an army of lower-class Mexicans and Indians, who sacked the important mining town of Guanajuato in late September 1810, exacting vengeance on the lives and property of the wealthy citizenry. The horrifying specter of social revolution sent a wave of fear through the upper classes of New Spain and quickly undermined Mexican creole support for the revolutionaries. Nonetheless, the rebellion was not thwarted until January 1811, when royalist forces won a decisive victory outside Mexico City. Hidalgo and the other rebel leaders were eventually captured and executed, their heads being displayed on poles throughout the countryside. News of the Hidalgo revolt reached Texas and crossed into Louisiana, exciting various groups who were interested in overturning the status quo.

Inspired by the news from Mexico and the political unrest in nearby West Florida, bondsmen residing among the sugar plantations at the German Coast rose up in the largest slave rebellion in the history of the United States just one month after American troops took possession of the Florida parishes. The uprising took place on the east bank plantations of the Mississippi River, where fifteen hundred slaves—more than half of whom had recently arrived from Africa, the Caribbean, or the eastern United States—greatly outnumbered the three hundred French and Anglo settlers. The rebellion began on the evening of January 8, 1811, when a group of creole slaves attacked the plantation of Colonel Manuel Andry, wounding the planter and killing his son while seizing a cache of public arms stored on the plantation. Fortified by liquor and well armed, the slaves proceeded downriver toward New Orleans, burning three plantations in the process and gathering about three hundred comrades, creoles and Africans alike. While the slaves rested at the Fortier plantation in Orleans Parish the following day, various groups of white citizens—including a detachment of army regulars and two companies of volunteers from New Orleans serving under General Wade Hampton—as well as a number of free people of color gathered their forces and converged on the rebels. Confronted by the white troops, the slaves retreated upstream to Bernard Bernoudy's plantation, where they made their stand with "colours displayed and full of arrogance." The free forces routed the slaves, killing dozens while wounding and capturing many others. Within a week local authorities in St. Charles and in New Orleans began interrogating prisoners, holding trials, and performing executions. At least thirty slaves were hung or shot to death, with their heads being placed on stakes along the levee "as a terrible example to all who would disturb the public tranquility in the future." In the wake of the slave revolt Claiborne urged the legislature to reestablish the free colored militia, citing their performance during the uprising as proof of their loyalty. Following Louisiana's entrance to the Union in 1812, the state legislature passed an act allowing for the formation of the Free Colored Battalion under the guidance of white officers.

Less than two weeks after the slave revolt on the Mississippi, sympathizers of Father Hidalgo, led by Juan Bautista de las Casas, seized power in Texas by orchestrating uprisings in San Antonio and Nacogdoches. By March 1811, however, royalists overthrew las Casas and effectively regained control of the province. A few rebel sympathizers, led by José Bernardo Gutiérrez de Lara, a rancher and merchant from northern Mexico, slipped across the international border into Louisiana and traveled to Washington. Arriving at the capital in December 1811, Gutiérrez met with President Madison and Secretary of State James Monroe, who, while not officially approving of his call for the overthrow of Spanish Texas, provided him with money and transportation by sea to New Orleans and a letter of introduction to Claiborne. The governor then sent the rebel to Natchitoches in the company of William Shaler, a special agent who was to monitor his activities. Arriving on the Louisiana-Texas frontier in April 1812, Gutiérrez, with Shaler's full support, began to gather volunteers for an invasion of Texas.

By August, Gutiérrez had assembled more than one hundred men, most of them Anglos, like Augustus William Magee, a West Point graduate and former lieutenant in the U.S. Army, and entered Texas at the head of the self-styled Republican Army of the North. The force, commanded by Magee, quickly captured Nacogdoches, where not a single civilian nor Indian answered the Spanish commander's appeal for volunteers to defend the town. The republicans then headed to La Bahía near the Texas coast and took control of the presidio there without a struggle. In February 1813, following Magee's mysteriously timed death, Samuel Kemper, one of the principals of the West Florida rebellion, assumed command. The republican army defeated the royalist forces outside San Antonio the following month. On April 2 the royalists surrendered Béxar to the invaders, who shockingly executed a group of officials, including Governor Manuel Salcedo and Lieutenant Colonel Herrera, a few days later. The republicans, following the example of the West Floridians, then proclaimed the independence of Texas and promulgated its first constitution. Their glory was short-lived, however, for a large, well-disciplined royalist army, commanded by Joaquín de Arredondo, marched upon San Antonio and crushed the unorganized republican mob in August. The victors then unleashed a wave of vengeance in Texas, using confiscation, detention, and execution to restore royal authority. The royalists did their work so thoroughly that the Euroamerican residents of Nacogdoches and East Texas abandoned their homes and ranches and fled to Louisiana for safety, while the population of La Bahía and San Antonio were severely reduced. Following a century of existence, the disastrous civil war in Texas returned the Spanish colony almost exclusively to Indian hands.

Mississippi Territory

While the international situation, along with American filibusters, resulted in the Spaniards virtually abandoning East Texas, Anglo pressures east of the Mississippi allowed the Americans to obtain even more land at the expense of Spain and the region's Native Americans. In the Mississippi Territory the peaceful acquisition of Louisiana prepared the way for a huge influx of settlers by securely opening the Mississippi River to western commerce. In order to encourage the migration, the federal government further developed the Natchez Trace and traffic grew considerably during the first decade of the nineteenth century. By 1810 the population of the Natchez district, lying mainly along the Mississippi River, had quadrupled since the turn of the century to reach thirty thousand people, just under half being slaves, as cotton was the region's principal crop. On the other hand, in the Tombigbee district, the ranching and farming area located just north of Spanish Mobile, the population only doubled to reach two thousand residents, few of whom were enslaved. The most impressive gains, however, took place in the newly opened Tennessee Valley in northeastern Mississippi Territory. Anglo settlement in the region began in 1804 when John Hunt moved his family from Tennessee to the springs that would soon bare his name, and by 1810 the newly created Madison County contained over forty-five hundred individuals, one fifth of them slaves. To govern the rapidly growing territory, President Jefferson appointed Robert Williams, a North Carolinian who already held office as land commissioner in Natchez, as Claiborne's replacement in 1804. Five years later, after struggling continually with the territorial legislature, Williams resigned and was replaced by Jefferson's fellow Virginian and Republican Party member, David Holmes. In contrast to his predecessor, Holmes worked well with the legislature while displaying a style perfectly suited to govern the infant territory, where politics was rooted in personalities rather than principles.

The rapid development of the Mississippi Territory caused American officials to reiterate the claim that the land between the Pearl and Perdido Rivers was part of the Louisiana Purchase and belonged to the United States. On April 14, 1812—just four days following Louisiana's entrance into the Union—Congress incorporated the region, consisting of about two thousand or so French creoles and their slaves living between Pass Christian and Mobile, into the Mississippi Territory. American forces, however, made no move to take possession of the area, due to the continued presence of 130 Spanish troops at Fort Charlotte. Action was further delayed by the United States' declaration of war against Great Britain in June, partly in response to British support of the Native Americans in the Ohio Valley, as well as attacks on neutral American shipping during the ongoing war against Napoleonic France. Following an uneasy truce of nearly a year, in February 1813 Secretary of War John Armstrong finally ordered General Wilkinson to move from New Orleans to take possession of Mobile. Two months later Wilkinson arrived at Mobile Bay with eight hundred men and five gunboats, meeting with four hundred American troops from Fort Stoddert, located just upstream. Spanish commander Cayetano Pérez quickly surrendered the fort without a fight, and Wilkinson allowed the garrison to evacuate to Pensacola. Luis de Onís, the Spanish ambassador in Washington, believed that his country could hope to retain Florida only through diplomacy and therefore forbid any counterattack from the troops at Pensacola. Instead, Onís made only a mild protest to the U.S. government concerning the capture of Mobile. It would not be long before the Americans proved Onís wrong, forcing him to cede the rest of Florida to the United States within a decade.

The influx of Anglos and their slaves into the Mississippi Territory initially provided the region's Native Americans with opportunities for profit. At the same time, it put pressure on the tribes to give up more land to the United States. By the early nineteenth century about thirty-five hundred Chickasaws resided in four districts located just west of the Tombigbee

River. Most of the Chickasaws had accepted parts of the American civilization policy, with the tribal men becoming stock raisers and the women raising crops, including cotton, that they spun into cloth. Whereas many Chickasaws entered the market economy and sold their goods to the incoming Anglos, mixed-bloods such as George Colbert, who American officials recognized as the official tribal chief, also opened profitable stands and ferries along the Natchez Trace. Nonetheless, the Chickasaws quickly ran up a huge debt to various trading firms and were forced to sell land to resolve the situation. In June 1805 American commissioners met with tribal leaders and negotiated the Treaty of Chickasaw Nation, in which the tribe ceded the fertile lands northeast of the Tennessee River—where John Hunt had recently settled—for $20,000. Half of the money went for the liquidation of their debts to Forbes and Company, the firm that succeeded Panton, Leslie, and Company as the main commercial traders of the Gulf South following Panton's death in 1801. The American commissioners, using a method that would soon become commonplace, bribed Chief Colbert with $1,000 in cash to use his influence to obtain Chickasaw approval for the treaty.

The twenty thousand or so Choctaws were in a situation similar to their Chickasaw brethren. By the first decade of the nineteenth century, most Choctaws, full-bloods as well as mixed-bloods, had taken up ranching and commercial farming and were well situated to sell the Anglos who arrived in the Mississippi Territory all the cattle, horses, and pigs they needed. However, as the sons of Euroamerican traders, Choctaw mixed-bloods were especially well placed to expand on the entrepreneurial efforts of their fathers. David Folsom, son of Nathaniel, attended an Anglo school that enabled him to take over his father's tavern on the Natchez Trace. Greenwood LeFlore left his father's plantation to live with an Anglo family in Nashville before returning home, while Peter Pitchlynn lived for a time with Andrew Jackson's good friend John Coffee in his home in Alabama. Whereas these mixed-bloods had the preparation to oversee taverns, stands, and cotton plantations manned by black slaves, important full-bloods in all three Choctaw divisions—who were also the kin of the mixed-blood entrepreneurs—became commercial livestock raisers who realized the market, rather than hunting, was the way of the future. For example, Mushulatubbee, chief of the Eastern district, owned livestock and slaves and was related to the mixed-blood Pitchlynn family. Pushmataha, the Sixtowns chief, was a member of the Jouzon mixed-blood clan, while Chief Puckshunubbee of the Western district was related to the Robert

Cole family. Due to their extended kinship ties, the Choctaws were able to avoid any serious conflict between the mixed- and full-bloods during the era. Despite the conversion from hunting to livestock raising, however, the Choctaws still owed Forbes and Company $48,000 by November 1805, when they ceded more than 4 million acres to the United States in the Treaty of Mount Dexter to pay off their debt. However, the Choctaws wisely sold the Americans a broad strip of infertile pinelands in southwestern Mississippi, just north of the border with Spanish West Florida, reserving for themselves the rich grazing lands in the center of the territory.

Internal Creek Conflict and War with the United States

In contrast to the Chickasaws and Choctaws, the division between mixed- and full-bloods, coupled with the Euroamericans' constant pressure for land and roads through their territory, caused the Creek Nation to erupt in a civil struggle that ultimately led to an incredibly destructive war with the United States. Following the escapades of Bowles and his Indian allies, the Upper and Lower Creeks, along with the Seminoles of Spanish West Florida, owed Forbes and Company over $100,000. In May 1804, with the approval of American and Spanish officials, Seminole and Lower Creek leaders formally ceded over 1 million acres lying between the Apalachicola and Wakulla Rivers to the company to cancel most of the debt. Forbes and Company also agreed to establish a new store at Prospect Bluff, located about forty miles from the Apalachicola's mouth. This treaty angered many tribesmen, for the land had been sold in order to cancel the huge debts the mixed-blood planters had incurred by purchasing goods from Forbes to sell at a profit to full-blooded Creek and Seminole hunters. Soon thereafter American officials began to pressure the Creeks to cede all their land east of the Ocmulgee River in Georgia, as well as giving the United States permission for a road to be built through the Lower Creek towns to Fort Stoddert on the Mobile River. Although William McIntosh, the Lower Creek mixed-blood who headed the delegation that traveled to the capital in November 1805 to discuss the matter, initially opposed the settlement, he signed the Treaty of Washington when the Americans promised that Creeks would have the sole right to operate ferries, inns, and taverns on the road, realizing that he and his mixed-blood supporters would personally profit from the pact. As a result of his acquiescence to the treaty, however, the Creek National Council removed McIntosh from office.

Work began on the so-called Federal Road in 1806, and it was completed in November 1811. The heavy flow of traffic on the road raised tensions between the Creeks and the United States, as did the blatant violation of the treaty by Americans who established stands and ferries along river crossings. Nonetheless, mixed-blood Lower Creek planters realized a profit from the Federal Road, as Agent Hawkins made sure they were paid for providing supplies during construction.

A drought that began in 1804 and lasted throughout the first decade of the nineteenth century also exacerbated the growing gulf between the mixed- and full-bloods. Traditionally, poorer Creeks relied on more fortunate kinsmen to help them through tough times, but those mixed-bloods who had adopted the civilization program had gradually resisted depositing crop surpluses into the communal supplies, choosing instead to sell them to the Americans. By 1811, as the drought wore on and the crops continued to fail, many Creeks had decided that the United States' civilization policy was only serving to dispossess them of their lands and undermine their sovereignty as a people, all for the benefit of a few tribesmen—mainly mixed-bloods—who had the resources and connections to profit from it.

Therefore, many tribesmen responded favorably to the message delivered by Tecumseh, a Shawnee warrior, at the Upper Creek town of Tuckabatchee in September 1811. Tecumseh told the Creek gathering that he had formed a strong alliance of Indian followers in the Ohio Valley—who obtained weapons from British traders in Canada—and with his brother, the prophet Tenskwatawa, had launched a religious and political movement destined to return the land to indigenous people. Following the conference, Tecumseh traveled throughout the Upper and Lower Creek towns and invited the tribesmen to signal their acceptance of the pan-Indian alliance by accepting the war pipe and a bundle of redsticks that he carried with him. Although most of the Lower Creek towns rejected Tecumseh's message, by spring 1812 a group of Upper Creeks and Seminoles responded favorably to the Shawnee call for resistance and killed a few American travelers on the Federal Road. Although the rebels, who became known as Red Sticks for the red-painted war clubs they wielded, were for the most part full-bloods, Josiah Francis (Hillis Hadjo) and William Weatherford were among the many mixed-bloods that also joined the uprising. Determined to have the criminals punished, Agent Hawkins induced William McIntosh and others to raise detachments of pro-American Creeks, who sought out the Red Sticks and killed them on the spot. In response to these murders, the

Creek civil war began in earnest, as the Red Sticks launched a full-scale campaign aimed at the wealthy mixed-bloods, killing many leaders and destroying spinning wheels and cattle, the symbols of the American civilization plan. By July 1813 the Red Sticks had surrounded Tuckabatchee, where three hundred Upper Creeks had taken refuge from the attacks.

As the Red Sticks besieged Tuckabatchee, a group of prophets—Jim Boy, Hillis Hadjo, and Peter McQueen—traveled to Pensacola and pressured the Spanish governor, Mateo González Manrique, to provide them with gunpowder, food, and blankets. Alerted to the transaction, Anglo militiamen and mixed-blood Creeks attacked the homeward-bound Red Sticks north of the international boundary line at Burnt Corn Creek and made off with their packhorses. Following this ambush, the Red Stick war chiefs and prophets could no longer restrain their warriors from seeking vengeance on the Americans and their allies. Therefore, the Red Stick leaders planned an assault on Fort Mims, a makeshift settlement of about four hundred Anglos and pro-American Creeks, located on the Tensaw River in the Tombigbee district. On August 30 about eight hundred Red Sticks, led by William Weatherford, attacked Fort Mims and killed more than half of its inhabitants while losing many of their own compatriots. The Fort Mims massacre, however, would cost the Red Sticks far more than the lives of their warriors, for the battle guaranteed that the United States and the land-hungry Anglos in the American strongholds that surrounded the Creeks would seek revenge and intervene in the indigenous civil struggle.

Unlike the French and Spanish, who failed in their eighteenth-century attacks upon the interior Indians' homelands, the United States had the men, material, and firm government support to successfully carry out an invasion of Creek territory. The Anglos in the states and territories immediately responded to the many calls for a war to "exterminate the Creek Nation and abettors." On September 20 the Tennessee governor ordered Andrew Jackson, a general in the state militia, to raise thirty-five hundred volunteers "to repel an approaching invasion . . . and to afford aid and relief to the suffering citizens of the Mississippi Territory." On October 7, although pale and weak from a bullet wound suffered in a barroom gunfight, Jackson took command of his army and marched to the Tennessee River, where he erected Fort Deposit, a stockade that was to serve him as a depot for his supplies. Jackson then cut a road through the mountains toward the Coosa River, where he established his base at Fort Strother. Jackson's troops destroyed the nearby Creek town of Tallushatchee, then a few days later defeated a force of over one thousand Red Sticks who had surrounded the pro-American Creek town of Talladega. Soon thereafter, the Hillabee town on the Tallapoosa River surrendered to Jackson, only to be attacked by eastern Tennessee militiamen who had not received word of the capitulation. Georgia forces, commanded by General John Floyd, supplemented the Tennessee victories by destroying the Tallapoosa town of Autosee in late November. The following month General Ferdinand L. Claiborne led Mississippi Territory militiamen into Creek territory from the south, where they burned William Weatherford's Holy Ground village on the Lower Alabama River, cutting the Red Sticks off from gaining supplies at Pensacola. The American invasion ground to halt at the end of December due to lack of supplies and the termination of most of the militiamen's terms of enlistment. Nonetheless, by this time the American forces had killed nearly one thousand Red Stick warriors while destroying a good part of their food supply.

In the face of the American attacks, the remaining core of the Red Sticks—about one thousand warriors, along with four hundred women and children—took refuge at the town of Tohopeka, a new settlement established by the prophetic leaders of the rebellion at Horseshoe Bend on the Tallapoosa River. Surrounded on three sides by the river, the Creeks constructed a sturdy breastwork on the land side, making Tohopeka an exceedingly well defended town. Receiving reinforcements from Tennessee, Jackson moved toward Horseshoe Bend in March 1814 with about twenty-seven hundred troops, five hundred Cherokees, and one hundred friendly Creeks. On the morning of March 27, Jackson positioned his troops opposite the barricade and opened fire with four cannons. At the same time his Indian troops crossed from the other side of the Tallapoosa and set fire to buildings near the shore, attacking the Red Sticks at the rear of their fortification. Jackson took advantage of the diversion and stormed the breastwork, enveloping the Red Sticks in a deadly pincer movement. Over the next five hours Jackson's troops killed eight hundred Creeks and captured another 350, effectively putting an end to all Creek resistance.

In the aftermath of the Battle of Horseshoe Bend, the remaining Red Sticks fled to Spanish Florida to join their Seminole kinsmen while other Creek refugees crowded into the Lower Creek towns, where the American army provided them with food and shelter. For the most part, the Upper Creek settlements had been completely abandoned. Following the battle the American army moved downstream near the juncture of the Coosa and the Tallapoosa, where the American flag was raised over the decrepit

Fort Toulouse, which was rebuilt and renamed Fort Jackson. In August 1814 Creek leaders convened at the fort and met with Jackson, who forced the headmen—most of whom had remained loyal to the United States—to cede 23 million acres in southern Georgia and central Alabama as reparations for American expenses incurred in the war. The Creeks and Agent Hawkins wrote letters to the secretary of war protesting the Treaty of Fort Jackson, but to no avail. As a result, Hawkins resigned his position as Indian agent in February 1815, only to die the following year in his home at the Creek Agency. Jackson, on the other hand, was rewarded by being appointed a major general in the U.S. Army and placed in command of the Seventh Military District, consisting of Tennessee, Louisiana, and the Mississippi Territory.

The British Invasion and the Battle of New Orleans

Jackson had little time to celebrate his appointment, for the British were making preparations for an invasion of the United States from the Gulf of Mexico. In early 1814 Vice Admiral Sir Alexander Forrester Inglis Cochrane, in command of the entire British North American naval station, put forth an invasion plan which, in his opinion, would not need more than a few thousand troops, for he was certain the attackers would be joined by Indians, slaves, and the Spaniards in Florida. Cochrane was also certain that New Orleans could easily be taken, as he believed the French creoles would turn on the Americans and welcome the British liberation. Planning to invade through Pensacola and Mobile, in May 1814 Cochrane sent Captain Hugh Pigot to Spanish West Florida to begin rounding up Indian and slave allies. Pigot, along with an interpreter named George Woodbine, established a camp near the Forbes and Company store at Prospect Bluff on the Apalachicola River and immediately took steps to obtain food and arms for the Seminoles and Red Stick Creeks who had sought refuge in the area following the Battle of Horseshoe Bend. In June, Pigot departed from Prospect Bluff and sailed for Nassau, where he made a report to Cochrane strongly recommending a British attack in the Gulf, and made arrangements to ship additional supplies and arms to the Indian allies. After receiving Pigot's favorable account, Cochrane sent Lieutenant Colonel Edward Nicholls to West Florida with two naval vessels, a small force of one hundred troops, and a huge supply of arms and ammunition. In August Nicholls first landed at Prospect Bluff, where he issued several proclamations stating that all slaves who joined him would be freed and all Indians who took up arms against the United States would regain the lands taken from them. Several hundred runaway slaves from Georgia answered Nicholls's call, as did two thousand or so Creeks and Seminoles. They gathered around Prospect Bluff, assisting Woodbine in the construction of a well-defended fort protected by artillery. Nicholls then sailed for Pensacola, where Governor Manrique allowed the British force to occupy Fort Barrancas at the entrance of the bay since he soon expected an American invasion.

Having learned of the British operations in Florida, General Jackson moved his troops to Mobile only two weeks after signing the treaty with the Creeks. Jackson's force, however, did not arrive in time to help American troops at Fort Bowyer, near the mouth of Mobile Bay, defeat a British amphibious assault from Pensacola in early September. Now convinced that the British planned their invasion with Pensacola as a base of operation, Jackson decided to invade Spanish Florida. Jackson left Mobile in late October with four thousand men, including regular troops, Tennessee volunteers, and several hundred Choctaw and Chickasaw warriors. The American force camped on the west side of Pensacola and demanded the surrender of the Spanish forts from Governor Manrique and the immediate evacuation of the British from Fort Barrancas. The governor rejected the demands, and Jackson attacked the town on November 7, surprising the Spaniards by moving his troops around Pensacola and attacking from the east. Resistance collapsed within minutes of the American assault and Manrique soon surrendered the city and its fortifications. The following day the British destroyed Fort Barrancas and sailed for Prospect Bluff. Jackson departed the defenseless Pensacola soon thereafter and returned to Mobile, certain that he had seriously disrupted the overall British strategy in the Gulf.

Jackson was correct, for the defeat at Mobile and the expulsion from Pensacola forced the British to change their invasion plans and target New Orleans directly as the point of invasion. On September 18, 1814, the British had launched an armada from Plymouth, England, consisting of sixty ships and about eleven thousand seasoned troops, many of whom had fought the French in Spain and Portugal under the command of the duke of Wellington. The fleet first sailed for Jamaica, where they met Admiral Cochrane, who was to direct operations from aboard his flagship, and then headed toward New Orleans on November 26. As the British force made its way north, General Jackson was en route from Mobile to New

Orleans with about two thousand American regular troops. Fearful of a British-Indian attack from Spanish Florida, Jackson sent Major Uriah Blue and a detachment of soldiers to attack the British base at Prospect Bluff. Although Blue was only able to destroy a few Red Stick camps near Pensacola before being forced to retreat because of a lack of supplies, his actions served to prevent Nicholls and his Indian allies from joining the British attack on New Orleans.

Jackson arrived in New Orleans on December 1 and immediately began to survey the situation and raise more men for the upcoming battle. Although the Americans at first doubted the loyalty of the French creoles—causing the general to place the city under martial law—the residents' hatred of the British and the belief that the invaders planned on initiating a slave uprising caused them to volunteer willingly to Jackson, who gladly accepted several hundred Louisiana militia troops into his army. Jackson also agreed to take on the services of the Free Colored Battalion, which now included a few Saint-Domingue refugees from Cuba. Volunteers from Tennessee and Kentucky arrived in New Orleans throughout December, as did about one hundred allied Choctaw warriors. Finally, despite his initial misgivings, Jackson acquired a pardon for Jean Lafitte and his Baratarians—who had only recently been arrested for smuggling—in return for their services, most important of which was the huge cache of arms and ammunition the pirates had at their disposal. Jackson rounded out his supplies by obtaining much needed artillery from the local U.S. naval depot. By early January 1815 General Jackson had about four thousand troops under his command.

The British armada arrived off the Louisiana coast on December 12 and, after defeating a small group of American gunboats, took possession of Lake Borgne, enabling them to use any of the numerous bayous and canals that approached the Mississippi River. After scouting the area, the British chose Bayou Bienvenue as their route, but shallow water forced them to row all troops and supplies for thirty miles in open boats during rainy, cold weather before reaching the swampy mainland. The ferrying operation began on December 17 and lasted six days, during which time about two thousand wet, cold, and demoralized British troops were disembarked. The attackers quickly seized the plantation of Jacques Villeré—a French creole who had lost the gubernatorial election to Claiborne in 1812—about ten miles downstream from the city and made it their headquarters. Learning of the British advance, on December 23 Jackson hurried troops southward, only to be repelled by the invaders, who decided not to consider any further advance until their entire force could be landed. Two days later Lieutenant General Sir Edward Michael Pakenham, the duke of Wellington's brother-in-law, arrived on the scene to take command of the British troops. Over the next two weeks, as the American forces established a line, reinforced with breastworks and artillery, on the Rodriguez Canal a few miles upstream from Pakenham's headquarters, the British landed another six thousand troops and prepared for battle.

By January 8, 1815, when Pakenham decided to launch his attack, British troop morale was exceedingly low because of their lack of adequate shelter, low rations, and rampant sickness among the soldiers. Dividing his troops into five groups for the assault—including a small force on the west bank of the Mississippi River—Pakenham led an attack across open fields upon Jackson's well-constructed line soon after sunrise. The American artillery opened fire when the British reached a range of about five hundred yards. With excellent discipline, the British columns continued to advance despite heavy losses. Jackson ordered his rifle companies to open fire when the enemy reached about three hundred yards, resulting in the deaths of many more attackers, including Pakenham and many of his officers. Thirty minutes after the assault began, General John Lambert, now in command of the British army, concluded the battle was lost and ordered a withdrawal. The British had suffered over two thousand casualties in the Battle of New Orleans, including just under three hundred men killed in action. The victorious Americans had only six men killed and seven wounded. The British forces remained in camp for ten more days before departing for Lake Borgne, from which they sailed into the Gulf of Mexico.

Learning of the British withdrawal, Jackson withdrew the greatest portion of his army to New Orleans, where the victory was celebrated on January 23. Jackson, however, feared the British might return and refused to suspend martial law in New Orleans until March 13, when news finally arrived that a peace treaty had been signed between Great Britain and the United States at the Belgian town of Ghent on December 24, 1814, two weeks prior to the fateful battle. Jackson was correct in questioning the intentions of the British, for Cochrane's force assaulted and captured Fort Bowyer at Mobile Bay in early February before learning of the Treaty of Ghent and withdrawing from the coast altogether. In June, Lieutenant Colonel Nicholls and the British troops abandoned Prospect Bluff on the Apalachicola River, as did most of the Creeks and Seminoles who had gathered in the area.

The Great Migration

Jackson's victories ended the threats from both the Creeks and the British, and thus allowed Anglo Protestants to pour confidently into the Gulf South during the final half of the decade, resulting in the establishment of firm American hegemony over the region by 1821. The migrants were driven, in part, by the end of the Napoleonic Wars in Europe, which brought rising commodity prices and invigorated opportunities to profit from the use of slave labor. Free migrants to the Gulf South, as well as planters and farmers already living in the area, responded by expanding their cultivation of cotton and sugar. Cotton production in the region almost tripled, rising from 54,000 bales in 1815 to 160,000 five years later. Sugar cultivation increased, too, as established Louisiana planters improved their productivity and new ones broadened the area of production to the north and the southwest. As a result, the amount of sugar arriving in New Orleans rose from twelve thousand hogsheads in 1815 to thirty thousand in 1818. The invention of the steamboat greatly facilitated the enormous growth in cotton and sugar production. Following the first steamboat's arrival on the Mississippi River in 1814, the number of vessels docking in New Orleans rose from fewer than twenty in 1815 to more than two hundred in 1820.

The great migration of planters and slaves—mainly from other southern states—caused the western section of the Mississippi Territory's population to more than double, reaching seventy-five thousand people by 1820, nearly half residing in the Natchez district. Thirty-three thousand bondspeople lived in Mississippi by the end of the decade, most of them toiling on cotton plantations near Natchez, where two-thirds of the inhabitants were unfree laborers. Because of the rapid influx of settlers, in March 1817 Congress passed an act that provided for admission of the territory's western half as the state of Mississippi and the reorganization of the rest as the territory of Alabama. In August, Mississippi territorial delegates authorized a constitution similar in nature to Louisiana's except that the governor was to be popularly elected. The following month the people chose David Holmes to continue as governor, and on December 10, 1817, President James Monroe signed the act admitting Mississippi into the Union as the nation's twentieth state. Alabama's population increased even more dramatically than Mississippi's during the period, as the number of free people rose eleven fold, from nine thousand in 1810 to ninety-nine thousand a decade later. The slave population gained at an even higher rate, growing from twenty-five hundred to forty-seven thousand in ten years. By August 1819 a convention at Huntsville had drafted a constitution more liberal than those of the surrounding states, as it removed all property qualifications for voting and for holding office. Congress readily approved the document, and Alabama became a state on December 14, 1819.

Many of the Anglos and slaves who migrated to Alabama established plantations in the fertile lands ceded by the Creeks in the Treaty of Fort Jackson. Following the War of 1812, however, American commissioners, led by General Jackson, became even more aggressive in extracting territory from the Gulf South Indians for the use of land hungry Anglos and their slaves. In September 1816 Jackson used bribes of land and money to obtain George and Levi Colbert's approval of a treaty in which the Chickasaws ceded territory between the Tombigbee and Tennessee Rivers to the United States. One month later the Choctaws sold their remaining ten thousand acres east of the Tombigbee River in return for an annuity of $6,000, to be paid for twenty years. Not yet satisfied, in August 1818 Jackson negotiated a second treaty with the Chickasaws through the Colbert brothers that turned over all the land between the Tennessee and Mississippi Rivers to the Americans, thus opening up the Chickasaw Bluffs for the establishment of the city of Memphis. In exchange for both Chickasaw land cessions, the United States agreed to provide the tribe with $420,000, to be paid in annual installments for twenty years.

Whereas the Choctaws, in contrast to the Creeks, had been able to avoid civil strife before the War of 1812, following the Battle of New Orleans the tribe divided into factions, leading to even more territorial cessions. Although many full-bloods had joined their mixed-blood brethren in entering the market economy, most of the former group remained devoted to the Choctaws' traditional political arrangement. Eastern district chief Mushulatubbee, along with Puckshunubbee and Pushmataha, his Western and Sixtowns counterparts, insisted that leadership positions should continue to be inherited through the female line, that each of the three divisions retain autonomy, and that chiefs would distribute goods and favors to their supporters. Opposition came from progressive mixed-bloods such as David Folsom and Greenwood LeFlore, who wanted to graft certain aspects of the American system onto Choctaw culture. Namely, these men sought a constitutional government that established a council of chiefs over the entire nation, supported private property ownership and the establishment of a police force, and promoted inheritance through the male line. In hope of furthering their agenda, in 1818 the mixed-bloods welcomed Protestant missionaries from the American Board of Foreign

Missions to Choctaw territory, where they established Eliot Mission on the Yalobusha River. The missionaries immediately formed a strong alliance with Folsom and LeFlore, as the mission farm and school reflected the mixed-bloods' desire for material improvement and for the accumulation of private property.

Threatened by the progressives' assault on their authority, the traditionalists proposed that the Choctaws should move across the Mississippi into the Arkansas Territory, where the real leaders could govern unchallenged. As a result of the Choctaws' suggestion, Secretary of War John C. Calhoun authorized Jackson and Thomas Hinds to discuss an exchange of land with the tribe. Although Folsom and his supporters tried to block the negotiations, in October 1820 the three traditionalist chiefs signed the Treaty of Doak's Stand, in which the Choctaws ceded 6 million acres—nearly one-third of their remaining territory—of extremely fertile land between the Mississippi and the Yazoo in return for 13 million acres between the Red and Arkansas Rivers in the Arkansas Territory. The treaty also continued the American civilization program by agreeing to further fund schools as well as promising to grant "enlightened" tribesmen U.S. citizenship in the future. The Anglo residents of Mississippi were jubilant over the treaty's terms and named its new capital city on the Pearl River after Jackson and the county in which it was located after Hinds. Despite the fact that few Choctaws relocated across the Mississippi following the ratification of the agreement, the Treaty of Doak's Stand would provide the model for the future removal of the remaining Indians of the Gulf South.

Little did Jackson and Hinds realize, however, that nearly five thousand American settlers had already established residences on the land granted to the Choctaws west of the Mississippi River, thus forcing a renegotiation of the treaty in 1825, for following the War of 1812 many Anglos and their slaves moved to Arkansas (mainly from Missouri), causing the population to increase to thirteen thousand whites and one thousand bondspeople by 1820. As a result of the migration, in March 1819 Arkansas became a separate territory after Missouri applied for statehood. Within a year its citizens had elected a territorial legislature and a delegate to represent them in Congress. In 1820 the U.S. government made its presence felt by constructing Fort Smith on the Arkansas River. In 1821 the territorial government moved its capital from Arkansas Post to Little Rock, which was closer to the center of the state and the locus of its population.

As with the tribes east of the Mississippi River, the influx of Anglos and slaves put enormous pressures on the Indians of the Arkansas Territory to cede their lands to the United States. In August 1818 American officials forced the four hundred remaining Quapaws to relinquish their claims to 30 million acres between the Arkansas and the Red Rivers, allowing them to remain on a small reserve surrounding their three towns. Continued conflict between the Cherokees and the Osages in northwestern Arkansas led William Lovely in September 1818 to negotiate an agreement with the latter tribe in which they ceded most of their remaining land in the territory to the Americans. At the same time, however, about three thousand Cherokees—who American officials considered to be more civilized than the Osages—were allowed to maintain their reservation between the Arkansas and the White Rivers. A different group of Cherokees, led by a chief named Duwali, along with some Shawnees, Delawares, and Kickapoos, moved to southwestern Arkansas after the Treaty of Ghent and set up farms and ranches on the north bank of the Red River. Although the emigrant Indians formed an anti-Osage alliance with the local Kadohadachos and Hasinais, the newcomers came into conflict with the one thousand Americans who had also recently settled in Miller County, Arkansas Territory, established north of the Red River. Whiskey peddlers continually hounded the Cherokees and their allies, forcing the two thousand or so tribesmen in 1821 to move into Spanish Texas, where they settled in the empty region north of Nacogdoches.

The great migration also affected Louisiana, as the state's population doubled to over 150,000 residents by 1820. Whereas the white and slave numbers grew twice as large—to seventy-two thousand and sixty-nine thousand, respectively—with settlers arriving predominantly from the United States, the free people of color's population rose more moderately, from seventy-five hundred to eleven thousand, mainly through natural increase. Anglos poured into New Orleans and the relatively undeveloped sections of Louisiana, allowing French creoles to maintain their dominance along the lower Mississippi river plantations. The white population of New Orleans rose from eight thousand to nineteen thousand during the decade, whereas the Euroamerican numbers downstream from Pointe Coupée increased from eight thousand to only eleven thousand. The white population in the rest of Louisiana, on the other hand, rose from eighteen thousand in 1810 to forty-two thousand a decade later. The planters along the Lower Mississippi did purchase most of the incoming slaves, as forty thousand bondspeople toiled in the region. Three-fourths of the state's free people of color lived in New Orleans—where they made up nearly 20 percent of the city's population—with most of the rest residing in the traditionally French-speaking regions of Natchitoches and Acadia. Only 250 free people of color lived in the Florida parishes, as this predominantly Anglo region maintained the simple white-black dichotomy characteristic of the rest of the United States. In fact, less than eleven hundred free people of color lived in Mississippi and Alabama in 1820—only one in two hundred people—most of them residing along the Gulf Coast in the French-settled areas, or in Natchez, developed under the liberal Spanish regime.

Spanish-American Diplomacy

Whereas the United States, along with the American political and racial systems, had taken full control of the Gulf South region bordering the Mississippi River by 1820, Spain still maintained nominal possession of East Texas and West Florida, even though Indians actually dominated both provinces. As a result, in 1817 President Monroe's secretary of state, John Quincy Adams, entered into negotiations with Spain's Minister Onís in an attempt to obtain Florida from Spain and settle once and for all the boundary between Louisiana and Texas. Even before the diplomatic discussions began, however, events took place in both territories that would heavily influence the outcome of the talks. Although a few hundred Euroamericans reestablished their farms and ranches near Nacogdoches late in the decade, official Spanish control in East Texas remained minimal. Jean Lafitte took advantage of the situation and moved his base of smuggling operations from Grand Terre in American-patrolled Louisiana to Galveston Island following the Battle of New Orleans. At the same time, Americans in New Orleans continued to support filibustering expeditions to Texas in hopes that they might result in the United States obtaining possession of the undeveloped province. Ignoring strong protests by Spanish diplomats, U.S. officials allowed Francisco Xavier Mina to purchase supplies and recruit a number of American soldiers in New Orleans for his badly organized invasion of Texas, which was defeated by Spanish royalists in April 1817. Following Mina's failure, President Monroe sent former Secretary of War George Graham to Galveston to try and win Lafitte's support for the American annexation of the Texas coast as far as the Rio Grande. Graham's negotiations with Lafitte had come to nothing by October 1818, by which time Secretary Adams began to consider seizing Galveston in an attempt to pressure Onís into ceding Texas to the United

States. The situation in West Florida, however, soon caused Adams to give up this idea, which even he realized was extreme.

Although Spanish troops remained in possession of Pensacola and San Marcos de Apalache following the War of 1812, they had little control over the Indians and runaway slaves in the province's backcountry. Perceiving the Native Americans and blacks as a threat, the Americans took advantage of the Spanish weakness to invade West Florida, ultimately forcing Minister Onís to turn the entire peninsula over to the United States. After the British abandoned Prospect Bluff following the Battle of New Orleans, most of the Lower Creeks who had gathered there took refuge either in the Miccosukee towns north of San Marcos de Apalache or farther east among the Indian settlements on the Suwannee River, where the Alachua Seminoles had relocated a few years prior. Several hundred runaway slave families, however, remained in possession of the fort and the great quantity of arms and ammunition contained within, much to the alarm of American officials. Because the so-called Negro Fort was located in Spanish West Florida, the Americans tried to persuade the Spaniards to launch an assault on the structure, but to no avail. Although the Negro Fort's inhabitants carried out no offensive operations against the Euroamericans, preferring instead to clear fields and plant crops, in September 1815 Agent Hawkins dispatched a force of Creeks under the command of William McIntosh to attack Prospect Bluff. The assault proved unsuccessful, but in the aftermath the blacks began to attack Spanish and American vessels on the Apalachicola River. Finally, in April 1816 General Jackson convinced West Florida governor Mauricio de Zúñiga to allow the Americans to reduce the Negro Fort. Jackson put General Edmund Pendleton Gaines in charge of the joint army-navy expedition, which began in July 1816. Colonel Duncan Clinch led one hundred American troops, accompanied by three hundred of McIntosh's Creeks, from Georgia to a point a few miles below the Negro Fort, where they met with naval vessels that had arrived from New Orleans. After the fort's inhabitants refused the Americans' call for surrender, naval gunboats were brought upriver under cover of darkness and began to fire. The fifth discharge struck the fort's largest powder magazine, causing an explosion that instantly destroyed the bastion and killed most of the three hundred defenders inside. The Americans turned over the survivors to a Forbes and Company representative before taking possession of the large cache of weapons and burning the fort.

Following the destruction of the Negro Fort, the Creeks and Seminoles (along with their black slave allies) in West Florida carried out retaliatory attacks on American troops and settlers in southern Georgia. Alexander Arbuthnot, a Scottish trader from the Bahamas, along with other British adventurers, such as Robert Ambrister, smuggled weapons to the Indians through stores they illegally maintained near San Marcos de Apalache. In response to the attacks, in December 1817 President Monroe and Secretary of War Calhoun authorized Jackson to invade West Florida and attack the Seminole towns. The orders were deliberately vague, leading Jackson to conclude that he also might take possession of the Spanish holdings in the province in order to put pressure on Spain to give up Florida altogether. In any case, Jackson gathered an army of three thousand men—many of them Tennesseans who had previously served with him—and traveled to the recently established Fort Scott at the head of the Apalachicola River, where two thousand Creeks under the ever-ready William McIntosh joined his force. Learning of Jackson's approach, in March 1818 the nearby Miccosukees under Kinache hurriedly abandoned their towns, which the Americans burned to the ground after taking possession of their food stores. Jackson's troops pressed on to San Marcos de Apalache, where they captured and swiftly hung Hillis Hadjo and another Red Stick leader and placed Arbuthnot under arrest. Turning eastward, the American and Creek force pursued the Miccosukees to the Seminole towns on the Suwannee River. Once again the Indians fled before the invaders, who destroyed the Seminole dwellings and their belongings. Led by Billy Bowlegs, Chief Payne's brother and successor, the Seminoles retreated farther down the Florida peninsula toward present Ocala, hundreds of miles from the Georgia border. While on the Suwannee River, Jackson captured Ambrister and took him back to San Marcos, where he was executed alongside Arbuthnot, following a speedy trial, for inciting the Indians. Having cleared West Florida of the Seminoles, in May 1818 Jackson took possession of Pensacola on the grounds that the Spaniards might use it to harbor other hostile Creeks.

Spain and Great Britain immediately protested Jackson's invasion and the execution of British citizens on Spanish soil. Although President Monroe and Secretary Calhoun denied granting Jackson permission to attack Spanish possessions, and Congress threatened to rebuke him for his ruthlessness in the whole affair, no actions were taken against the general. In fact, instead of apologizing for Jackson's violations of Spanish sovereignty, Secretary Adams blamed Spain for not keeping better order in West Florida and used the invasion to pressure Minister Onís to settle their negotiations. Finally, on February 22, 1819, Adams and Onís signed the treaty that bears their names, in which Spain ceded East Florida to the United States and recognized its de facto control of West Florida. In return, Adams relinquished his demand for Texas, drawing the boundary between the province and Louisiana at the Sabine River, only a few miles west of the border that had been established between the Spanish and French territories in the early eighteenth century. The two ministers continued to draw the boundary between Spain and the United States westward up the Red and Arkansas Rivers, then moving due west to the Pacific along the 42nd Parallel, the northern border of Spanish California. Although the U.S. Senate unanimously ratified the treaty two days later, officials in Spain hesitated to sign it until October 1820. Since the treaty had expired for want of ratification within the agreed upon six-month period, President Monroe resubmitted it to the Senate and it was approved on February 22, 1821, two years to the day after it had first been signed.

Although the Adams-Onís Treaty gave the United States complete possession over most of the Gulf South region, a few Americans were angry that the agreement had not included Texas. Therefore, in the spring of 1819, before the treaty's final ratification, a Natchez merchant named James Long followed in the illustrious footsteps of other filibusters by organizing an expedition designed to wrest control of Texas from the Spanish royalists. Using the West Florida rebellion as a model, Long desired to establish the province as an independent republic in hope of American annexation. With about three hundred followers, Long occupied Nacogdoches in June 1819 and held it for a few months before Spanish troops drove him back into Louisiana. The following year Long established a new base on Galveston Island, from which he led an expedition against La Bahía in the fall of 1821. This time, Spanish troops captured Long and sent him to Mexico City, where he died six months later. Although Long's effort, like those of the other filibusters in Texas, had ended in abject failure, it would not be long before other Anglo Protestants from the United States would follow his lead and take possession of the province, ultimately extending American hegemony over the entire Gulf South by 1845.

Epilogue

The Extension of Anglo Protestant Hegemony 1821–1845

Anglo Protestant settlers, along with their slaves, continued to pour into the Gulf South following the February 1821 ratification of the Adams-Onís Treaty, many intending to pursue the cultivation of cotton. As a result, within two decades the incredible diversity of the region had been replaced by the strict biracial system that dominated the rest of the American South, ultimately leading to the Civil War by the 1860s. Alabama experienced the greatest amount of growth, as the white population nearly doubled to 190,000 during the 1820s, with the slave numbers almost tripling to reach 117,000. The greatest increases took place in the counties located along the Coosa and Alabama Rivers, containing the rich lands that had been wrested from the Creeks in 1814. Nearly one-third of the state's slave population resided in this region—soon to be designated as the Black Belt—where they comprised almost half of the residents. As a result of the influx, Alabama more than doubled its cotton production during the decade, increasing from 65,000 to 160,000 bales by 1830. Except for the cotton grown in the Tennessee River Valley (which traveled downstream to New Orleans), most of the bales went to Mobile, transforming the backwater, French creole town into a bustling port. By the end of the decade Mobile's population had grown to over six thousand residents, thirty-four hundred being slaves, along with 550 free people of color, one-third of the state's total.

Mississippi lagged behind Alabama a bit, as the white population rose from forty-two thousand in 1820 to seventy thousand ten years later, with the number of enslaved people doubling to reach sixty-five thousand by 1830. Even more than in Alabama, the state's slaves were heavily concentrated in the cotton-producing counties located along the Mississippi River downstream from Vicksburg: the forty thousand bondspeople residing there outnumbered the white residents by a ratio of two to one. Although many of the migrants who moved to Alabama and Mississippi came from Georgia, that state's population also increased during the decade. Georgia's white residents increased their numbers by one-third, reaching nearly 300,000 people by 1830. The slave population rose at the same rate during the 1820s, attaining 220,000 by the end of the decade. Only forty-five hundred free people of color—about 1 percent of the entire free population—resided in Alabama, Mississippi, and Georgia by 1830. The increase in the amount of slaves during the decade allowed Mississippi planters to more than double their cotton production, from 50,000 to 120,000 bales, while Georgia's yields increased from 165,000 to 260,000 bales.

Georgia also provided settlers for the newly acquired territory of Florida. In July 1821 Andrew Jackson formally accepted the transfer of Florida from Spain in a ceremony held in Pensacola. As Florida's first territorial governor, Jackson established an effective governing structure within a few months, creating two vast administrative units, Escambia and St. Johns Counties, nearly coterminous with the old West and East Floridas, with the boundary being the Suwannee River. In October 1821, as soon as the provisional government was functioning, Jackson resigned as governor and was succeeded by William P. Duval, a Kentuckian who maintained the position until 1834. In March 1822 Congress replaced the provisional structure with a single territorial government consisting of a governor, secretary, and legislative council all appointed by the president. Tallahassee, the ancient homeland of the Apalaches, and most recently the site of the Miccosukee Seminole towns destroyed by Jackson in 1818, was chosen as the permanent capital because of its central location.

Migration into Florida, however, was hindered by the six thousand or so Seminoles who still resided in the north-central portion of the territory. In September 1823 federal officials responded to Governor Duval's demands for the removal of the Seminoles by pressuring thirty-two chiefs to sign the Treaty of Moultrie Creek, in which the tribe ceded 24 million acres in North Florida in exchange for 4 million acres located farther south. Anglo Protestant settlers began to flood into the territory soon thereafter, particularly in the Middle Florida region, the fertile lands lying between the Apalachicola and Suwannee Rivers. As with the rest of the Gulf South, Florida's main cash crop was cotton, raised by the toil of black slaves. Sixteen thousand people resided in Middle Florida by

1830, more than half being in bondage. Ten years later the white population of all of Florida had risen to twenty-seven thousand, with the slave numbers growing to twenty-five thousand. By 1840 the twelve thousand slaves in Middle Florida constituted nearly two-thirds of the region's entire population. Pensacola, situated in the pine barrens of West Florida, lagged behind the rich, north-central counties despite being the former British and Spanish capital. By 1840 only twenty-three hundred whites and thirteen hundred slaves resided in Escambia County. However, three hundred free people of color, or 40 percent of Florida's total free black population, lived in Pensacola.

Whereas Florida had extraneous territory on which to relocate the Seminoles, the Anglo Protestant residents of Georgia, Alabama, and Mississippi strongly desired the fertile lands that the fifty thousand Creeks, Choctaws, and Chickasaws still possessed, but they had nowhere to send the tribes within their state boundaries. Consequentially, President Monroe proclaimed that his administration planned on removing all the eastern Indians to the region west of the Mississippi River in order to open up their territory to white cultivators. Not only would this provide succor to the hordes of land-hungry Americans who maintained the vote, it also fit well with the hardening racial views whites were developing about blacks and Indians. Although the United States' "civilization" program initiated in the 1790s had optimistically hoped to assimilate the Indians into American society on an equal footing with whites, following the War of 1812 most southern Anglos had come to see the Native Americans as being members of an inferior, subordinate race, situated just a notch above blacks, who were suited only for enslavement. Following this logic, since Indians were racially inferior to whites, they could never be assimilated into American society as equals, thus they should give up their lands in the eastern states and be moved westward as wards of the federal government. The 1820 Treaty of Doak's Stand, in which the Choctaws had ceded land in Mississippi in exchange for territory in the West, provided the blueprint for what the Monroe administration had in mind for the other eastern tribes.

In the 1820s the Creeks, Choctaws, and Chickasaws responded to the intensified pressure for removal by attempting to transfer authority from the individual towns to a more centralized form of government that would have the means and power to act as a counterweight to the Americans. Ironically, the leadership for the movement to centralize authority came from the growing numbers in each tribe that had most fully embraced the "civilization" program and the market-oriented economy that had come with it. Prior to the War of 1812, Creek progressives—most of whom were mixed-bloods, but certainly not all—had established a weak national council that had passed laws to protect their private property and had appointed police forces to enforce them. By the third decade of the nineteenth century, the progressives in each tribe hoped that by strengthening the central authority even further they could protect the tribal domain as a whole from the incursions of the state and federal governments. They also hoped to fight the Americans' demands for removal by allowing Protestant missionaries to establish churches in their midst, and by sending their children to schools in which they were taught English. As a result of these progressive initiatives, in the 1820s the Creeks and Chickasaws established strong national councils that established written legal codes, including laws forbidding the unauthorized sale of land by any individual and the prohibition of tribal members' receiving private reservations of land in treaty negotiations with the United States. In 1826 the Choctaws, led by progressives David Folsom and Greenwood LeFlore, went so far as to adopt a written constitution, establishing a national executive committee composed of the chiefs of the Eastern, Western, and Sixtowns districts and authorizing the committee to draft laws in conjunction with a national council that would protect private property, encourage education, and unify political opposition to the Americans in order to fight calls for land cessions and removal to territory west of the Mississippi River.

The southern tribes' movement to centralize their governmental institutions in order to forestall removal only served to strengthen the resolve of the Anglo Protestant residents of Georgia, Alabama, and Mississippi to force them off their lands, leading to a crisis by the middle of the decade. In 1824 Secretary of War Calhoun responded to Georgia's demands for the acquisition of all Creek territory in the state—basically, the land between the Flint and Chattahoochee Rivers—by appointing a commission to negotiate a treaty of removal. The Creek National Council, however, turned down the American commissioners' proposal. Nonetheless, the Creek mixed-blood William McIntosh met with the Americans and, in return for a large bribe, signed the Treaty of Indian Springs in February 1825, which ceded all the tribe's land in Georgia and about two-thirds of their holdings in Alabama to the United States in exchange for territory west of the Mississippi River. The Creek National Council responded by finding McIntosh guilty of the tribal law forbidding the unauthorized sale of land and ordered his execution, which was carried out in April 1825. Georgia governor George M. Troup and the state legislature protested the execution of McIntosh and threatened to invade Creek country with state militia to arrest the council members. The newly inaugurated president, John Quincy Adams, further enraged the Georgians by recognizing McIntosh's execution as the legal act of a sovereign nation and warned Governor Troup to desist. In order to defuse the explosive situation, President Adams then met with a Creek delegation in Washington, resulting in a second treaty being signed in January 1826. In return for maintaining their holdings in Alabama, the Creeks—who continued to fear an invasion by the Georgia militia—sold all their lands in the state for over $200,000, plus a perpetual annuity of $20,000.

Whereas the Treaty of Washington forced the Lower Creeks to move northward to join their brethren in the Upper Creek towns, President Adams's actions demonstrated his belief that the federal government maintained sole jurisdiction over Indian affairs, and that the Native Americans exercised exclusive sovereign power within their own country through their tribal governments. Thwarted by the claims of the federal government and the tribes' assertions of sovereignty, in the late 1820s Georgia, Alabama, and Mississippi sought to obtain title to the Indians' lands by enacting legislation extending state law over lands occupied by the Indians, while at the same time denying them political or civil rights, such as the rights to vote or testify in court on their own behalf. Although tribal leaders appealed to the federal government for protection from the states, Andrew Jackson, who became president in March 1829, announced that he sided with the states on the matter. In December 1829 Jackson recommended legislation calling for the negotiation of removal treaties with all the eastern tribes, in which they would give up their lands in exchange for reservations in the Indian Territory, to be established west of Arkansas and Missouri. The tribes would be transported at government expense to their new country, supported for one year upon arrival, and be compensated for any improvements they were forced to leave behind. President Jackson insisted that the Indian Removal Act would solve the impasse between the states and the tribes, and thus ensure the survival of the Indians, who would certainly suffer under state law. In addition, the act would open up the Indians' territory to further cotton cultivation, as demanded by the southern Anglos. Despite intense opposition to the bill by northern legislators, it passed both houses with full southern support, and was signed into law in May 1830.

Secretary of War John Eaton, along with General John Coffee, negotiated the first removal treaty with the Choctaws in September 1830. With most of the tribe gathered at the council ground located at Dancing Rabbit Creek, the progressive Choctaw leaders shifted their previous anti-removal stance and indicated their willingness to accept the treaty—mainly due to having exhausted all of their options—but they were vehemently shouted down by the rank-and-file members of the tribe, and the negotiations broke down. The American commissioners then met in private with LeFlore and Folsom, among others, and threatened to repossess the western lands the Choctaws had received in the Treaty of Doak's Stand, leaving them at the mercy of the state of Mississippi if they did not agree to the treaty. Following LeFlore's lead, the Choctaw chiefs grudgingly accepted the removal treaty as the best chance to have some control in the final dispossession of the nation, and signed the Treaty of Dancing Rabbit Creek, ceding the Choctaws' last 10 million acres in Mississippi to the United States. Many of the leaders, including LeFlore, were also induced to sign by being granted generous land allotments in the treaty, which they could then sell for a considerable profit.

Although most of the tribe opposed the treaty, the first removal party left the Choctaw lands in Mississippi via steamboats during the unusually harsh winter of 1831–1832, suffering greatly from the lack of warm clothes and supplies that had been promised by government officials. Two subsequent removals proceeded more smoothly, despite cholera striking the Choctaw migrants during the 1832 trek. In the meantime, Anglo Protestant settlers swarmed onto the ceded lands in Mississippi, stealing livestock, confiscating homes and improvements, and abusing the remaining tribal members. By the end of 1833 nearly eighteen thousand Choctaws had moved to their new lands, located between the Red and Canadian Rivers, in the Indian Territory. Twenty-five hundred Choctaws, however, had perished on the "Trail of Tears." Even though they were the first of the southern tribes to move to the Indian Territory, the Choctaws had the easiest time once they had arrived. After landing in the Indian Territory, in 1834 the Choctaws mended their differences by writing a new constitution that reestablished the tribe's three traditional divisions. Progressive Choctaws maintained their allegiance to the market economy and set up ranches and cotton plantations, in addition to allowing Protestant missionaries to open schools on the reservation, which ultimately found widespread support from most of the tribal members.

The Chickasaws, on the other hand, experienced the least traumatic move westward, despite having their removal document delayed until October 1832 by the tribal scouts' inability to find a suitable homeland for the nation in the West. In the Treaty of Pontotoc Creek, each Chickasaw adult received a tract of land. Upon his or her removal, it would be sold and the allottee would receive the money. The United States would then sell surplus lands and deposit the proceeds into a tribal fund. Despite signing the treaty of removal, the tribe did not settle on an acceptable homeland until January 1837, when, under pressure from Mississippi settlers, they signed the Treaty of Doaksville, in which the Choctaws allowed the Chickasaws to settle on the western portion of their Indian Territory lands in return for $500,000, one-sixth of the tribal allotment money. Nearly five thousand Chickasaws, along with one thousand black slaves, then relocated to the Indian Territory, where they became the fourth division of the Choctaw Nation. In 1855 the Chickasaws, in return for $150,000, purchased their independence from the Choctaws and created their own sovereign nation.

Despite the fact that the Seminoles had been forced southward far from white settlements in the 1823 Treaty of Moultrie Creek, Floridians and President Jackson insisted that the tribe sign a treaty of removal and relocate to the Indian Territory. As a result, in May 1832 American commissioners convinced various Seminole chiefs to sign the Treaty of Payne's Landing, in which the tribe agreed to move westward and unite with the Creeks, who had been granted lands between the Arkansas and Canadian Rivers in the 1826 Treaty of Washington. Seven Seminole leaders headed west to inspect the land, which their agent stated they agreed to move to in the Treaty of Fort Gibson, signed in March 1833. Although the Seminoles in Florida denounced the treaty, the federal government insisted on its validity and gave the tribe until 1836 to move. Instead, Osceola, a mixed-blood Creek who as a child had fled to Florida with the Red Sticks in 1814, led a December 1835 Seminole uprising in which they killed their agent and destroyed Major Francis Dade's detachment of over one hundred federal troops, thus initiating the Second Seminole War. During the war, which cost the United States more than fifteen hundred lives, American leaders resorted to seizing Seminole leaders, including Osceola, under a flag of truce and holding them captive. Finally, in August 1842, in return for allowing five hundred or so Seminoles to remain on a small reserve of land in Florida, the war came to an end with four thousand tribal members, along with one thousand black allies, accepting removal to the Indian Territory, where they settled on the Creek lands. Three years after the Seminoles moved westward, Florida entered the Union as a state, with an economic and social system firmly based on white superiority and black slavery.

The removal of the Creeks from Alabama was connected with the events taking place with the Seminoles in Florida. Despite having obtained land in the West by treaty in 1826, only about three thousand Creeks, most of whom were followers of William McIntosh, had settled on the Indian Territory lands by 1832. The remaining fifteen thousand Creeks, led by Opothleyahola, the speaker of the National Council, preferred to remain on their lands in Alabama, located east of the Coosa River. Therefore, in March 1832 Opothleyahola met with President Jackson's new secretary of war, Lewis Cass, and negotiated the Treaty of Washington, which allowed the Creeks to stay in Alabama temporarily. The treaty called for the cession of all the Creek lands in Alabama and the allotment of half sections, clustered together to form towns, to every family head. The excess territory would then be sold to the United States and opened up to white settlement. Although Alabama Anglos and their slaves poured into the ceded lands and tried to intimidate the Indians into giving up their remaining allotments, the Creeks held onto their allotted lands and maintained the peace until early 1836, when the warriors finally rose up against the white hostility, threatening the newly founded city of Columbus, Georgia, situated in the heart of the former Lower Creek towns. Fearing that the enraged Creeks might join with their Seminole brethren in Florida, Secretary Cass ordered federal troops to subdue and remove the tribe to the Indian Territory. By July 1836 the military had restored peace and begun evacuating the Creeks, with many of the warriors being handcuffed and chained. By early 1837 nearly fifteen thousand Creeks had arrived in the Indian Territory, most with no possessions but what they could carry.

Unlike the Choctaws, the Creeks remained bitterly divided in their new homeland. The tribal members who had migrated westward prior to 1836—most of whom were market-oriented types like the followers of William McIntosh—established farms and plantations along the Arkansas River. Many of the newcomers, however, were traditionalists like Opothleyahola, and they chose to reconstitute tribal towns in the Canadian River Valley, fifty miles to the south, and to maintain their communal values. The two Creek divisions governed themselves separately until 1840, when they established a National Council that met annually at a halfway point between them. In addition, the Seminoles clashed with the Creeks on the Arkansas River, not only because they had fought against them in 1814, but also due to the attempt by McIntosh's followers to regain possession of the slaves who had previously escaped from their plantations to join with the Seminoles in Florida. As a result, some Seminoles and their black allies followed Coacoochee (Wild Cat), first to Texas and then to Mexico, in search of independence. Eventually, the Creeks allowed the Seminoles to establish their own independent towns, and in 1856, following the example set by the Chickasaws, the tribe created an independent nation west of the Creeks.

With the Indians' removal to the West, the Anglo Protestants of Georgia, Alabama, and Mississippi were free to establish the strict biracial system that would remain in place for more than a century. By 1840 Georgia's white population had risen by a quarter to reach 400,000 people, with the number of slaves growing at the same rate, to 280,000. Settlers poured onto the former Creek lands east of the Coosa River, increasing Alabama's white population by more than a third to 335,000, with the slave numbers rising more than half to reach 250,000. In Mississippi, the white numbers more than doubled to 180,000, while the slave figures tripled to 195,000, thus creating a black majority. Much of the newly acquired Indian lands were used for the cultivation of cotton, as worldwide demand and prices remained astoundingly high. As a result, Mississippi planters increased their cotton production fivefold to 580,000 bales, Alabama increased two and a half times to nearly 400,000 bales, while Georgia nearly doubled its output, reaching 450,000 bales. In the wake of the Indians' departure, all three states enacted even harsher slave codes and dramatically reduced whatever rights the few free people of color had previously enjoyed, prohibiting manumission altogether by the 1850s.

Although the Anglo Protestant influx to the Gulf South was a bit slower west of the Mississippi River, the results were basically the same, as the Native Americans were forced westward in order to free more lands for cash crop cultivation by black slaves. With all the former Indian territory opened up for settlement in Georgia, Alabama, and Mississippi, Anglo Protestants hesitated to relocate to French Catholic Louisiana, and the white population only increased by one-sixth during the 1820s, reaching ninety thousand settlers by 1830. Slave numbers, on the other hand, rose to 110,000, an increase of more than 50 percent during the decade. The number of free people of color grew at the same rate as slaves, attaining seventeen thousand residents by 1830. More than half of Louisiana's population continued to reside along the Mississippi River downstream from Pointe Coupée, as forty-two thousand whites, sixty-eight thousand slaves, and fourteen thousand free people of color lived in the region. New Orleans, despite the great wealth it was attaining by becoming a major world port, grew at a measured pace, increasing its population by only seven thousand people during the 1820s, reaching forty-eight thousand inhabitants by the end of the decade, one-fourth of whom were free people of color. Most of Louisiana's other free people of color lived in French creole-dominated Acadia and Natchitoches alongside twenty-six thousand whites and twenty-four thousand slaves. Anglo Protestants only maintained a majority of the Euroamerican population in Louisiana's recently developed northern parishes, as twenty-two thousand whites, eighteen thousand slaves, and only five hundred free people of color lived in this area. Despite the French Catholic majority in the state, the conservative Constitution of 1812 allowed Louisiana's few voters to choose an Anglo Protestant as governor in the elections of 1820 and 1824. Both French and Anglos shared an affinity for the booming plantation economy, and cotton production nearly tripled during the decade to reach 140,000 bales produced in 1830, while sugar production more than doubled to reach 66,000 pounds.

Louisiana's French Catholics and Anglo Protestants also agreed on the necessity of removing the few remaining Indians from the state. By the 1820s most of Louisiana's Native Americans resided along the Red River. About two hundred Pascagoulas, Biloxis, Apalaches, and Taensas lived between Alexandria and Natchitoches, while another eight hundred or so Indians resided upstream from Natchitoches and the Great Raft. This latter group consisted of five hundred Kadohadachos, two hundred Coushattas, and one hundred Yatasis, Natchitoches, and Adaes. Because of pressure from white citizens, in 1825 the federal government arranged for all of the Red River Indians to congregate in Kadohadacho territory, which Chief Dehahuit and Agent George Gray officially delineated as being nearly six hundred thousand acres located west of the Red River above the Great Raft. In spite of the arrangement, the Indians living downstream from Natchitoches were violently driven off their lands before they could relocate to Kadohadacho country. In 1826 Anglo planters launched a campaign of terror against the tribes, using slaves to burn their cabins and destroy their crops. Rather than stay within the United States, most of the Pascagoulas, Apalaches, Biloxis, and Taensas fled to Texas to join their kinsmen in the Alabama and Coushatta villages. About thirty Pascagoulas and Apalaches stayed near Alexandria, only to be wiped out by a cholera epidemic in 1832.

Although the Kadohadachos and the Coushattas remained on American soil, increasing pressure in the late 1820s greatly demoralized the tribes, causing them to turn to alcohol for solace, which threatened the agricultural base of the tribes. By the mid-1820s the federal Indian agent was forced to supply the Kadohadachos with food, since their drunkenness and depression made them neglect their fields. Game near the Kadohadacho village was scarce, and the influx of American and Indian settlers forced the tribe to travel even farther west for their winter hunts. Pressure on the tribes to give up their lands completely increased following the 1830 arrival of Jehiel Brooks, President Jackson's appointee as Indian agent, and the announcement three years later that engineer Henry Shreve planned on clearing the Red River for navigation by removing the Great Raft, thus opening up the region for cotton cultivation. At this point most of the Coushattas moved to Texas and entered their kinsmen's Trinity River villages, while a few others joined with their fellow Creeks in the lands that had recently been set aside for the tribe in the Indian Territory. Following the death of Dehahuit in 1833, Brooks pressured the starving Kadohadachos to sign a treaty in July 1835 in which the tribe agreed to sell all their land and move at their own expense to Texas within one year. Soon thereafter, only a few Indians—mainly Biloxis, Tunicas, Choctaws, and Houmas—remained in Louisiana, residing in lowland swamps and marshlands unfit for plantation agriculture.

Following the removal of most of the state's Indians, Louisiana's population grew in the explosive manner of the Gulf South states located east of the Mississippi River. The white population nearly doubled to 160,000, while the slave numbers rose by half to reach 170,000. Although the free black population of twenty-five thousand—four-fifths of whom resided in New Orleans—also represented an increase of nearly 50 percent, hardening racial attitudes among the consolidated French Catholics and Anglo Protestants resulted in the passage of increasingly restrictive legislation. In 1830 Louisiana legislators passed an act requiring all free people of color who had come to the state after 1825 to leave within sixty days. The act also forced those masters who freed their slaves to post a $1,000 bond to guarantee that the former slave would move within one month of manumission. Four years later the state legislature disbanded the free black militia, which had continued to muster and train following the Battle of New Orleans. The consequences of these acts were fully demonstrated in the 1840s, when the free black population of Louisiana actually declined, dropping to seventeen thousand people by 1850. New Orleans's free black numbers dropped from nineteen thousand in 1840 to just nine thousand ten years later. Still unhappy with the number of free blacks in their midst, Louisiana's white legislators banned manumission altogether in 1857, thus falling in line completely with the other slave states of the Gulf South.

During the 1820s the white population in the Arkansas Territory rose from fourteen thousand to twenty-five thousand residents, while the number of slaves tripled to reach forty-five hundred, as many of the new immigrants established cotton plantations along the Mississippi, Arkansas, White, and Red Rivers. As a result, cotton production increased five-fold, from three hundred to fifteen hundred bales, during the decade. As with the residents of the Florida Territory, the newcomers to Arkansas felt the region's Indians stood in the way of further development of the cotton culture, and they put pressure on their politicians to remove them. Although the four hundred remaining Quapaws had ceded most of their lands on the Lower Arkansas River to the United States in 1818, seven years later Arkansas politicians convinced U.S. officials to relocate the tribe westward to Kadohadacho lands in Louisiana. Chief Heckaton begged the government to rescind the order, but his petition was denied and in December 1825 the Quapaws unwillingly walked alongside their horses to northwestern Louisiana. Things did not go well in Kadohadacho country, and by 1830 nearly one-third of the Quapaws had returned to Arkansas, where they were considered squatters by the local residents. Finally, in May 1833 American officials negotiated a treaty with the Quapaws in which they were granted eighty-six thousand acres on the Neosho River in the extreme northwestern part of the Indian Territory. Within a few years half of the Quapaws had relocated to the reservation, while the other half had drifted to East Texas, where they established settlements near the Cherokees, Shawnees, and Delawares just north of Nacogdoches.

In the latter half of the 1820s, American officials obtained the lands of the other Indian residents of Arkansas by negotiating treaties granting them reservations west of the territorial boundary. By 1825 most of the six thousand Osages had been driven out of Arkansas by the Cherokees and their allies. Therefore, in June Great Osage chief Pawhuska, along with Clermont II, leader of the Arkansas Osages, agreed to cede all claims to lands in the state of Missouri and the territory of Arkansas in exchange for a reservation located along the Neosho and Verdigris Rivers in present southeastern Kansas. Although a few Osages continued to hunt in the Ozark and Ouachita Mountains of Arkansas, by the early 1830s most of them had permanently relocated to the new reservation. Despite having favored the supposedly more "civilized" three thousand Western Cherokees over the Osages in the treaty negotiations of 1818, which resulted in the so-called Lovely's Purchase, in 1828 American officials forced the tribe to exchange their lands in Arkansas for territory located to the west in the Indian Territory. By 1836 only a few Indians remained in Arkansas when President Jackson signed the bill transforming the territory into a slave state.

Not even international boundaries could contain the Anglo Protestant sweep across the Gulf South following the ratification of the Adams-Onís Treaty, as Texas was brought into the fold by 1845. This was particularly surprising, for East Texas had become one of the most diverse areas in the Gulf South following the end of the War of 1812. As the Anglo Protestants poured into the Southeast after the Battle of New Orleans, many Indians sought refuge in Spanish Texas and relocated near Nacogdoches, which had been abandoned by Euroamericans in the aftermath of the royalist victory over the revolutionaries in 1814. By August 1821, when Mexico declared independence from Spain, about two thousand Cherokees, Shawnees, Delawares, and Kickapoos had settled in East Texas along the upper reaches of the Neches, Angelina, and Sabine Rivers, where they established farms and cattle ranches. About seven hundred Hasinais, the Caddoan-speaking natives of the region, lived nearby, as did thirteen hundred Alabamas, Coushattas, and other refugees from Louisiana, who had recently established villages along the Lower Trinity and Neches Rivers. Westward, between the Brazos and the Trinity, resided about seventeen hundred Wichita Indians, dispersed among the Tawakoni, Waco, and Kichai agricultural villages. All of these Indians visited the newly reconstituted town of Nacogdoches to carry out trade with the one hundred or so settlers—people of Spanish, French, Irish, African, and Native American descent—who had reestablished their farms and ranches by 1820. The newly independent state of Mexico initially welcomed the Indian settlement of East Texas in hopes of establishing a buffer against Anglo Protestant encroachment from the United States. In November 1822 Richard Fields, a literate one-eighth Cherokee, traveled to San Antonio and concluded a treaty with Governor José Felix Trespalacios granting his tribe official permission to settle in Texas. The Cherokees, led by Chief Duwali, formed an alliance with most of the Indians in East Texas and began to act as if the Trespalacios-Fields agreement was in force for all of the newcomers.

The Native American domination of East Texas, however, proved to be very short lived. In 1824 Mexico adopted a constitution providing the nation with a federalist form of government that permitted considerable regional autonomy and left the central government relatively weak. In the new arrangement, underpopulated Texas was joined with the more developed province to the south to form the state of Coahuila y Texas, with its capital at Saltillo. In an attempt to promote economic development, Mexican liberals did away with the restrictive, mercantilist trading policies maintained under Spanish rule and implemented a system of free trade, designed to foster commercial relations with the United States. Realizing that Texas would not profit from this liberal system of trade without settlers, the Mexican government and the state of Coahuila y Texas passed a series of colonization laws in the 1820s designed to promote American immigration into the relatively empty province. These laws allowed foreigners to purchase as much as forty-five hundred acres of land at much lower prices than could be found in the United States. As a result, by the early 1830s nearly eight thousand Anglo Protestants—most of whom were from the Gulf South region that was in the midst of forcibly moving that area's Native American population to the Indian Territory—had established settlements in East Texas. About one thousand slaves resided in East Texas, where they produced two thousand bales of cotton, as that crop continued to be the key incentive for settlement. The Anglo Protestants clashed with the Mexican Catholics on a variety of issues, including a threat by Mexico to abolish slavery altogether, which led to rebellion and the independence of Texas by 1836. The Texans immediately wrote a constitution providing for slavery, while at the same time forbidding manumission or the residence of free blacks within the republic without the consent of the legislature. Independence opened an era of rapid growth for Anglo Protestant settlement and slavery in Texas. By the mid-1840s the region mirrored the rest of the Gulf South, as about one hundred thousand whites and forty thousand slaves resided in the republic.

Texas also resembled the other Gulf South states in its desire for Indian removal. Although the Anglo Protestant settlers in East Texas had formed an alliance with the Cherokees in the 1820s that resulted in the forced expulsion of the Wichitas from the Brazos and Trinity Valleys, following independence the call for Indian removal increased dramatically. Whereas the republic's first president, the Tennessean Sam Houston, had promoted peace with the tribes—in part because Indian wars were costly—his successor, Mirabeau Buonaparte Lamar, called for the "total extinction or total expulsion" of all the Native Americans from Texas. Lamar, who had been the private secretary of Georgia's Governor Troup during the Creek crisis of the mid-1820s, used the failed August 1838 Córdova Rebellion, as an excuse for action. Vicente Córdova, a former East Texas judge, had tried to organize an uprising of the Hispanics and Indians residing near Nacogdoches, aimed at freeing the region from Anglo Protestant domination. The plot was uncovered before the planned attack could be launched, but in the immediate aftermath Texas Rangers drove the Kickapoos, Hasinais, and Kadohadachos—who had just recently moved into Texas from Louisiana—northwestward into the Indian Territory. In July 1839 Texas Rangers killed Chief Duwali and destroyed the remaining Cherokee and Delaware villages near Nacogdoches, and signed a treaty forcing the Shawnees to join the refugees who had relocated north of the Red River. Encouraged by the events in northeastern Texas, citizens along the Lower Trinity and Neches Rivers acted on their own to try and force the region's few remaining Indians from their midst. By early 1840 only a few hundred Native Americans were still living in the Alabama and Coushatta villages when the Texas Congress passed an act establishing small reservations for the tribes in the Big Thicket, an area considered unfit for cultivation. In the next two years, Lamar ordered Texas Rangers to drive the few remaining Wichitas into the Indian Territory and forced the equestrian Comanches far to the west beyond the settlements of the Anglo Protestants. By the end of 1841, the Texans had removed nearly all the Indians from the boundaries of the republic. Four years later, Texas entered the United States as the fifteenth and final slave state. Anglo American hegemony throughout the Gulf South was now complete. Although the Civil War would bring an end to slavery twenty years later, the strict biracial system implemented throughout the Gulf South by the Anglo Protestants in the aftermath of the Adams-Onís Treaty would remain in place for yet another century.

FURTHER READING

This brief discussion of secondary sources includes the most influential works written in the past two and a half decades. Works relevant to multiple chapters are mentioned only once, and articles in scholarly journals are not included. The most important previously published works as well as published and unpublished primary documents can be found in the footnotes and bibliographies of these books. While this work relies primarily on the many excellent works that have been published on the Native Americans, Europeans, and Africans residing in Louisiana and the Gulf South prior to the establishment of United States' hegemony, few actually deal with all three groups at the same time. The exception, however, is Daniel H. Usner Jr., *Indians, Settlers, and Slaves in a Frontier Exchange Economy: The Lower Mississippi Valley Before 1783* (Chapel Hill: Univ. of North Carolina Press, 1992), the book that provided an introduction to this field of study for many of the scholars mentioned below. Another highly influential work, David J. Weber, *The Spanish Frontier in North America* (New Haven: Yale Univ. Press, 1992), was published the same year as Usner's—the five hundredth anniversary of the first voyage of Christopher Columbus—and includes the region as part of an overview of Spain's activities in the area located within the present boundaries of the United States. For collections of essays that deal with all three groups throughout the region, see Richmond F. Brown, ed., *Coastal Encounters: The Transformation of the Gulf South in the Eighteenth Century* (Lincoln: Univ. of Nebraska Press, 2007), and Gene Allen Smith and Sylvia L. Hinton, eds., *Nexus of Empire: Negotiating Loyalty and Identity in the Revolutionary Borderlands, 1760s–1820s* (Gainesville: Univ. Press of Florida, 2010).

1. INITIAL ENCOUNTERS, 1500–1670

The best introductions to the Mississippians of the Gulf South are Charles Hudson, *The Southeastern Indians* (Knoxville: Univ. of Tennessee Press, 1976), and Theda Perdue and Michael D. Green, *The Columbia Guide to American Indians of the Southeast* (New York: Columbia Univ. Press, 2001). More detailed archaeological studies of the early period include Patricia Galloway, ed., *The Southeastern Ceremonial Complex: Artifacts and Analysis* (Lincoln: Univ. of Nebraska Press, 1989); Mark Williams and Gary Shapiro, eds., *Lamar Archaeology: Mississippian Chiefdoms in the Deep South* (Tuscaloosa: Univ. of Alabama Press, 1990); Bruce D. Smith, ed., *Mississippian Emergence: The Evolution of Ranked Agricultural Societies in Eastern North America* (Washington, D.C.: Smithsonian Institution Press, 1990); David H. Dye and Cheryl Anne Cox, eds., *Towns and Temples along the Mississippi* (Tuscaloosa: Univ. of Alabama Press, 1990); Timothy K. Perttula, *"The Caddo Nation": Archaeological and Ethnohistoric Perspectives* (Austin: Univ. of Texas Press, 1992); Marvin T. Smith, *Coosa: The Rise and Fall of a Southeastern Mississippian Chiefdom* (Gainesville: Univ. Press of Florida, 2000); Ian W. Brown, ed., *Bottle Creek: A Pensacola Culture Site in South Alabama* (Tuscaloosa: Univ. of Alabama Press, 2003); Thomas J. Pluckhahn and Robbie Ethridge, eds., *Light on the Path: The Anthropology and History of the Southeastern Indians* (Tuscaloosa: Univ. of Alabama Press, 2006); and Christopher Morris, *The Big Muddy: An Environmental History of the Mississippi and Its Peoples from Hernando de Soto to Hurricane Katrina* (Oxford: Oxford Univ. Press, 2012).

Early Spanish activities in the Gulf South are examined in Robert S. Weddle, *Spanish Sea: The Gulf of Mexico in North American Discovery, 1500–1685* (College Station: Texas A&M Univ. Press, 1985); Andrés Reséndez, *A Land So Strange: The Epic Journey of Cabeza de Vaca* (New York: Basic Books, 2007); Charles Hudson, *Knights of Spain, Warriors of the Sun: Hernando de Soto and the South's Ancient Chiefdoms* (Athens: Univ. of Georgia Press, 1997); Gloria A. Young and Michael P. Hoffman, eds., *The Expedition of Hernando de Soto West of the Mississippi, 1541–1543* (Fayetteville: Univ. of Arkansas Press, 1993); Patricia Galloway, ed., *The Hernando de Soto Expedition: History, Historiography, and "Discovery" in the Southeast* (Lincoln: Univ. of Nebraska Press, 1997); and Paul E. Hoffman, *A New Andalucia and a Way to the Orient: The American Southeast During the Sixteenth Century* (Baton Rouge: Louisiana State Univ. Press, 1990).

For the sixteenth- and seventeenth-century aftermath of the Spanish intrusion into the Gulf South, see John H. Hann, *Apalachee: The Land between the Rivers* (Gainesville: Univ. Press of Florida, 1988); Amy Turner Bushnell, *Situado and Sabana: Spain's Support System for the Presidio and Mission Provinces of Florida* (Athens: Univ. of Georgia Press, 1994); Charles Hudson and Carmen Chavez Tesser, eds., *The Forgotten Centuries: Indians and Europeans in the American South, 1521–1704* (Athens: Univ. of Georgia Press, 1994); Patricia Galloway, *Choctaw Genesis, 1500–1700* (Lincoln: Univ. of Nebraska Press, 1995); Jerald T. Milanich, *Florida Indians and the Invasion from Europe* (Gainesville: Univ. Press of Florida, 1995); Bonnie McEwan, ed. *Indians of the Greater Southeast: Historical Archaeology and Ethnohistory* (Gainesville: Univ. Press of Florida, 2000); Robbie Ethridge and Charles Hudson, eds., *The Transformation of the Southeastern Indians, 1540–1760* (Jackson: Univ. Press of Mississippi, 2002); Jerald T. Milanich, *Laboring in the Fields of the Lord: Spanish Missions and Southeastern Indians* (Gainesville: Univ. Press of Florida, 2006); and Robbie Ethridge, *From Chicaza to Chickasaw: The European Invasion and the Transformation of the Mississippian World, 1540–1715* (Chapel Hill: Univ. of North Carolina Press, 2010).

2. INITIAL EUROPEAN SETTLEMENTS, 1670–1712

For the establishment of British South Carolina and the Indian slave trade, see Steven J. Oates, *A Colonial Complex: South Carolina's Frontiers in the Era of the Yamasee War, 1680–1730* (Lincoln: Univ. of Nebraska Press, 2004), and Allan Gallay, *The Indian Slave Trade: The Rise of the English Empire in the American South, 1670–1717* (New Haven: Yale Univ. Press, 2002). The Great Smallpox Epidemic of 1696 and its aftermath, including Indian population figures, are dealt with by Paul Kelton, *Epidemics and Enslavement: Biological Catastrophe in the Native Southeast, 1492–1715* (Lincoln: Univ. of Nebraska Press, 2007); Daniel H. Usner Jr., *American Indians in the Lower Mississippi Valley: Social and Economic Histories* (Lincoln: Univ. of Nebraska Press, 1998); Peter Wood, Gregory Waselkov, and M. Thomas Hadley, eds., *Powhatan's Mantle: Indians in the Colonial Southeast* (Lincoln: Univ. of Nebraska Press, 2006); and Robbie Ethridge and Sheri M. Shuck-Hall, eds., *Mapping the Mississippian Shatter Zone: The Colonial Indian Slave Trade and Regional Instability in the American South* (Lincoln: Univ. of Nebraska Press, 2009).

French activities in Canada, the Caribbean, and in the Gulf South have been investigated by William J. Eccles, *The Canadian Frontier, 1534–1760* (Albuquerque: Univ. of New Mexico Press, 1983); James Pritchard, *In Search of Empire: The French in the Americas, 1670–1730* (Cambridge: Cambridge Univ. Press, 2004); Marcel Giraud, *A History of French Louisiana*, vol. 1, *The Reign of Louis XIV* (Baton Rouge: Louisiana State Univ. Press, 1974); Robert S. Weddle, *The French Thorn: Rival Explorers in the Spanish Sea, 1682–1762* (College Station: Texas A&M Univ. Press, 1991); Robert S. Weddle, *The Wreck of the Belle: The Ruin of La Salle* (College Station: Texas A&M Univ. Press, 2001); Patricia K. Galloway, ed., *La Salle and His Legacy: Frenchmen and Indians in the Lower Mississippi Valley* (Jackson: Univ. Press of Mississippi, 1982); Joseph G. Dawson III, ed., *The Louisiana Governors: From Iberville to Edwards* (Baton Rouge: Louisiana State Univ. Press, 1990); François Lagarde, ed., *The French in Texas: History, Migration, Culture* (Austin: Univ. of Texas Press, 2003); Jay Higginbotham, *Old Mobile: Fort Louis de la Louisiane, 1702–1711* (Tuscaloosa: Univ. of Alabama Press, 1977); and Michael V. R. Thomason, ed., *Mobile: The New History of Alabama's First City* (Tuscaloosa: Univ. of Alabama Press, 2001).

On the Spanish response to the French encroachment and the establishment of Texas, see William C. Foster, *Spanish Expeditions into Texas, 1689–1768* (Austin: Univ. of Texas Press, 1995), and Donald E. Chipman and Harriet Denise Joseph, *Spanish Texas, 1519–1821* (Austin: Univ. of Texas Press, 2010). For Pensacola, see Michael Gannon, ed., *The New History of Florida* (Gainesville: Univ. Press of Florida, 1996); Paul Hoffman, *Florida's Frontiers* (Bloomington: Indiana Univ. Press, 2002); and Judith A. Bense, ed., *Presidio Santa María de Galve: A Struggle for Survival in Colonial Spanish Pensacola* (Gainesville: Univ. Press of Florida, 2003).

Many excellent works deal with the Native American response to the initial British, French, and Spanish settlements and beyond. These include Kathryn E. Holland Braund, *Deerskins and Duffels: Creek Indian Trade with Anglo-America, 1685–1815* (Lincoln: Univ. of Nebraska Press, 1993); Steven C. Hahn, *The Invention of the Creek Nation, 1670–1763* (Lincoln: Univ. of Nebraska Press, 2004); Joshua Piker, *Okfuskee: A Creek Indian Town in Colonial America* (Cambridge: Harvard Univ. Press, 2004); Sheri M. Shuck-Hall, *Journey to the West: The Alabama and Coushatta Indians* (Norman: Univ. of Oklahoma Press, 2008); Mary Ann Wells, *Native Land: Mississippi, 1540–1798* (Jackson: Univ. Press of Mississippi, 1994); James R. Atkinson, *Splendid Land, Splendid People: The Chickasaw Indians to Removal* (Tuscaloosa: Univ. of Alabama Press, 2004); Richard White,

The Roots of Dependency: Subsistence, Environment, and Social Change Among the Choctaws, Pawnees, and Navajos (Lincoln: Univ. of Nebraska Press, 1983); James Taylor Carson, *Searching for the Bright Path: The Mississippi Choctaws from Prehistory to Removal* (Lincoln: Univ. of Nebraska Press, 1999); Jim Barnett, *The Natchez Indians: A History to 1735* (Jackson: Univ. Press of Mississippi, 2007); Fred B. Kniffen, Hiram F. Gregory, and George A. Stokes, *The Historic Indian Tribes of Louisiana* (Baton Rouge: Louisiana State Univ. Press, 1987); David W. Baird, *The Quapaw Indians: A History of the Downstream People* (Norman: Univ. of Oklahoma Press, 1980); Jeannie Whayne, ed., *Cultural Encounters in the Early South: Indians and Europeans in Arkansas* (Fayetteville: Univ. of Arkansas Press, 1995); Morris S. Arnold, *The Rumble of a Distant Drum: The Quapaws and Old World Newcomers, 1673–1804* (Fayetteville: Univ. of Arkansas Press, 2000); Kathleen Duval, *The Native Ground: Indians and Colonists in the Heart of the Continent* (Philadelphia: Univ. of Pennsylvania Press, 2006); Willard H. Rollings, *The Osage: An Ethnohistorical Study of Hegemony on the Prairie-Plains* (Columbia: Univ. of Missouri Press, 1992); F. Todd Smith, *The Caddo Indians: Tribes at the Convergence of Empires, 1542–1854* (College Station: Texas A&M Univ. Press, 1995); Cecile Elkins Carter, *Caddo Indians: Where We Come From* (Norman: Univ. of Oklahoma Press, 1995); David La Vere, *The Caddo Chiefdoms: Caddo Economics and Politics, 700–1835* (Lincoln: Univ. of Nebraska Press, 1998); F. Todd Smith, *The Wichita Indians: Traders of Texas and the Southern Plains, 1540–1845* (College Station: Texas A&M Univ. Press, 2000); David La Vere, *The Texas Indians* (College Station: Texas A&M Univ. Press, 2004); and Pekka Hämäläinen, *The Comanche Empire* (New Haven: Yale Univ. Press, 2009).

3. ESTABLISHING LOUISIANA, 1713–1731 *and* 4. STABILITY AND MATURATION OF THE GULF SOUTH, 1732–1763

For the establishment of Louisiana under the direction of Crozat, the Company of the Indies, and the French Crown, see Glenn R. Conrad, ed., *The French Experience in Louisiana* (Lafayette: Center for Louisiana Studies, University of Southwestern Louisiana, 1995); Bradley G. Bond, ed., *French Colonial Louisiana and the Atlantic World* (Baton Rouge: Louisiana State Univ. Press, 2005); Carl A. Brasseaux, *French, Cajun, Creole, Houma: A Primer on Francophone Louisiana* (Baton Rouge: Louisiana

State Univ. Press, 2005); Marcel Giraud, *A History of French Louisiana*, vol. 2, *Years of Transition, 1715–1717* (Baton Rouge: Louisiana State Univ. Press, 1993); and Marcel Giraud, *A History of French Louisiana*, vol. 5, *The Company of the Indies, 1723–1731* (Baton Rouge: Louisiana State Univ. Press, 1991). For an excellent look at the French military in Louisiana, see Carl A. Brasseaux, *France's Forgotten Legion* (Baton Rouge: Louisiana State Univ. Press, 2000). The various French settlements in Louisiana have been examined in the works of John G. Clark, *New Orleans, 1718–1812: An Economic History* (Baton Rouge: Louisiana State Univ. Press, 1970); Arnold R. Hirsch and Joseph Logsdon, eds., *Creole New Orleans: Race and Americanization* (Baton Rouge: Louisiana State Univ. Press, 1992); Craig E. Colten, ed., *Transforming New Orleans and Its Environs: Centuries of Change* (Pittsburgh: Univ. of Pittsburgh Press, 2000); Emily Clark, *Masterless Mistresses: The New Orleans Ursulines and the Development of a New World Society, 1727–1834* (Chapel Hill: Univ. of North Carolina Press, 2007); Shannon Lee Dawdy, *Building the Devil's Empire: French Colonial New Orleans* (Chicago: Univ. of Chicago Press, 2008); Richard Campanella, *Bienville's Dilemma: A Historical Geography of New Orleans* (Lafayette: Center for Louisiana Studies, 2008); Jennifer M. Spear, *Race, Sex, and Social Order in Early New Orleans* (Baltimore: Johns Hopkins Univ. Press, 2009); Lawrence N. Powell, *The Accidental City: Improvising New Orleans* (Cambridge: Harvard Univ. Press, 2012); Samuel C. Hyde Jr., ed., *A Fierce and Fractious Frontier: The Curious Development of Louisiana's Florida Parishes, 1699–2000* (Baton Rouge: Louisiana State Univ. Press, 2004); Reinhart Kondert, *Charles Frederick D'Arensbourg and the Germans of Colonial Louisiana* (Lafayette: Center for Louisiana Studies, 2008); Morris Arnold, *Unequal Laws Unto a Savage Race: European Legal Traditions in Arkansas, 1686–1836* (Fayetteville: Univ. of Arkansas Press, 1985); Morris Arnold, *Colonial Arkansas, 1686–1804: A Social and Cultural History* (Fayetteville: Univ. of Arkansas Press, 1991); Carl J. Ekberg, *French Roots in Illinois Country: The Mississippi Frontier in Colonial Times* (Urbana: Univ. of Illinois Press, 1998); H. Sophie Burton and F. Todd Smith, *Colonial Natchitoches: A Creole Community on the Louisiana-Texas Frontier, 1714–1803* (College Station: Texas A&M Univ. Press, 2008); and Daniel H. Thomas, *Fort Toulouse: French Outpost at the Alabamas on the Coosa* (Tuscaloosa: Univ. of Alabama Press, 1989).

For two different opinions on African slavery in Louisiana, see Gwendolyn Midlo Hall, *Africans in Colonial Louisiana: The Development of Afro-Creole Culture in the Eighteenth Century* (Baton Rouge: Louisiana

State Univ. Press, 1992), and Thomas Ingersoll, *Mammon and Manon in Early New Orleans: The First Slave Society in the Deep South, 1718–1819* (Knoxville: Univ. of Tennessee Press, 1999).

Developments in Texas during this period have been examined by Jack Jackson, *Los Mesteños: Spanish Ranching in Texas, 1721–1821* (College Station: Texas A&M Univ. Press, 1986); Jack Jackson and William C. Foster, eds., *Imaginary Kingdom: Texas as Seen by the Rivera and Rubí Military Expeditions, 1727 and 1767* (Austin: Texas State Historical Association, 1995); Donald E. Chipman and Harriet Denis Joseph, *Notable Men and Women of Spanish Texas* (Austin: Univ. of Texas Press, 1998); and Robert S. Weddle, *After the Battle: The Violent Legacy of the San Saba Mission* (Lubbock: Texas Tech Univ. Press, 2007).

5. TRANSFORMATION OF THE GULF SOUTH, 1763–1783 *and* 6. THE ANGLO PROTESTANT INFLUX AND THE CONSEQUENCES OF THE FRENCH REVOLUTION, 1783–1803

For British West Florida, see Robert L. Gold, *Borderlands Empires in Transition: The Triple-Nation Transfer of Florida* (Carbondale: Southern Illinois Univ. Press, 1969); Robin F. A. Fabel, *The Economy of British West Florida, 1763–1783* (Tuscaloosa: Univ. of Alabama Press, 1988); Robert R. Rea, *Major Robert Farmar of Mobile* (Tuscaloosa: Univ. of Alabama Press, 1990); and Christopher Morris, *Becoming Southern: The Evolution of a Way of Life, Warren County and Vicksburg, Mississippi, 1770–1860* (Oxford: Oxford Univ. Press, 1995).

The Spanish accession of Louisiana has been examined by John Preston Moore, *Revolt in Louisiana: The Spanish Occupation, 1766–1770* (Baton Rouge: Louisiana State Univ. Press, 1976), and Carl A. Brasseaux, *Denis-Nicolas Foucault and the New Orleans Rebellion of 1768* (Ruston, La.: McGinty Publications, 1987). For Louisiana under the dominion of Spain, see Gilbert C. Din, ed., *The Spanish Presence in Louisiana, 1763–1803* (Lafayette: Center for Louisiana Studies, University of Southwestern Louisiana, 1996); Jack D. L. Holmes, *Gayoso: The Life of a Spanish Governor in the Mississippi Valley, 1789–1799* (Baton Rouge: Louisiana State Univ. Press, 1965); Carl A. Brasseaux, *The Founding of New Acadia: The Beginnings of Acadian Life in Louisiana, 1765–1803* (Baton Rouge: Louisiana State Univ. Press, 1987); Samuel Wilson Jr., *The Architecture of Colonial*

Louisiana (Lafayette: Center for Louisiana Studies, University of Southwestern Louisiana, 1987); Gilbert C. Din, *The Canary Islanders of Louisiana* (Baton Rouge: Louisiana State Univ. Press, 1988); Carl A. Brasseaux and Glenn R. Conrad, eds., *The Road to Louisiana: The Saint-Domingue Refugees, 1792–1809* (Lafayette: Center for Louisiana Studies, University of Southwestern Louisiana, 1992); Gilbert C. Din, *Francisco Bouligny: A Bourbon Soldier in Spanish Louisiana* (Baton Rouge: Louisiana State Univ. Press, 1993); Russ E. Williams Jr., *Spanish Poste d'Ouachita: The Ouachita Valley in Colonial Louisiana, 1783–1804, and Early American Statehood, 1804–1820* (Monroe: Williams Genealogical Publications, 1995); Robert S. Weddle, *Changing Tides: Twilight and Dawn in the Spanish Sea, 1763–1803* (College Station: Texas A&M Univ. Press, 1995); Gilbert C. Din and John E. Harkins, *The New Orleans Cabildo: Colonial Louisiana's First City Government, 1769–1803* (Baton Rouge: Louisiana State Univ. Press, 1996); Nathalie Dessens, *From Saint-Domingue to New Orleans: Migration and Influences* (Gainesville: Univ. Press of Florida, 2007); and Gilbert C. Din, *War on the Gulf Coast: The Spanish Fight against William Augustus Bowles* (Gainesville: Univ. Press of Florida, 2012).

Slaves and free people of color are discussed in Gilbert C. Din, *Spaniards, Planters, and Slaves: The Spanish Regulation of Slavery in Louisiana, 1763–1803* (College Station: Texas A&M Univ. Press, 1999); Gary B. Mills and Elizabeth Shown Mills, *The Forgotten People: Cane River's Creoles of Color* (1977; rev. ed., Baton Rouge: Louisiana State Univ. Press, 2013); Carl A. Brasseaux, Keith P. Fontenot, and Claude F. Oubre, eds., *Creoles of Color in the Bayou Country* (Jackson: Univ. Press of Mississippi, 1994); James H. Dormon, ed., *Creoles of Color of the Gulf South* (Knoxville: Univ. of Tennessee Press, 1996); and Kimberley S. Hanger, *Bounded Lives, Bounded Places: Free Blacks in Colonial New Orleans, 1769–1803* (Durham: Duke Univ. Press, 1997).

The impact of the American Revolution on Louisiana and the Gulf South has been examined by J. Barton Starr, *Tories, Dons, and Rebels: The American Revolution in British West Florida* (Gainesville: Univ. Press of Florida, 1976); Light Townsend Cummins, *Spanish Observers and the American Revolution, 1775–1783* (Baton Rouge: Louisiana State Univ. Press, 1991); and Thomas E. Chávez, *Spain and the Independence of the United States: An Intrinsic Gift* (Albuquerque: Univ. of New Mexico Press, 2002).

Anglo American expansion into Tennessee and Mississippi, as well as the diplomacy of the Louisiana Purchase, has been studied by John R. Finger, *Tennessee Frontiers: Three Regions in Transition* (Bloomington:

Indiana Univ. Press, 2001); David J. Libby, *Slavery and Frontier Mississippi, 1720–1835* (Jackson: Univ. Press of Mississippi, 2004); Robert V. Haynes, *The Mississippi Territory and the Southwest Frontier, 1795–1817* (Lexington: Univ. Press of Kentucky, 2010); Arthur H. DeRosier Jr., *William Dunbar: Scientific Pioneer of the Old Southwest* (Lexington: Univ. Press of Kentucky, 2007); and Jon Kukla, *A Wilderness So Immense: The Louisiana Purchase and the Destiny of America* (New York: Knopf, 2003).

For Native Americans in the period, see William S. Coker and Thomas D. Watson, *Indian Traders of the Southeastern Borderlands: Panton, Leslie and Company and John Forbes and Company, 1783–1847* (Gainesville: Univ. Press of Florida, 1986); Florette Henri, *The Southern Indians and Benjamin Hawkins* (Norman: Univ. of Oklahoma Press, 1988); Joel W. Martin, *Sacred Revolt: The Muskogees' Struggle for a New World* (Boston: Beacon Press, 1991); Claudio Saunt, *A New Order of Things: Property, Power, and the Transformation of the Creek Indians, 1773–1816* (Cambridge: Cambridge Univ. Press, 2003); Robbie Ethridge, *Creek Country: The Creek Indians and Their World* (Chapel Hill: Univ. of North Carolina Press, 2003); Greg O'Brien, *Choctaws in a Revolutionary Age, 1750–1830* (Lincoln: Univ. of Nebraska Press, 2002); Greg O'Brien, ed., *Pre-Removal Choctaw History: Exploring New Paths* (Norman: Univ. of Oklahoma Press, 2008); Charles A. Weeks, *Paths to a Middle Ground: The Diplomacy of Natchez, Boukfouka, Nogales, and San Fernando de las Barrancas, 1791–1795* (Tuscaloosa: Univ. of Alabama Press, 2005); Gilbert C. Din and Abraham P. Nasatir, *The Imperial Osages: Spanish-Indian Policy in the Mississippi Valley* (Norman: Univ. of Oklahoma Press, 1983); Maurine T. Wilson and Jack Jackson, *Philip Nolan and Texas: Expeditions to the Unknown Land, 1791–1801* (Waco: Texian Press, 1987); and F. Todd Smith, *From Dominance to Disappearance: The Indians of Texas and the Near Southwest, 1786–1859* (Lincoln: Univ. of Nebraska Press, 2005).

7. THE ESTABLISHMENT OF ANGLO PROTESTANT HEGEMONY 1804–1821

The American takeover of Louisiana and the integration of slave policies have been examined by Dolores Egger Labbé, ed., *The Louisiana Purchase and Its Aftermath, 1800–1830* (Lafayette: Center for Louisiana Studies, University of Southwestern Louisiana, 1998); Peter Kastor, *The Nation's Crucible: The Louisiana Purchase and the Creation of America* (New Haven: Yale Univ. Press, 2004); Adam Rothman, *Slave Country: American Expansion and the Origins of the Deep South* (Cambridge: Harvard Univ. Press, 2005); Daniel Rasmussen, *American Uprising: The Untold Story of America's Largest Slave Revolt* (New York: HarperCollins, 2011).

For the areas outside of New Orleans, see Samuel C. Hyde Jr., *Pistols and Politics: The Dilemma of Democracy in Louisiana's Florida Parishes, 1810–1899* (Baton Rouge: Louisiana State Univ. Press, 1996); Andrew McMichael, *Atlantic Loyalties: Americans in Spanish West Florida, 1785–1810* (Athens: Univ. of Georgia Press, 2008); Charles S. Bolton, *Territorial Ambition: Land and Society in Arkansas, 1800–1840* (Fayetteville: Univ. of Arkansas Press, 1993); Patrick G. Williams, Charles S. Bolton, and Jeannie M. Whayne, eds., *A Whole Country in Commotion: The Louisiana Purchase and the American Southwest* (Fayetteville: Univ. of Arkansas Press, 2005); and Carl A. Brasseaux, *Acadian to Cajun: Transformation of a People, 1803–1877* (Jackson: Univ. Press of Mississippi, 1992).

The Creek War, the Battle of New Orleans, and the diplomacy of the Gulf Borderlands have been dealt with by Frank L. Owsley Jr., *Struggle for the Gulf Borderlands: The Creek War and the Battle of New Orleans, 1812–1815* (Gainesville: Univ. Press of Florida, 1981); Frank L. Owsley Jr. and Gene A. Smith, *Filibusters and Expansionists: Jeffersonian Manifest Destiny, 1800–1821* (Tuscaloosa: Univ. of Alabama Press, 1997); Robert V. Remini, *The Battle of New Orleans: Andrew Jackson and America's First Military Victory* (New York: Penguin, 1999); Gregory Waselkov, *A Conquering Spirit: Fort Mims and the Redstick War of 1812–1814* (Tuscaloosa: Univ. of Alabama Press, 2006); and Angela Pulley Hudson, *Creek Paths and Federal Roads: Indians, Settlers, and Slaves and the Making of the American South* (Chapel Hill: Univ. of North Carolina Press, 2010).

INDEX